GED MATH

LearningExpress's

GED MATH ▶

LearningExpress ®

NEW YORK

Copyright © 2008 LearningExpress, LLC.

All rights reserved under International and Pan-American Copyright Conventions. Published in the United States by LearningExpress, LLC, New York.

Library of Congress Cataloging-in-Publication Data:
GED math.
    p. cm.
  ISBN 978-1-57685-623-9
    1. Mathematics—Examinations, questions, etc.   2. Mathematics—Problems, exercises, etc. 3. General educational development tests—Study guides.   I. LearningExpress (Organization)
  QA43.L419   2008
  510.76—dc22   2008010721

Printed in the United States of America

9 8 7 6 5 4 3 2 1

First Edition

Regarding the Information in This Book
We attempt to verify the information presented in our books prior to publication. It is always a good idea, however, to double-check such important information as the test format, application and testing procedures, and deadlines, as such information can change from time to time.

For more information or to place an order, contact LearningExpress at:
  2 Rector Street
  26th Floor
  New York, NY 10006

Or visit us at:
  www.learnatest.com

Contents ▶

Introduction   **1**

About *GED Math*   1

GED Test Overview   2

GED Scoring   4

GED Testing Information   4

GED Test-Taking Tips   5

The GED Mathematics Exam   6

Using a Calculator   7

Alternative-Format Questions   8

Graphics on the GED   10

Pretest   **11**

Chapter 1: Numbers and Operations   **27**

Numbers and Operations Pretest   28

Whole Numbers and Their Place Value   29

Rounding Whole Numbers   29

Whole Number Addition and Subtraction   29

Whole Number Multiplication and Division   30

Choosing an Operation   31

Odd and Even Numbers   32

Order of Operations   33

Properties of Real Numbers   33

Number Lines and Signed Numbers   34

CONTENTS

Prime and Composite Numbers 36

Absolute Value 37

Numbers and Operations Posttest 37

Chapter 2: Fractions and Decimals 39

Fractions and Decimals Pretest 40

Writing and Recognizing Fractions 41

Reducing Fractions to Lowest Terms 41

Raising Fractions to Higher Terms 42

Comparing Fractions 42

Operations with Fractions—Overview 43

Adding and Subtracting Fractions 43

Multiplying and Dividing Fractions 44

Improper Fractions 45

Mixed Numbers 45

Writing and Recognizing Decimals 45

How to Read a Decimal 46

Adding and Subtracting Decimals 47

Multiplying Decimals 48

Dividing Decimals 49

Decimal Operations: Multiplying or Dividing by the Powers of 10 49

Converting between Fractions and Decimals 49

Common Fraction and Decimal Equivalents 49

Fractions and Decimals Posttest 50

Chapter 3: Measurement 53

Measurement Pretest 54

Types of Measurements 56

Converting Units 58

Conversions within the Metric System 58

Addition with Measurements 59

Subtraction with Measurements 59

Multiplication with Measurements 60

Division with Measurements 60

Temperature 60

Ratios 61

Solving Ratio Problems 62

Proportions 63

Solving Proportion Word Problems 64

CONTENTS

Scale   64

Rates   65

Calculating Simple Interest   65

Measurement Posttest   66

Chapter 4: Percentages   69

Percentages Pretest   70

Percents   71

Converting Percents to Decimals   71

Converting Decimals to Percents   71

Converting Percents to Fractions   72

Converting Fractions to Percents   72

Solving Percent Problems   73

Finding a Part of a Whole   73

Finding a Percent   73

Finding the Whole   75

Percentages Posttest   75

Chapter 5: Exponents and Roots   77

Exponents and Roots Pretest   78

Powers and Exponents Review   79

Finding Squares   79

Negative Exponents   80

Square Roots   80

Working with Square Roots   80

Fractional Exponents   81

Scientific Notation   81

Laws of Exponents   82

Exponents and the Order of Operations   82

Exponents and Roots Posttest   83

Chapter 6: Algebra and Functions   85

Algebra and Functions Pretest   86

What Are Algebraic Expressions?   87

Evaluating Algebraic Expressions   88

Simplifying Algebraic Expressions   89

Equations   90

Solving Multiple-Step Algebraic Equations   91

Polynomials   92

CONTENTS

Operations with Polynomials   92

FOIL   93

Factoring   93

Removing a Common Factor   93

Quadratic Equations   94

Inequalities   94

Solving Linear Inequalities   94

Functions   94

Domain   95

Range   95

Nested Functions   95

Algebra and Functions Posttest   95

Chapter 7: Geometry   97

Geometry Pretest   98

What Are Angles?   99

Measuring Angles   100

Classifying Angles   101

Relationships between Lines and Angles   102

Polygons   103

Quadrilaterals   103

Finding Perimeter and Circumference   104

Finding Area   104

Finding Volume   105

Surface Area   105

Triangles   106

Types of Triangles   106

Congruent Triangles   107

Similar Triangles   108

Parts of a Right Triangle   108

The Pythagorean Theorem   109

Coordinate Geometry   109

Slope   110

Midpoint   110

Distance   110

Geometry Posttest   111

Chapter 8: Data Analysis, Statistics, and Probability — 113

Data Analysis, Statistics, and Probability Pretest — 114

Measures of Central Tendency — 115

Finding the Mean — 115

Finding the Median — 116

Finding the Mode — 117

Measures of Dispersion — 117

Range — 117

Standard Deviation — 117

Frequency Distribution — 117

What Is Probability? — 118

Data Representation and Interpretation — 120

Getting Information from Tables and Charts — 121

Data Analysis, Statistics, and Probability Posttest — 122

Posttest — 125

GED Math Answers and Explanations — 141

Formula Cheat Sheet — 167

Glossary — 169

GED MATH

Introduction ▶

▶ About *GED Math*

GED Math has two main goals: first, to prepare you to take the General Educational Development examination (GED®), and second, to help you learn math concepts with an organized, user-friendly guide. The skills covered represent the type and difficulty level of skills tested on the official GED.

    GED Math is divided into four main components:

1. **Pretest:** These 50 questions will allow you to check your understanding of the core GED math skills. These questions will help you identify your strengths and weaknesses in math concepts, procedures, and applications across the four content areas highlighted on the GED (for concepts, see page 3).

2. **Instructional Chapters:** Instruction and practice on GED math skills provide the review you need to be prepared for the official GED Mathematics Exam. Each instructional chapter represents a content area that you will encounter on the official GED. The practice questions and examples are chosen to increase your understanding, extend your knowledge, and make connections with related skills. They show different ways the skills may be approached on the official GED.

3. **Posttest:** A two-part GED practice test will show your readiness to take the official test. For best results, take this posttest under timed, testlike conditions.

4. **Additional Material:** Lessons and practices aside, this book also provides supporting material for test success—extensive answer keys with thorough answer explanations, a formula cheat sheet, and a glossary of key math terms.

This test-preparation guide can be used in a variety of ways—with individual-directed self-study, one-on-one instruction, or group instruction.

Create a calendar that represents the time you have until the actual test day and what you will study during that time. You may want to use this book's table of contents to determine how long you can spend with each chapter. Some chapters may take you longer than others, so build in extra time. You can revise your calendar down the road, but it's always good to start with some kind of study plan.

Contents at a Glance

Content	Chapter
Numbers and Operations	1
Fractions and Decimals	2
Measurement	3
Percentages	4
Exponents and Roots	5
Algebra and Functions	6
Geometry	7
Data Analysis, Statistics, and Probability	8

If you set a realistic study plan for yourself using *GED Math* and stick to it, you will have the know-how necessary to conquer the GED Mathematics Exam.

▶ GED Test Overview

If you didn't finish high school, and you now wish to expand your educational and professional opportunities, the best way to remedy that is to earn a General Equivalency Diploma, or GED. Approximately a million people a year earn a GED, and it's accepted as equal to a high school diploma by almost all companies and colleges in the United States. Also, once you've gotten a GED, if you decide to go to college, you're eligible for as much government financial aid as a high school graduate.

Reasons for Taking the GED

The American Council on Education (ACE), which oversees the GED exams, reports that the two most common reasons for taking the GED are to gain further education at the college level and to advance a career—either by improving a present job or getting something totally different.

In the United States, 61% of those taking the GED take it for educational reasons and 49% for employment reasons, while some take it for both reasons.

The GED covers five major subject areas—mathematics, reading, writing, social studies, and science, which are also the main subjects high school students must take. Test scores range from 200 to 800, and you'll need to score an average of 450 to earn your diploma in most states. You'll have to write a short essay to demonstrate your vocabulary and grammar skills for the Writing section of the GED Language Arts exam, but all the other sections of the GED test consist of multiple-choice or alternative-format questions.

GED at a Glance

Mathematics
50 items, 75 minutes

Content areas:		
	Numbers, Number Sense, and Operations	25%
	Measurement and Geometry	25%
	Data Analysis, Statistics, and Probability	25%
	Algebra, Functions, and Patterns	25%

Language Arts, Reading
40 items, 65 minutes

Content areas:		
	Nonfiction Texts	25%
	Literary Texts (Poetry, Prose, Drama)	75%

Language Arts, Writing, Part I
50 items, 75 minutes

Content areas:		
	Organization	15%
	Sentence Structure	30%
	Usage	30%
	Mechanics	25%

Language Arts, Writing, Part II
Essay, about 250 words, 45 minutes

Social Studies
50 items, 80 minutes

Content areas:		
	U.S. History	25%
	World History	15%
	Civics and Government	25%
	Geography	15%
	Economics	20%

Science
50 items, 80 minutes

Content areas:		
	Life Science	45%
	Earth and Space Science	20%
	Physical Science	35%

The GED is jointly administered by the General Education Development Testing Service, a program of the American Council on Education (ACE) Center for Adult Learning and Education Credentials, and the education department of each participating state or province. The ACE and participating states/provinces have set eligibility requirements for GED candidates. You are eligible if you meet the following requirements:

- are not enrolled in high school *and*
- have not graduated from high school *and*
- are at least 16 years of age *and*
- meet the requirements of your state/province about age, residency, and length of time since leaving school

You're in Good Company

More than 16 million people have taken the GED since it was first given in 1942!

▶ GED Scoring

Your scores on the GED will be reported as separate standard scores ranging from 200 to 800 for each test. The number of questions answered correctly, or raw score, is converted to a score so that all GED subject tests can be evaluated similarly. In other words, each correct answer is worth one point, but because the individual tests have different numbers of questions, the score for each test is converted to this 200–800 standard.

A Tough Exam

According to the American Council on Education, only 60% of high school graduates pass the GED exam.

How you receive your scores will depend on what state you take the test in. Most testing centers will mail

your test results within two to four weeks. The Language Arts essay score, however, takes a little longer— typically four to six weeks.

GED Statistics

The American Council on Education oversees the GED exams, and reports the following:

- 680,874 people took the test in 2005 in the United States alone; 715,365 took it worldwide.
- 423,714 passed in the United States; 443,607 passed worldwide.
- 25% of GED test takers are between the ages of 20 and 24.

To pass the GED in most states, besides getting a total minimum average score of 450 overall, you must get a minimum score per test of 410. (This is the passing score set by the GED Testing Service, and most jurisdictions follow this scoring.)

▶ GED Testing Information

The GED test is offered almost everywhere in the United States and Canada, as well as in about 100 international testing sites.

"Smarter Than the Average Bear"

The GED exam is deliberately designed to be more difficult than many high school courses. Passing the GED proves that you're in the upper percentiles!

In the United States, GED testing centers are typically operated by local school boards, community colleges, or centers for adult education. If you're thinking of taking the GED, you can locate local testing centers in the United States and Canada by contacting the GED toll-free hotline at 800-626-9433, or 800-62-MY-GED. A GED contact person will be able to help you determine dates, locations, and costs. Your state department of education or local community college might have the information, too.

To find an international testing center, foreign nationals and U.S. citizens abroad can contact Prometric, a Baltimore-based corporation that has a partnership with the GED Testing Service. The website for Prometric is www.prometric.com.

Military personnel can take the GED at DANTES (Defense Activity for Non-Traditional Education Support) testing centers. Family members of military personnel are allowed to take the GED tests only at DANTES centers located overseas. See www.dantes .doded.mil/dantes_web/danteshome.asp?Flag=True for more information.

▶ GED Test-Taking Tips

As you prepare to take the GED, consider the following test-taking tips:

- Combat test anxiety. Remember, a *little* test anxiety is a good thing. Everyone gets nervous before a big exam—and if that nervousness motivates you to prepare thoroughly, so much the better. Some keys to bringing your anxiety level down before the test day include being prepared, practicing self-confidence, fighting negative messages, visualizing success, and exercising. To bring your anxiety level down on the test day, try deep breathing, moving your body (i.e., roll your head in a circle or rotate your shoulders), and visualize again (i.e., think of the place where you are most relaxed).
- The night before the exam, lay out the clothes you will wear and the materials you will need (i.e., photo ID, admission card, pencils). Plan on dressing in layers, because you won't have any control over the temperature of the exam room. Have a sweater or jacket you can take off if it's warm.
- On the day of the exam, don't skip breakfast, even if you don't usually eat breakfast. Avoid sweet foods like doughnuts; a sugar high will leave you with a sugar low in the middle of the test. A mix of proteins and carbohydrates is best (i.e., cereal with milk, or eggs with toast).
- Pace yourself. The time limit for each test is always announced or written on the blackboard of the testing room. Consider bringing a watch to the exam, so you can keep track of your own progress.

Contacting the GED Administrators

Here is how to obtain further information on disabilities, test times, locations, and so on.

1. Begin by contacting your local high school or adult education office.
2. Contact the American Council on Education, which oversees the GED: GED—General Educational Development American Council on Education One Dupont Circle NW, Suite 250 Washington, D.C. 20036 800-626-9433
3. Visit the ACE website at www.ged test.org, or e-mail ACE at comments @ace.nehu.edu.

- Carefully read every question before you attempt to answer it. Take note of words like *but*, *not*, *however*, *always*, *only*, and *never*. Be careful of absolutes like *greatest*, *least*, or *lowest*.
- Answer the easiest questions first. If you run into a difficult question that has you stumped, go on to the next question and come back to it later.
- Avoid careless errors. Read each question thoroughly, so you will understand exactly what is being asked. Make sure that you mark in the correct circle for the correct corresponding question number.
- Answer every question. On the GED, you are not penalized for an incorrect answer, so you should always at least make a guess. By eliminating obvious incorrect choices, you improve your chances of choosing the right answer.
- Use any time you have left. Go back to questions that you earmarked to return to later and try them again. Check your work. Review your answer sheet to make sure you've put the answers in the right places and you've marked only one answer for each question. If you've erased an answer, make sure you've done a good job of removing any mark. Also, check for stray marks on your answer sheet that could distort your score.

A Large Percentage

More than 39 million adults in the United States over the age of 16 (18% of the adult population) did not complete their high school education and are not enrolled in any education program.

If you've been out of school for a while, remember that any determined person can earn a GED, and doing so can open up a whole new world of previously unavailable opportunities.

► The GED Mathematics Exam

The GED Mathematics Exam is a test used to measure your understanding of the mathematical knowledge needed in real life. The questions are based on information presented in words, diagrams, charts, graphs, and pictures. In addition to testing your math skills, you will also be asked to demonstrate your problem-solving skills. Here are some examples of the skills needed for the mathematical portion of the GED:

- understanding the question
- organizing data and identifying important information
- selecting problem-solving strategies
- knowing when to use appropriate mathematical operations
- setting up problems and estimating
- computing the exact, correct answer
- reflecting on the problem to ensure the answer you choose is reasonable

The GED Mathematics Exam is divided into two equally weighted parts, each containing 25 questions. The time limit for the GED is 90 minutes, meaning that you have 45 minutes to complete each section. The sections are timed separately but weighted equally. This means that you must complete both sections in one testing session to receive a passing grade. If only one section is completed, the entire test must be retaken.

The GED Mathematics Exam assesses your understanding of math concepts and the application of those concepts to various real-world situations. The following four major areas are tested on the exam:

1. Number Operations and Number Sense (20%–30%)
2. Measurement and Geometry (20%–30%)
3. Data Analysis, Statistics, and Probability (20%–30%)
4. Algebra, Functions, and Patterns (20%–30%)

The 50 questions on the test fit into three different category types:

1. conceptual (15 questions identifying and applying math definitions, facts, and principles)
2. procedural (10 questions using math procedures)
3. application (25 questions applying math in real-life situations)

The test contains 40 multiple-choice questions and 10 alternative-format questions for a total of 50 questions overall. Each multiple-choice question has five answer choices, **a** through **e**. (Alternative-format questions will be discussed in the section "Alternative-Format Questions.")

On Part I of the test, you may use the Casio fx-260SOLAR calculator to compute answers. Because estimation and mental math are critical skills, you are not permitted to use the calculator on Part II of the test.

For both math sections, a formula sheet will be provided to the test taker. You are allowed to use this page when you are taking the test; however, you should become familiar with the formulas and understand when and how to use them prior to the test day. (When tackling the practice tests or questions in this book, you can consult the "Formula Cheat Sheet" on page 167.)

The structure of the GED Mathematics Exam ensures that for no more than two questions is "Not enough information is given" the correct answer choice. Given this fact, it is important for you to pay attention to how many times you select this answer choice. If you find yourself selecting "Not enough information is given" for the third time, be sure to check the other questions for which you have selected this choice, because one of them must be incorrect.

Additionally, the current GED has an increased focus on math in everyday life. This is emphasized by allowing the use of a calculator on Part I as well as by an increased emphasis on data analysis and statistics.

▶ Using a Calculator

A Casio fx-260SOLAR calculator will be provided for your use at the official GED testing center. The Casio fx-260SOLAR calculator is shown on the left. The calculator on the right shows only those keys you may find helpful for questions on the GED Mathematics Exam.

 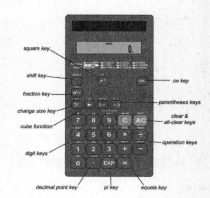

The ON key is used each time you begin a new question or make an error entering a number or an operation. It is used to clear the display and to clear all parts of a calculation. Other keys to know include the following:

■ +/−: the change sign key, used to enter a negative number

- $a^{b/c}$: the fraction key, used to enter a fraction
- x^2: the square key, used to square a number
- $[(---$ and $---)]$: the parentheses keys, used for performing calculations involving parentheses (i.e., questions for which the order of operations is very important)
- SHIFT: the shift key, used to access the functions listed above the other keys

The Casio fx-260SOLAR performs additional functions outside of those indicated on the keys. These functions are indicated by the symbols placed above the keys. To access a function key, press the SHIFT key, release it, and then press the key below the desired function.

Calculator Hints

Although you are given a calculator for Part I, you are not required to use it. Some questions can be solved just as easily without a calculator. Use the calculator only for questions where it is helpful or time-efficient. You will need to recognize questions for which a calculator is helpful and questions for which it is not.

▶ Alternative-Format Questions

Although 80% of the mathematics questions are multiple-choice, 20% of the questions require you to construct your own answer. Rather than select from five choices, you must record answers on either standard or coordinate-plane grids. (Alternative-format questions are always referred to as grid-in questions or constructed-response questions.) Both Parts I and II of the test have multiple-choice, standard-grid, and coordinate-plane-grid questions.

Standard grids record numerical answers.

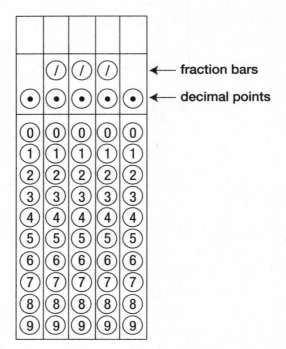

← fraction bars
← decimal points

When you are given a question with a grid, first write your answer in the blank boxes at the top of the grid. This will help keep you organized as you "grid in" the bubbles and ensure that you fill them out correctly. (You are not required to fill in the blank boxes at the top, but it will help you avoid making a careless mistake.)

You can start in any column, but leave enough columns for your whole answer. Answers can be left justified or right justified. One-digit or three-digit answers can also be centered. The number 149, for example, can be recorded on the standard grid in three ways:

You do not have to use all of the columns. If your answer takes up only two or three columns, leave the others blank.

You can write your answer by using either fractions or decimals. For example, if your answer is $\frac{1}{4}$, you can enter it as a fraction or as a decimal, 0.25. The slash "/" is used to signify the fraction bar of the fraction. The numerator should be "bubbled in" to the left of the fraction bar and the denominator should be "bubbled in" to the right. Here are five ways to correctly record either answer.

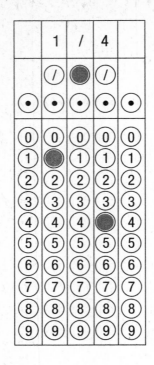

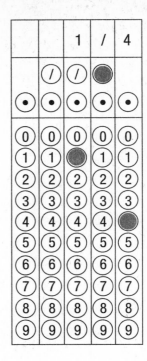

When your answer is a mixed number, it must be represented on the standard grid in the form of an improper fraction. For example, for the answer $1\frac{1}{4}$, grid in 5/4.

A coordinate-plane grid is a grid on which a number is recorded by filling in one circle that represents a point. Negative numbers are possible, but fractions, mixed numbers, and decimals are not.

When you are asked to plot a point on a coordinate grid like the one shown, simply fill in the bubble where the point should appear. For example, the point (1,3) is recorded as one filled-in circle (or point) on the coordinate grid. Make sure that you completely erase all marks except the answer.

▶ Graphics on the GED

At least 25 out of the 50 questions on the GED Mathematics Exam use diagrams, pie charts, graphs, tables, and other visual stimuli as references. Sometimes, more than one of these questions will be grouped under a single graphic. Do not let this confuse you. Learn to recognize question sets by reading both the questions and the directions carefully.

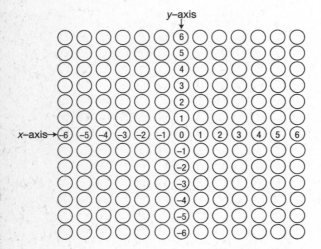

Pretest

BEFORE REVIEWING MATH topics common to the GED Mathematics Exam, test your existing skills by taking the pretest that follows. You will encounter 50 questions that are similar to the types you will find on the GED. The questions are organized by the four content areas tested by the GED Testing Service:

1. Number Operations and Number Sense
2. Measurement and Geometry
3. Data Analysis, Statistics, and Probability
4. Algebra, Functions, and Patterns

Unlike the official GED Mathematics Exam, this pretest is not divided into a calculator part and a non-calculator part. You are encouraged to use a calculator for any problem for which you find it helpful. For now, we also suggest that you ignore the time restraints of the official GED and take as much time as you need to complete each problem.

Answer every question; however, if you are not sure of an answer, put a question mark by the question number to note that you are making a guess. On the official GED, an unanswered question is counted as incorrect, so making a good guess is an important skill to practice.

When you are finished, check the answer key on page 142 carefully to assess your results. Your pretest score will help you determine how much preparation you need and in which areas you need the most careful review and practice.

▶ Pretest Answer Sheet

1. ⓐ ⓑ ⓒ ⓓ ⓔ
2. ⓐ ⓑ ⓒ ⓓ ⓔ
3. ⓐ ⓑ ⓒ ⓓ ⓔ
4. ⓐ ⓑ ⓒ ⓓ ⓔ
5. ⓐ ⓑ ⓒ ⓓ ⓔ
6. ⓐ ⓑ ⓒ ⓓ ⓔ
7. ⓐ ⓑ ⓒ ⓓ ⓔ
8.
9.
10. ⓐ ⓑ ⓒ ⓓ ⓔ
11. ⓐ ⓑ ⓒ ⓓ ⓔ
12. ⓐ ⓑ ⓒ ⓓ ⓔ
13. ⓐ ⓑ ⓒ ⓓ ⓔ
14. ⓐ ⓑ ⓒ ⓓ ⓔ
15. ⓐ ⓑ ⓒ ⓓ ⓔ
16. ⓐ ⓑ ⓒ ⓓ ⓔ
17.

18. ⓐ ⓑ ⓒ ⓓ ⓔ
19. ⓐ ⓑ ⓒ ⓓ ⓔ
20. ⓐ ⓑ ⓒ ⓓ ⓔ
21. ⓐ ⓑ ⓒ ⓓ ⓔ
22.
23. ⓐ ⓑ ⓒ ⓓ ⓔ
24. ⓐ ⓑ ⓒ ⓓ ⓔ
25. ⓐ ⓑ ⓒ ⓓ ⓔ
26. ⓐ ⓑ ⓒ ⓓ ⓔ
27.
28. ⓐ ⓑ ⓒ ⓓ ⓔ
29. ⓐ ⓑ ⓒ ⓓ ⓔ
30. ⓐ ⓑ ⓒ ⓓ ⓔ
31. ⓐ ⓑ ⓒ ⓓ ⓔ
32. ⓐ ⓑ ⓒ ⓓ ⓔ
33. ⓐ ⓑ ⓒ ⓓ ⓔ
34. ⓐ ⓑ ⓒ ⓓ ⓔ

35. ⓐ ⓑ ⓒ ⓓ ⓔ
36. ⓐ ⓑ ⓒ ⓓ ⓔ
37. ⓐ ⓑ ⓒ ⓓ ⓔ
38. ⓐ ⓑ ⓒ ⓓ ⓔ
39. ⓐ ⓑ ⓒ ⓓ ⓔ
40. ⓐ ⓑ ⓒ ⓓ ⓔ
41.
42. ⓐ ⓑ ⓒ ⓓ ⓔ
43. ⓐ ⓑ ⓒ ⓓ ⓔ
44. ⓐ ⓑ ⓒ ⓓ ⓔ
45. ⓐ ⓑ ⓒ ⓓ ⓔ
46. ⓐ ⓑ ⓒ ⓓ ⓔ
47. ⓐ ⓑ ⓒ ⓓ ⓔ
48.
49. ⓐ ⓑ ⓒ ⓓ ⓔ
50. ⓐ ⓑ ⓒ ⓓ ⓔ

Directions: Read each of the following questions carefully and determine the best answer. Record your answers by circling the answer letter choice for multiple-choice questions and by filling in the circles for alternative-format questions.

Note: On the GED, you are not permitted to write in the test booklet. For this pretest, practice by making any notes or calculations on a separate piece of paper.

Number Operations and Number Sense

1. The price of an iPod has been reduced to $224.99. Round $224.99 to the nearest $10.
   a. $200
   b. $220
   c. $225
   d. $230
   e. $250

2. Bernadette has to mail gift cards to several friends. The gift cards have the following weights: 0.76 lb., 0.6 lb., 0.07 lb., and 0.8 lb. Which of the following lists the weights from least to greatest?
   a. 0.6, 0.8, 0.76, 0.07
   b. 0.6, 0.8, 0.07, 0.76
   c. 0.07, 0.6, 0.8, 0.76
   d. 0.07, 0.6, 0.76, 0.8
   e. 0.07, 0.76, 0.6, 0.8

3. At the beginning of the month, Natalie's checking account balance was $589.86. She then wrote checks in the amounts of $18.12 and $50.43. She also made a deposit of $40.11. What is the balance in the checking account right now?
   a. $481.20
   b. $561.42
   c. $618.30
   d. $661.42
   e. $698.52

4. Paul is ordering workout clothes from an online catalog. He selects three T-shirts and two sweatshirts. If Paul pays an $11 shipping cost, which expression gives the total cost of his order?

▶ Item	Price
○ T-shirt	$16.00
○ Sweatshirt	$22.00
○ Hooded sweatshirt	$26.00
○ Running pants	$29.00

   a. $(3 + 2) \times (\$16 + \$22 + \$11)$
   b. $(3 + 2) \times (\$16 + \$22 - \$11)$
   c. $(3 \times \$16) + (2 \times \$22) \times \$11$
   d. $(3 \times \$16) + (2 \times \$22) + \$11$
   e. $(3 \times \$16) + (2 \times \$22) - \$11$

5. Chris and three friends have coffee at the Coffee Klatch. Their bill is $22. If they share the cost equally, how much is each person's share?
   a. $5
   b. $5.50
   c. $7.33
   d. $18.00
   e. $19.00

6. To train for a marathon, five friends ran as far as they could for ten minutes. The distance each friend ran is recorded in the table. Who was the fastest runner?

NAME	DISTANCE
Tsahai	$1\frac{1}{2}$ mi.
Andrea	$1\frac{1}{4}$ mi.
Cleo	$1\frac{5}{8}$ mi.
Denise	$1\frac{3}{4}$ mi.
Jennifer	$\frac{7}{8}$ mi.

   a. Tsahai
   b. Andrea
   c. Cleo
   d. Denise
   e. Jennifer

7. Jerome walked $\frac{1}{8}$ mile to the library. He then walked $2\frac{3}{4}$ miles to school. Later in the day, Jerome walked $2\frac{1}{3}$ miles home. Which is the best estimate of the total number of miles Jerome walked?

a. 2

b. 3

c. 4

d. 5

e. 6

8. Alexia bought three pounds of chocolate. She plans to distribute the chocolate to her classmates. How many $\frac{1}{4}$-pound pieces can Alexia make from the three pounds of chocolate? Mark your answer in the circles in the grid.

9. Within three hours after the polls opened, $\frac{3}{8}$ of the registered voters had voted in the presidential election. A news report stated that 80% of the registered voters were expected to vote. What percent are still expected to vote? Mark your answer in the circles in the grid.

10. Which expressions show how to find the sale price of a $250 car stereo that is being offered at 25% discount?

I. $0.25 \times \$250$

II. $0.75 \times \$250$

III. $(1 + 0.25) \times \$250$

IV. $(1 - 0.25) \times \$250$

a. I and III

b. I and IV

c. II and III

d. II and IV

e. III and IV

11. A summary of Palvik's paycheck is shown below. What percent of Palvik's gross earnings goes to paying taxes? Round your answer to the nearest whole percent.

Gross Earnings	$2,000.00
Federal Tax	$300.00
State Tax	$100.00
Social Security Tax	$124.00
Medical Insurance	$150.00
Net Earnings	$1,326.00

a. 34%
b. 26%
c. 20%
d. 15%
e. 11%

12. In New York City, two out of every five people surveyed bicycle to work. Out of a population sample of 200,000 people, how many bicycle to work?
a. 4,000
b. 8,000
c. 40,000
d. 80,000
e. 100,000

13. Lena's Touch of Italy recently raised the price of lasagna from $14.00 to $15.50. To the nearest whole percent, by what percent has the price increased?
a. 11%
b. 14%
c. 15%
d. 18%
e. 21%

Measurement and Geometry

14. What is the approximate distance from New Orleans to Biloxi, MS?
a. 135 centimeters
b. 135 meters
c. 135 millimeters
d. 135 kilometers
e. 135 liters

15. On Sundays, Mike gives half-hour drum lessons from 10:30 A.M. to 5:30 P.M. He takes a half-hour lunch break at noon. If Mike is paid $20 for each lesson, what is the total amount he makes on Sunday?
a. $260
b. $190
c. $170
d. $140
e. $110

16. Jamal bought 2 feet of material for a costume. The price of the material is $.80 per yard. What fraction of a yard did Jamal purchase?
a. $\frac{3}{2}$
b. $\frac{2}{3}$
c. $\frac{2}{5}$
d. $\frac{5}{2}$
e. $\frac{1}{2}$

17. If Ming walks at a rate of 4.5 miles per hour, how many miles can she walk in 5 hours? Mark your answer in the circles in the grid.

	/	/	/	
●	●	●	●	●
⓪	⓪	⓪	⓪	⓪
①	①	①	①	①
②	②	②	②	②
③	③	③	③	③
④	④	④	④	④
⑤	⑤	⑤	⑤	⑤
⑥	⑥	⑥	⑥	⑥
⑦	⑦	⑦	⑦	⑦
⑧	⑧	⑧	⑧	⑧
⑨	⑨	⑨	⑨	⑨

18. You borrow $7,000 from Washington Bank to buy a new car. You agree to pay the entire amount owed, including interest, as one payment at the end of 15 months. About how much must you pay the bank at that time?

Washington Bank Car Loan Rate

Type of car

New 5%

Used 8%

All rates are computed as simple interest.

a. $7,842.25
b. $7,437.50
c. $7,180.94
d. $7,120.30
e. $7,074.75

19. Pierre wants to reduce an 8″ × 10″ vertical photograph to wallet size. At most, the copy can be 4 inches high. At this height, what will be the width of the copy?

10 in.

8 in.

Original Photograph

4 in.

?

Wallet-Size Copy

a. 2.4 inches
b. 2.8 inches
c. 3.1 inches
d. 3.2 inches
e. 3.7 inches

20. A map of Nevada has the following scale: 0.5 inches = 15 miles. Which expression tells the actual distance, d, between points that are 5.25 inches apart on the map?

a. $\frac{0.5}{15} = \frac{5.25}{d}$
b. $\frac{15}{0.5} = \frac{5.25}{d}$
c. $\frac{0.5}{d} = \frac{15}{5.25}$
d. $\frac{d}{2.5} = \frac{0.5}{15}$
e. $\frac{d}{15} = \frac{0.5}{5.25}$

21. A CD plays 75 minutes of music. Which expression can be used to find the maximum number of songs, s, that can be recorded on one CD if the average length of a recorded song is 2 minutes 20 seconds?

a. $s = 75 \div 2.2$
b. $s = 75 \times 2.2$
c. $s = 75 \div 2\frac{1}{5}$
d. $s = 75 \times 2\frac{1}{3}$
e. $s = 75 \div 2\frac{1}{3}$

22. The measure of ∠*ABC* is 55.3°. What is the measure in degrees of an angle that is the complement to ∠*ABC*?

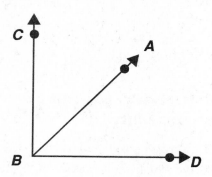

Mark your answer in the circles in the grid.

```
        ⊘  ⊘  ⊘
  ⊙  ⊙  ⊙  ⊙  ⊙
  0  0  0  0  0
  1  1  1  1  1
  2  2  2  2  2
  3  3  3  3  3
  4  4  4  4  4
  5  5  5  5  5
  6  6  6  6  6
  7  7  7  7  7
  8  8  8  8  8
  9  9  9  9  9
```

23. Annie is making a memory quilt for her grandmother. One of the quilt pieces is shown here. Which expression tells you how to find the measure in degrees of ∠*x*?

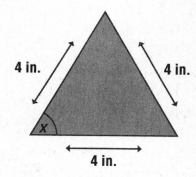

a. $(3 \times 4) \div 360$
b. $(3 \times 4) \div 3$
c. $180 \div 3$
d. $180 \div (3 \times 4)$
e. $180 \div 4$

24. Which is the best estimate of the length of side *AB*?

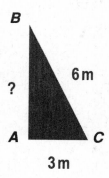

a. less than 3 meters
b. equal to 3 meters
c. between 3 and 6 meters
d. equal to 6 meters
e. greater than 6 meters

25. Molly is using square tiles measuring 8 inches on each side to cover the floor of a pantry. Which expression tells the number of tiles needed if the pantry is 6 feet long and 4 feet wide?

a. $(6 \times 4) \times (\frac{2}{3} \div \frac{2}{3})$

b. $(6 + 4) \div (\frac{2}{3})$

c. $(6 + 4) \div (\frac{2}{3} \times \frac{2}{3})$

d. $(6 \times 4) \div (\frac{2}{3})$

e. $(6 \times 4) \div (\frac{2}{3} \times \frac{2}{3})$

26. Travis is making a concrete driveway. The rectangular driveway is 25 feet long and 16 feet wide; the concrete will be 6 inches thick. Which expression gives the number of cubic feet of concrete Travis will need?

a. $25 \times 16 \times 0.5$

b. $25 \times 16 \times 0.6$

c. $25 \times 16 \times 0.12$

d. $25 \times 16 \times 2$

e. $25 \times 16 \times 6$

27. The coordinates of three vertices of a parallelogram are $(-3,-2)$, $(-1,2)$, and $(3,2)$. Plot the fourth vertex on the coordinate plane grid.

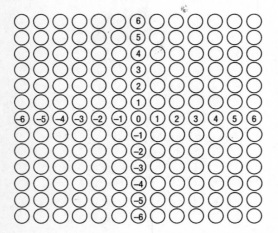

28. Two points are on a graphed line: $(5,1)$ and $(2,0)$. Which expression gives the slope of this line?

a. $(5 - 1) \div (2 - 0)$

b. $(2 - 1) \div (5 - 0)$

c. $(5 - 2) \div (1 - 2)$

d. $(1 - 0) \div (5 - 2)$

e. none of the above

Data Analysis, Statistics, and Probability

29. On two 100-point math exams, Haley scored 80 and 100. If she scores 90 on the next exam, which of the following data measures would change: mean, median, mode, or range?

a. mean only

b. median only

c. mode only

d. range only

e. none will change

30. Avi's final math grade is based on his scores on four tests. To get an A, Avi needs an average test score of 88 or higher. His scores for the first three tests are:

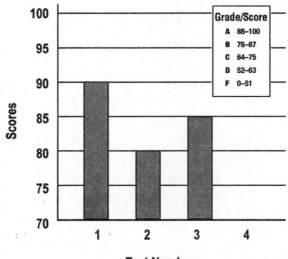

What is the lowest score Avi can get on the fourth test and still earn an A?

a. 99
b. 97
c. 95
d. 93
e. 91

Use the following information and graph to answer questions 31 and 32.

The Tibetan Tea House sells hot and iced tea. The graph shows how average total sales of each drink depend on the outdoor average temperature.

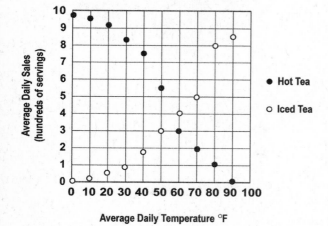

31. At approximately what temperature are the sales of iced tea and hot tea equal?

a. 30° F
b. 40° F
c. 50° F
d. 55° F
e. 60° F

32. Which is the best estimate of hot tea sales at a temperature of 45° F?

a. about 3 servings
b. about 3.5 servings
c. about 6.5 servings
d. about 65 servings
e. about 650 servings

Use the following information and line graph to answer questions 33 and 34.

Brenna took an eight-hour road trip. She made a line graph to show the distance she traveled.

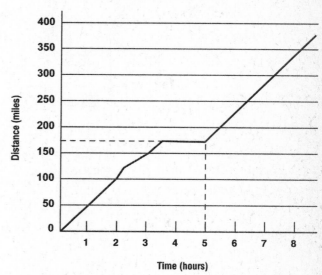

33. What was Brenna's average speed during the first five hours?

   a. 55 mph

   b. 45 mph

   c. 35 mph

   d. 30 mph

   e. Not enough information is given.

34. How far did Brenna travel during the first hour of her trip?

   a. about 10 miles

   b. about 25 miles

   c. about 50 miles

   d. about 65 miles

   e. about 85 miles

35.

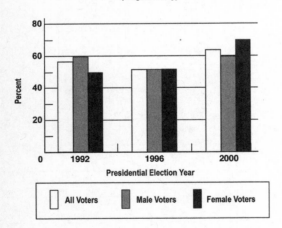

Percent of Registered Voters
Voting in Presidential Elections
(Bergen County)

In 2000, there were 40,400 registered male voters in Bergen County. That same year, there were 36,200 registered female voters. About how many more women voted that year than men?

   a. about 4,000

   b. about 3,000

   c. about 2,000

   d. about 1,000

   e. Not enough information is given.

Use the following pie chart to answer questions 36–38.

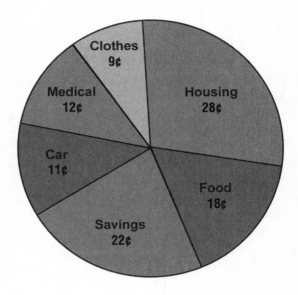

Ricardo's Budget
(cents per $1.00)

36. For which item does Ricardo spend half as much as he puts in his savings account?

   a. car

   b. clothes

   c. housing

   d. food

   e. Not enough information is given.

37. For which two items does Ricardo spend 50% of each budgeted dollar?

   a. savings and housing

   b. clothes and housing

   c. car and medical

   d. medical and food

   e. savings and car

38. Last year, Ricardo made $46,500. About how much more did he spend on housing during the year than he put away in savings?
   a. $2,000
   b. $2,600
   c. $2,800
   d. $3,000
   e. $3,200

39. Hillary, Mark, and Jomarie are attending a benefit. A drawing will be held for a door prize for all of those attending. If 390 people attend the benefit, what is the probability that Hillary, Mark, or Jomarie will win the door prize?
   a. $\frac{1}{3}$
   b. $\frac{1}{13}$
   c. $\frac{1}{39}$
   d. $\frac{1}{130}$
   e. $\frac{1}{180}$

40. During a basketball game, Jack has made 20 free-throw shots out of his 50 tries. How many of his next 25 free-throw attempts is Jack most likely to make?
   a. 5
   b. 10
   c. 15
   d. 20
   e. 25

Algebra, Functions, and Patterns

41. What is the value of j in the formula $j = 2(4h - 3w)^2$ where $h = 3$ and $w = 2$? Mark your answer in the circles in the grid.

42. On an exam, Bart is asked to choose two ways to determine $n\%$ of 40. He is given these four choices:
   I. $n \div 100 \times 40$
   II. $(n \times 0.01) \times 40$
   III. $(n \times 100) \div 40$
   IV. $(n \div 0.01) \times 40$
   Which two ways are correct?
   a. I and II
   b. I and IV
   c. II and III
   d. II and IV
   e. III and IV

43. Terrell is paying a math tutor a $30 one-time fee plus $40 per hour for time spent tutoring. Which of the following equations tells how to find x, the total amount Terrell will be charged for h hours?

   a. $x = \$30h + \$40$

   b. $x = \$30 + \$40h$

   c. $x = (\$30 + \$40)h$

   d. $x = \$30h - \$40$

   e. $x = (\$30 - \$40)h$

44. Which expression gives the area of this triangle?

3x

4x

   a. $7x$

   b. $12x$

   c. $6x^2$

   d. $12x^2$

   e. $12x^3$

45. Serena has to choose between two jobs. One is at Books R Us and pays $18,000 with yearly raises of $800. The other, at Readers Galore, pays $16,400 per year with yearly raises of $1,200. In how many years will the two yearly salaries be equal?

   a. 6

   b. 5

   c. 4

   d. 3

   e. 2

46. When you know the temperature in degrees Celsius (°C), the formula that tells you how to find degrees in Fahrenheit (°F) is $°F = \frac{9°}{5} C + 32°$. According to the formula, which of the following is NOT true?

   a. $212° \text{ F} = 100° \text{ C}$

   b. $86° \text{ F} = 30° \text{ C}$

   c. $50° \text{ F} = 10° \text{ C}$

   d. $32° \text{ F} = 0° \text{ C}$

   e. $0° \text{ F} = 32° \text{ C}$

47. Bernie's monthly rent is r. For each day he pays the rent before it is due, he is given a small discount. Which equation tells how the value of r depends on the value of d, the number of days early that Bernie pays his rent?

d	0	1	2	3	4
r	$485	$482	$479	$476	$473

   a. $r = \$485d - \$3$

   b. $r = (\$485 + \$3)d$

   c. $r = (\$485 - \$3)d$

   d. $r = \$485 + 3d$

   e. $r = \$485 - \$3d$

48. The point (2,2) is on a line that passes through the origin (0,0). What is the point on this line that has a *y*-coordinate of –5? Mark your answer on the following coordinate plane grid.

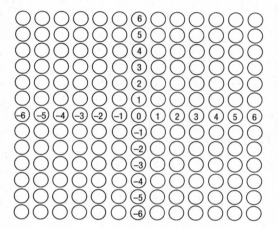

49. The simple interest formula is interest earned = principal × rate × time, or *I* = *prt*. Maria leaves $3,500 in the bank for 1 year and 6 months. If the total interest earned is $210, what is the interest rate?

a. 2%

b. 3%

c. 4%

d. 5%

e. 6%

50. Crystal keeps her winter clothes in two storage boxes during the hotter months. Each edge of the larger box, including the height, is 1.25 yards long. Each edge of the smaller box is 1 yard long or high. By about what percent is the volume of the larger box greater than the volume of the smaller box?

a. 150%

b. 95%

c. 66%

d. 50%

e. 33%

Now, check your answers on page 142.

1 ▶ Numbers and Operations

THIS CHAPTER COVERS the basics of numbers and operations. Basic problem solving in mathematics is rooted in number math facts. Your ability to work with numbers depends on how quickly and accurately you can do simple mathematical computations.

► **Numbers and Operations Pretest**

1. $10 - 5 + 2 =$
   a. 3
   b. −3
   c. −7
   d. 7
   e. 10

2. $32 - 40 \div 4 =$
   a. −2
   b. −18
   c. 22
   d. 12
   e. 42

3. Estimate the answer to the nearest 10:
   $7 + (4 + 52) \times (4 + 3) =$
   a. 70
   b. 390
   c. 400
   d. 440
   e. 2,740

4. Which choice shows the prime factorization of 60?
   a. $3 \times 4 \times 5$
   b. 6×10
   c. $6 \times (8 + 2)$
   d. 1×60
   e. $2 \times 2 \times 3 \times 5$

5. Find the greatest common factor of 20 and 30.
   a. 60
   b. 20
   c. 5
   d. 600
   e. 10

6. Find the least common multiple of 40 and 50.
   a. 10
   b. 5
   c. 100
   d. 200
   e. 2,000

7. Which choice shows an example of the distributive property?
   a. $7 \times (8 \times 6) = (7 \times 8) \times 6$
   b. $7(40 + 8) = 7 \times 40 + 7 \times 8$
   c. $7 \times 48 = 48 \times 7$
   d. $7(40 + 8) = 7 \times 20 + 7 \times 28$
   e. $7 \times 40 + 8 = 7 \times (40 + 8)$

8. $100 \div 5 + |{-5} \times 3| =$
   a. 35
   b. 75
   c. 5
   d. 45
   e. $33\frac{1}{3}$

9. Which choice shows an example of the associative property?
   a. $12 + (49 + 51) = (49 + 51) + 12$
   b. $49 + (51 + 12) = (49 + 51) + 12$
   c. $49 + (51 + 12) = 49 + 51 + (49 + 12)$
   d. $12 + 49 + 51 = 51 + 49 + 12$
   e. $12(49 + 51) = 12 \times 49 + 12 \times 51$

10. Which example shows the commutative property?
   a. $29 \times 7 \times 21 = (29 \times 7) \times 7 \times 21$
   b. $(29 \times 7) \times 21 = 29 \times (7 \times 21)$
   c. $29 \times 7 \times 21 = 29 \times 21 \times 7$
   d. $29 \times 7 \times 21 = 203 \times 21$
   e. $29(7 + 21) = 29 \times 7 + 29 \times 21$

11. Which of the following will result in an even-number answer?

a. 3×7

b. $2 + 3$

c. 5×9

d. $7 + 5$

e. 1×7

12. $|3 \times -7| =$

a. -21

b. -4

c. 4

d. 10

e. 21

Now, check your answers on page 146.

▶ Whole Numbers and Their Place Value

Whole numbers are the counting numbers and zero: 0, 1, 2, 3, 4, 5, 6, 7, 8, 9, . . . Whole numbers are also sometimes called **digits**.

Each digit has a specific value. The position, or place, of a digit in a number written in standard form determines the value the digit represents.

PLACE (UNDERLINED)	NAME OF POSITION
1,00<u>0</u>	ones
1,0<u>0</u>0	tens
1,<u>0</u>00	hundreds
<u>1</u>,000	thousands
1,<u>0</u>00,000	ten thousands
1,<u>0</u>00,000	hundred thousands
<u>1</u>,000,000	millions
1,0<u>0</u>0,000,000	ten millions
1,<u>0</u>00,000,000	hundred millions
<u>1</u>,000,000,000	billions

The number 543,210 has a 5 in the hundred thousands place, a 4 in the ten thousands place, a 3 in the thousands place, a 2 in the hundreds place, a 1 in the tens place, and a 0 in the ones place.

The **expanded form** of a number is the sum (addition) of its various place values: $500,000 + 40,000 + 3,000 + 200 + 10 + 0$.

▶ Rounding Whole Numbers

On the GED, you may be asked to estimate your answer, which means to find an approximate answer. You can estimate by using **rounded numbers**. Numbers can be rounded to different place values. For example, to round to the nearest ten means to find the closest number having all zeros to the right of the tens place.

TO THE NEAREST . . .	TEN	HUNDRED	THOUSAND
27,239 rounds to	27,240	27,200	27,000
691 rounds to	690	700	1,000
38 rounds to	40	0	0

When the digit 5, 6, 7, 8, or 9 appears to the right of the place you are rounding to, round up. When the digit 0, 1, 2, 3, or 4 appears to the right of the place you are rounding to, round down.

▶ Whole Number Addition and Subtraction

Addition is used when you need to combine amounts. The answer in an addition problem is called the **sum** or **total**.

It is helpful to stack the numbers in a column when adding. Be sure to line up the place-value columns and to work from right to left, starting with the ones column.

Example

20 + 529 + 24 =

First, align the numbers you want to add on the ones column. Because it is necessary to work from right to left, begin to add starting with the ones column. The ones column equals 13, so write the 3 in the ones column and regroup or carry the 1 to the tens column:

$$
\begin{array}{r}
{}^{1} \\
20 \\
529 \\
+\ 24 \\
\hline
3
\end{array}
$$

Now, add the tens column, including the regrouped 1.

$$
\begin{array}{r}
{}^{1} \\
20 \\
529 \\
+\ 24 \\
\hline
73
\end{array}
$$

Finally, add the hundreds column. Because there is only one value, write the 5 in the answer.

$$
\begin{array}{r}
{}^{1} \\
20 \\
529 \\
+\ 24 \\
\hline
573
\end{array}
$$

Subtraction is used when you want to find the difference between amounts. Write the greater number on top, and align the amounts on the ones column. You may also need to regroup as you subtract. The answer in subtraction is called the **difference**.

Example

Find the difference between 36 and 75.

Start with the ones column. Because 5 is less than the number being subtracted (6), regroup or borrow a

10 from the tens column, leaving 6 tens. Add the regrouped amount to the ones column. Now, determine 15 – 6 in the ones column.

$$
\begin{array}{r}
{}^{6}{}^{1} \\
\cancel{7}5 \\
-\ 36 \\
\hline
9
\end{array}
$$

Regrouping 1 ten from the tens column left 6 tens. Subtract 3 from 6, and write the result in the tens column of your answer.

$$
\begin{array}{r}
{}^{6}{}^{1} \\
\cancel{7}5 \\
-\ 36 \\
\hline
39
\end{array}
$$

▶ Whole Number Multiplication and Division

In **multiplication**, you combine the same amount multiple times. In some cases, multiplication can be used instead of addition. For example, instead of adding 60 four times, 60 + 60 + 60 + 60, you could simply multiply 60 by 4. If a problem asks you to find the **product** of two or more numbers, you should multiply.

Example

Find the product of 12 and 16.

Line up the place value as you write up the problem in columns. Multiply the ones of the top number by the ones of the bottom number: $2 \times 6 = 12$. Write the 2 in the ones place in the first partial product. Regroup the 10.

$$
\begin{array}{r}
{}^{1} \\
12 \\
\times\ 16 \\
\hline
2
\end{array}
$$

Multiply the tens place in the top number by 6: $6 \times 1 = 6$. Then add the regrouped amount: $6 + 1 = 7$. Write the 7 in the tens column of the partial product.

$$
\begin{array}{r}
1 \\
12 \\
\times\,16 \\
\hline
72
\end{array}
$$

Now multiply by the tens place of 16. Write a placeholder 0 in the ones place in the second partial product, because you're really multiplying the top number by 10. Then multiply the top number by 1: $1 \times 2 = 2$. Write 2 in the partial product next to the zero. Multiply 1 by the top number in the tens place: $1 \times 1 = 1$. Your total second partial product is 120.

$$
\begin{array}{r}
12 \\
\times\,16 \\
\hline
72 \\
120
\end{array}
$$

Add 72 and 120. Your answer is 192.

In **division**, the answer is called the **quotient**. The number you are dividing by is called the divisor and the number being divided is the dividend. The operation of division is finding how many equal parts an amount can be divided into.

Example

Find the quotient of 72 divided by 3.

Set up a long division problem with 3 as the divisor and 72 as the dividend:

$$3\overline{)72}$$

What times 3 equals 7, or a whole number closest to 7? $3 \times 2 = 6$, so this is your best choice. Write a 2

over the 7 in the dividend. $7 - 6 = 1$, which is the remainder. Bring down the 2.

$$
\begin{array}{r}
2 \\
3\overline{)72} \\
6 \\
\hline
12
\end{array}
$$

What times 3 equals 12? $3 \times 4 = 12$. Write a 4 over the 2 in the dividend.

$$
\begin{array}{r}
24 \\
3\overline{)72} \\
6 \\
\hline
12 \\
12 \\
\hline
0
\end{array}
$$

The quotient of 72 divided by 3 is 24.

▶ Choosing an Operation

Often a problem will tell you exactly which operation you should do. However, sometimes you will have to translate the words in a word problem into the operations. Look for these clues when you have to choose the operations.

You add (+) when you are asked to

- find a sum
- find a total
- combine amounts

Key words to look for:

- sum
- total
- all together

You subtract (−) when you are asked to

- find a difference
- take away an amount
- compare quantities

  Key words to look for:

- difference
- take away
- how many more than
- how many fewer than
- how much less than
- how much is left over

You multiply (×, ×) when you are asked to

- find a product
- add the same number over and over

  Key words to look for:

- product
- times

You divide (÷) when you are asked to

- find a quotient
- split an amount into equal parts

  Key words to look for:

- quotient
- per

Examples

1. Add the product of 6 and 3 to the sum of 10 and 4.

To solve this problem, begin by translating the words into math symbols. You know from the list of clues that the word *product* indicates multiplication. So you will need to multiply 6 and 3. You also know that *sum* indicates addition. You could write the problem like this: $6 \times 3 + 10 + 4$.

Now, follow the order of operations. Multiply 6 and 3: $18 + 10 + 4$.

Add in order from left to right: $28 + 4 = 32$. The answer is 32.

2. Missy and Amy went to a movie at the theater. They shared a large popcorn. Each girl paid for her own drink. The movie cost $6.25. The popcorn cost $4.50. Each drink cost $2. How much did each girl pay?

Begin by translating the words into math symbols. The cost of the popcorn should be divided between the two girls. So, each girl paid the following: $6.25 + ($4.50 ÷ 2) + $2.

Now, follow the order of operations. Do operations in parentheses first: $6.25 + ($2.25) + $2. Add in order from left to right: $8.50 + $2 = $10.50.

Each girl paid $10.50 for the movie and refreshments.

> **GED Tip**
> Addition and subtraction are *inverse operations*. (They undo each other; for example, if 3 + 6 = 9, then 9 − 6 = 3 and 9 − 3 = 6.) Multiplication and division are also inverse operations. (They also undo each other; for example, if 30 ÷ 6 = 5, then 5 × 6 = 30.) So, when addition is on the variable side of the equation, you should subtract to isolate the variable. When you see subtraction on the variable side, you should add. When you see multiplication, you should divide, and when you see division, you should multiply to isolate the variable. Got it? (For more on variables, see Chapter 6.)

▶ Odd and Even Numbers

An **even number** is a number that can be divided by the number 2: 2, 4, 6, 8, 10, 12, 14, . . . An **odd number** cannot be divided by the number 2: 1, 3, 5, 7, 9, 11, 13, . . . The even and odd numbers listed are also examples of consecutive even numbers and consecutive odd numbers, because they differ by two.

Here are some helpful rules for how even and odd numbers behave when added or multiplied:

even + even = even	and	even × even = even
odd + odd = even	and	odd × odd = odd
odd + even = odd	and	even × odd = even

▶ Order of Operations

The basic operations of real numbers include addition, subtraction, multiplication, division, and exponentiation. Often, in expressions, there are grouping symbols—usually shown as parentheses—which are used to make a mathematical statement clear. In math, there is a predefined order in which you perform operations. This is an agreed-upon order that must be used. For the five basic operations, the order is:

- First, perform all operations enclosed in parentheses.
- Second, evaluate all exponents. (See Chapter 5 for a discussion of exponents.)
- Third, perform any multiplication and division, in order, working from left to right.
- Finally, evaluate any addition and subtraction, in order, working from left to right.

GED Tip
The order of operations rules can be remembered by the visual aid:

P parentheses
E exponents
MD multiplication and division
AS addition and subtraction
or by the verbal clue: **P**lease **E**xcuse **M**y **D**ear **A**unt **S**ally.

Examples

1. $8 + 15 \times 3$

There are no parentheses or exponents, so evaluate multiplication first: $15 \times 3 = 45$. Now perform the addition: $8 + 45 = 53$.

2. $7 + 24 \div 6 \times 10$

There are no parentheses or exponents, so evaluate multiplication and division from left to right. First, do the division: $24 \div 6 = 4$. Next, perform multiplication: $4 \times 10 = 40$. Finally, perform addition: $7 + 40 = 47$.

3. $(36 + 64) \div (18 - 20)$

First, evaluate the parentheses, from left to right: $(36 + 64) = 100$ and $(18 - 20) = -2$. Now, do the division: $100 \div -2 = -50$.

▶ Properties of Real Numbers

Real numbers are all numbers, positive and negative, on the number line: . . . , $-3, -2, -1, 0, 1, 2, 3,$ . . . (See the next section for an explanation of number lines.)

The real numbers share properties with which you should be familiar. These properties allow you to change the rules for the order of operations. They can be used to increase speed and accuracy when doing mental math. These properties are also used extensively in algebra when solving equations (for algebra information, see Chapter 6).

Two properties, the commutative and associative properties, deal with expressions that involve a string of all addition operations or a string of all multiplication operations. These properties are for addition and multiplication only.

The **commutative property** states that when performing a string of addition operations or a string of multiplication operations, the order does not matter: $a + b = b + a$.

Recall that the order of operations directs you to add or multiply working from left to right.

When you balance your checkbook and have to add up a string of outstanding checks, you can list them all and use the commutative property to arrive at the total by changing the order of addends to add pairs whose ones digits add to 10.

Example

$17 + 64 + 35 + 43 + 96 =$

Change the order: $17 + 43 + 64 + 96 + 35$.

Add 17 and 43 first, because $7 + 3 = 10$:

$17 + 43 = 60$.

The problem becomes $60 + 64 + 96 + 35$.

Add 64 and 96 next, because $4 + 6 = 10$:

$64 + 96 = 160$.

The problem becomes $60 + 160 + 35$.

Work left to right: $60 + 160 + 35 = 220$

$+ 35 = 255$.

In the same way, the commutative property is helpful when multiplying several numbers terms. Change the order to find pairs of numbers whose product would be 10, 100, or 1,000.

Example

$4 \times 2 \times 70 \times 50 \times 25 =$

Change the order to: $4 \times 25 \times 2 \times 50 \times 70$.

Multiply 4 and 25 first: $4 \times 25 = 100$.

The problem becomes $100 \times 2 \times 50 \times 70$.

Multiply 2 and 50 together: $2 \times 50 = 100$.

The problem becomes $100 \times 100 \times 70$.

Finish left to right: $10,000 \times 70 = 700,000$.

The **associative property** is used when grouping symbols are present. This property states that when you perform a string of addition operations or a string of multiplication operations, you can change the grouping: $(a \times b) \times c = a \times (b \times c)$.

Examples

1. $19 + (7 + 16) + 34 =$

Change grouping to add 16 and 34 first, because $6 + 4 = 10$: $19 + 7 + (16 + 34)$.

Evaluate the parentheses: $16 + 34 = 50$.

The problem becomes $19 + 7 + 50$.

Finish, working left to right: $19 + 7 = 26$,

then $26 + 50 = 76$.

2. $15 \times (8 \times 20) \times 5 =$

Change grouping to multiply 20 and 5 first, because $20 \times 5 = 100$: $15 \times 8 \times (20 \times 5)$.

Evaluate parentheses first: $20 \times 5 = 100$.

The problem becomes $15 \times 8 \times 100$.

Finish, working left to right: $15 \times 8 = 120$,

then $120 \times 100 = 12,000$.

The **distributive property** states that multiplication distributes over addition or subtraction. It deals with two operations—multiplication and addition or multiplication and subtraction. The equation $5(10 + 2)$ $= 5(12) = 60$ could also be evaluated as $5(10 + 2) = 5 \times 10 + 5 \times 2 = 50 + 10 = 60$.

The distributive property makes it easy to solve certain math problems quickly.

Example

$17 \times 5 =$

You know that $7 + 10 = 17$: $17 \times 5 = 5(10 + 7)$.

Use the distributive property: $5 \times 10 + 5 \times 7$.

Follow the order of operations: $50 + 35 = 85$.

► Number Lines and Signed Numbers

A **signed number** is a number with a positive (+) or a negative (−) sign in front of it. Any number can have a sign in front of it. If a number has no sign in front of it, it is + (positive).

Signed whole numbers (and zero) make up a group of numbers called **integers**. Integers are often represented on a **number line**. Zero (0) is in the center of the line, and numbers to the left of the zero are negative, while the numbers to the right of zero are positive.

You can use a number line to add and subtract signed whole numbers. Here's how it works.

Example

8 + (–4) =

The number 8 is positive because there is no negative sign in front of it.

Start at zero. Then, move eight units in the positive direction (to the right), as shown here.

The sign in front of the 4 is – (negative). So you need to move four units in the negative direction (to the left) as shown here.

The answer is 4.

Here are some basic rules to help you add, subtract, multiply, and divide signed numbers.

What Sign Is the Answer?

Rule	Example
When adding	
If the numbers have the same sign, just add them together. The answer has the same sign as the numbers being added.	$5 + 6 = 11$ $-5 + (-6) = -11$ $1 + 2 + 3 = 6$ $-1 + (-2) + (-3) = -6$
If two numbers have different signs, subtract the smaller number from the larger one. The answer has the same sign as the larger of the two numbers.	$5 + (-6) = -1$ $-5 + 6 = 1$
If you are adding more than two numbers, add the positive numbers and the negative numbers separately. Then, follow the preceding rule.	$2 + (-5) + (-7) + 4 + 3 = -3:$ $2 + 4 + 3 = 9$ $(-5) + (-7) = -12$ $9 + (-12) = -3$
When subtracting	
Change the sign of the number that follows the minus sign. Then, add. (Notice that two negative signs next to each other make a positive sign.)	$3 - 5 = 3 + (-5) = -2$ $-3 - 5 = -3 + (-5) = -8$ $-3 - (-5) = -3 + (+5) = 2$

(Continued)

What Sign Is the Answer?

Rule	Example
When multiplying	
If you are multiplying two numbers and the numbers have the same sign, then the answer is positive. (This also applies to any even number of numbers being multiplied together.)	$2 \times 6 = 12$ $-2 \times (-6) = 12$
If you are multiplying two numbers and the numbers have the opposite signs, then the answer is negative.	$-2 \times 6 = -12$ $2 \times (-6) = -12$
When multiplying more than two numbers together, two negative signs make a positive sign.	$-2 \times (-6) = 12$ $-1 \times (-2) \times (-3) = -6$ $-1 \times (-2) \times (-3) \times (-4) = 24$
When dividing	
If the numbers have the same sign, then the answer is positive.	$15 \div 3 = 5$ $-15 \div (-3) = 5$
If the numbers have different signs, then the answer is negative.	$-15 \div 3 = -5$ $15 \div (-3) = -5$

▶ Prime and Composite Numbers

A positive integer that is greater than the number 1 is either **prime** or **composite**, but not both. A **factor** is an **integer** that divides evenly into a number.

- A *prime number* has only two factors: itself and the number 1.
  Examples: 2, 3, 5, 7, 11, 13, 17, 19, 23, . . .
- A *composite number* is a number that has more than two factors.
  Examples: 4, 6, 8, 9, 10, 12, 14, 15, 16, . . .
- The number 1 is neither prime nor composite.

Prime factorization is the expression of a positive integer as a product of prime numbers. For example, the prime factor of $72 = 2 \times 2 \times 2 \times 3 \times 3$.

If the same prime factor occurs more than once, it can be written in exponential form. For instance, the prime factorization of 99 is $3 \times 3 \times 11$. It can also be written as $3^2 \times 11$. (See Chapter 5 for a discussion of exponents.)

Prime factorization is usually applied to find the greatest common factor (GCF) or the least common multiple (LCM) of two or more integers.

The **greatest common factor (GCF)** is the greatest factor that divides into two numbers. To find the GCF of two numbers, list the prime factors of each number. Then, multiply together those factors both numbers have in common. If there are no common prime factors, the GCF is 1.

Example

Find the GCF of 18 and 24.

Prime factors of 18: $2 \times 3 \times 3$

Prime factors of 24: $2 \times 2 \times 2 \times 3$

There is one 2 and one 3 in common. The GCF is $2 \times 3 = 6$.

The **least common multiple (LCM)** is the smallest number that divides two numbers. To find the LCM of two or more whole numbers, make a list of multiples for each whole number. Continue your lists until at least two multiples are common to all lists. Identify the common multiples. The LCM is the smallest of these common multiples.

Example

Find the least common multiple of 4 and 10.

4: 4, 8, 12, 16, 20, 24, . . .

10: 10, 20, 30, 40, . . .

The LCM of 4 and 10 is 20.

don't get

▶ Absolute Value

The **absolute value** of a number or expression is its numerical value without regard to its sign. The absolute value is always positive because it is the *distance* of a number from zero on a number line. Absolute value is indicated by the symbol | before and after the number or expression.

Example

$|-1| = 1$

$|2 - 4| = |-2| = 2$

For order of operations, the absolute value symbol is treated at the same level as parentheses.

Example

$5 \times |-13 + 3|$

First, evaluate the expression inside the absolute value symbol: $5 \times |-10|$.

Second, evaluate the absolute value: 5×10.

Now, perform the multiplication: $5 \times 10 = 50$.

▶ Numbers and Operations Posttest

1. $25 + 15 \times 3 =$
   a. 120
   b. 30
   c. 15
   d. 70
   e. $13\frac{1}{3}$

2. $8 - 10 \div 2 =$
   a. −1
   b. 1
   c. 3
   d. −3
   e. 9

$10 \div 2 = 5$
$8 - 5 = 3$

3. $5 \times (6 + 19) =$
   a. 49
   b. 125
   c. 115
   d. 5
   e. −5

$6 + 19 = 25$
$5 \times 25 = 125$

4. $12 + 144 \div (8 + 4) =$
   a. 24
   b. 16
   c. 144
   d. 32
   e. 34

$8 + 4 = 12$
$12 \overline{)144} = 12$
$12 + 12 = 24$

5. $120 \div 5 \times -2 =$
   a. 12
   b. −50
   c. −48
   d. 48
   e. 50

$5 \times -2 = -10$
$120 \div 10 = -12$

6. Which example shows the prime factorization of 90?

　a. 9×10

　b. 90×1

　c. $2 \times 3 \times 3 \times 5$

　d. $2 \times 5 \times 9$

　e. $3 \times 3 \times 10$

7. Which choice shows an example of the distributive property?

　a. $5 \times 27 = 27 \times 5$

　b. $5(20 + 7) = 5 \times 20 + 5 \times 7$

　c. $5 \times (9 \times 3) = (5 \times 9) \times 3$

　d. $5(20 + 7) = 2 \times 15 + 5 \times 7$

　e. $5 \times 20 + 7 = 5 \times (20 + 7)$

8. What is the greatest common factor of 48 and 120?

　a. 12

　b. 2

　c. 240

　d. 3

　e. 24

9. What is the least common multiple of 20 and 30?

　a. 20

　b. 30

　c. 600

　d. 60

　e. 10

10. Estimate the answer to the nearest ten: $35 - 5 + 7 =$

　a. 20

　b. 30

　c. 35

　d. 40

　e. 50

11. Which of the following will result in an odd-number answer?

　a. $36 + 48$

　b. 20×8

　c. $37 + 47$

　d. 7×12

　e. $13 + 12$

12. $-25 \div |9 - 4| =$

　a. -30

　b. -20

　c. -5

　d. 5

　e. 13

Now, check your answers on page 147.

2 ▶ Fractions and Decimals

FRACTIONS AND DECIMALS are the most common ways that numbers are represented. An understanding of how to perform operations on these types of numbers is essential to your success on the GED.

▶ **Fractions and Decimals Pretest**

1. $\frac{4}{9} - \frac{7}{9} =$
  a. $\frac{3}{9}$
  b. $-\frac{1}{3}$
  c. $-\frac{3}{18}$
  d. $-\frac{11}{9}$
  e. $-\frac{11}{18}$

2. $\frac{8}{15} + \frac{9}{30} =$
  a. $\frac{7}{30}$
  b. $\frac{26}{30}$
  c. $\frac{5}{6}$
  d. $\frac{17}{45}$
  e. $\frac{6}{15}$

3. $2\frac{3}{4} - 3\frac{2}{4} =$
  a. $-\frac{3}{4}$
  b. $-1\frac{1}{4}$
  c. $\frac{3}{4}$
  d. $5\frac{1}{4}$
  e. $6\frac{1}{4}$

4. $\frac{7}{9} \times \frac{3}{4} =$
  a. $\frac{27}{28}$
  b. $\frac{21}{9}$
  c. $\frac{28}{27}$
  d. $\frac{7}{12}$
  e. $\frac{36}{21}$

5. $4\frac{2}{3} \div 6 =$
  a. $\frac{14}{6}$
  b. $\frac{84}{3}$
  c. $24\frac{2}{3}$
  d. 28
  e. $\frac{7}{9}$

6. $\frac{3}{4} \div \frac{7}{8} =$
  a. $\frac{7}{6}$
  b. $\frac{21}{32}$
  c. $\frac{6}{7}$
  d. $\frac{32}{21}$
  e. $\frac{21}{24}$

7. $1{,}036.09 + 2.4 + 17 =$
  a. 1,036.50
  b. 1,055.49
  c. 103.650
  d. 105.549
  e. 1,077.09

8. $26.19 \times 0.3 =$
  a. 7.857
  b. 7,857
  c. 7.837
  d. 7,837
  e. 0.7857

9. Which is greatest?
  a. $\frac{7}{12}$
  b. $\frac{5}{7}$
  c. 0.079
  d. 0.63
  e. 0.0108

10. $540 \div 2.7 =$
  a. 2
  b. 20
  c. 2,000
  d. 0.2
  e. 200

Now, check your answers on page 147.

▶ Writing and Recognizing Fractions

What exactly is a fraction? Imagine that you and a friend order a whole pizza for yourselves. The pizza is cut into nine slices.

If one of you eats the whole pizza and doesn't share with the other one, then you would eat nine of the nine slices, or $\frac{9}{9}$. But what if you ate two slices and your friend ate three slices? Then you ate $\frac{2}{9}$ of the pizza, your friend ate $\frac{3}{9}$ of the pizza, and $\frac{4}{9}$ of the pizza is left over. The numbers $\frac{2}{9}$, $\frac{3}{9}$, and $\frac{4}{9}$ are all fractions.

Notice that **fractions** are two numbers that represent a part of a whole. The two numbers are separated by a bar. The bar means to divide the top number by the bottom number.

The top number is called the **numerator**. The numerator tells you how many parts of the whole are being talked about. For example, $\frac{2}{9}$ of the pizza refers to two slices of a pizza that has been cut into nine slices.

The bottom number in a fraction is called the **denominator**. The denominator tells you how many equal parts the whole has been divided into. The pizza has been divided into nine slices, so the denominator is 9. What if you cut the pizza into eight slices? Then the denominator would be 8.

Think about some other common fractions.

- You use fractions to talk about money. For example, a quarter is 25 cents, or $\frac{1}{4}$ of a dollar. Four quarters, or $\frac{4}{4}$, equal one dollar.
- You also use fractions to talk about time. An hour is a fraction of a day. One hour is $\frac{1}{24}$ of a whole day. One day is a fraction of a week: $\frac{1}{7}$. What fraction of a year is one month?
- Sometimes you'll see fractions in ads. A department store might have a sale of "one-half off" last season's styles. That means that you pay only $\frac{1}{2}$ of the whole original price.

▶ Reducing Fractions to Lowest Terms

The numerator and the denominator of a fraction are called **terms**. On the GED, the directions might ask you *to reduce fractions to lowest terms*. This is the standard and usual way to write fractions.

To reduce a fraction to lowest terms, you need to find a fraction that is equal to the one you have but has a smaller numerator and denominator. Divide both the numerator and the denominator by the same whole number. The whole number must divide evenly into both numbers. Continue to divide the numerator and denominator until there is no number other than 1 that can divide evenly into both numbers. If only 1 can divide into both numbers evenly, then the fraction is said to be reduced to lowest terms.

Examples

1. Reduce $\frac{7}{28}$ to lowest terms.

Begin by thinking of a number that will divide evenly into both the numerator and the denominator. You know that $4 \times 7 = 28$, so you can divide both numbers by 7.

$$\frac{7 \div 7}{28 \div 7} = \frac{1}{4}$$

The fraction $\frac{1}{4}$ is equal to $\frac{7}{28}$. No number other than 1 can divide into both 1 and 4 evenly; so $\frac{1}{4}$ is reduced to lowest terms.

> **GED Tip**
> To reduce a fraction where both the numerator and the denominator end in zero, cross out the same number of zeros in each number. If you cross out one zero in each number, you are dividing by 10. Crossing out two zeros at the end of each number is dividing by 100.
>
> $$\frac{2\cancel{0}}{4\cancel{0}} = \frac{2}{4} = \frac{1}{2} \qquad \frac{3\cancel{00}}{9\cancel{00}} = \frac{3}{9} = \frac{1}{3}$$

2. Reduce $\frac{12}{22}$ to lowest terms.

Both numbers are even, so you can begin by dividing by 2:

$$\frac{12 \div 2}{22 \div 2} = \frac{6}{11}$$

Often when you begin reducing a fraction by dividing by a small number, you will have to divide more than one time. If you can find the largest number that divides into both numbers, you can reduce the fraction faster—often in only one step.

Example

Reduce $\frac{8}{24}$ to lowest terms.

If you begin by dividing by 2, you will have to divide again by 4:

First, divide by 2:
$$\frac{8 \div 2}{24 \div 2} = \frac{4}{12}$$
Then divide by 4:
$$\frac{4 \div 4}{12 \div 4} = \frac{1}{3}$$

If you begin by dividing by 8, you can reduce the fraction in only one step:

$$\frac{8 \div 8}{24 \div 8} = \frac{1}{3}$$

Notice that you get the same answer either way.

► Raising Fractions to Higher Terms

You raise a fraction to higher terms by multiplying both the numerator and the denominator by the same number. For example, if you multiply $\frac{5}{6}$ by $\frac{4}{4}$, you will get $\frac{20}{24}$.

$$\frac{5 \times 4}{6 \times 4} = \frac{20}{24}$$

Both $\frac{5}{6}$ and $\frac{20}{24}$ have the same value; they are equal fractions. You sometimes need to raise a fraction to higher terms when you are comparing fractions. You will also have to raise fractions to higher terms when you are adding and subtracting fractions that have different denominators.

When raising a fraction to higher terms, you will usually need to find an equal fraction with a specific denominator. Here's how to raise a fraction to higher terms with a specific denominator.

Step 1 Divide the denominator of the fraction into the new denominator.

Step 2 Multiply the quotient, or the answer to step 1, by the numerator.

Step 3 Write the product, or the answer to step 2, over the new denominator.

Example

$\frac{1}{3} = \frac{?}{9}$

This problem asks you to raise $\frac{1}{3}$ to 9ths. Divide the denominator into the new denominator, which is 9: $9 \div 3 = 3$.

Multiply 3 by the numerator: $3 \times 1 = 3$.

Write 3 over the new denominator: $\frac{3}{9}$.

► Comparing Fractions

Sometimes you will be asked to compare two or more fractions. You might be asked which of two fractions is larger, for example. Or you could be asked if two fractions are equal. If the two fractions have the same denominator, you simply compare the numerators; the number with the higher numerator is larger.

Example

Which fraction is larger, $\frac{5}{12}$ or $\frac{8}{12}$?
You know that 8 is larger than 5, so $\frac{8}{12}$ is larger than $\frac{5}{12}$.

What if the fractions do not have the same denominator? One way to answer this type of question is to convert both fractions so that they have the same denominator. This is called finding a **common denominator**. If the two fractions have the same denominator, you can compare their numerators.

Example

Which fraction is larger, $\frac{5}{6}$ or $\frac{3}{4}$?

To answer this question, you can raise both fractions to higher terms with a common denominator. First, you need to find a denominator that both 6 and 4 can divide into. You could choose 24 ($6 \times 4 = 24$), but 12 is the **least common denominator (LCD)**. Then raise each fraction to higher terms with the same denominator.

$\frac{5 \times 2}{6 \times 2} = \frac{10}{12}$

$\frac{3 \times 3}{4 \times 3} = \frac{9}{12}$

Then compare the numerators of the two fractions. Because 10 is greater than 9, you know that $\frac{10}{12}$ is larger than $\frac{9}{12}$. This means that $\frac{5}{6}$ is larger than $\frac{3}{4}$.

▶ Operations with Fractions—Overview

To do well when working with fractions, it is necessary to understand some basic concepts. Here are some math rules for fractions using variables:

$\frac{a}{b} \times \frac{c}{d} = (a \times c) \div (b \times d)$

$\frac{a}{b} \div \frac{c}{d} = \frac{a}{b} \times \frac{d}{c} = (a \times d) \div (b \times c)$

$\frac{a}{b} + \frac{c}{d} = (ad + bc) \div bd$

▶ Adding and Subtracting Fractions

How would you add 2 hours and $5? You can't. You can add and subtract only *like* objects: You can add $2 to $5

or 2 hours to 5 hours. It's the same with fractions. To add and subtract fractions, you need **like fractions**. Like fractions are fractions that have the same denominator. If the denominators are already the same, add or subtract the numerators and keep the denominator. Then, simplify if needed.

Example

$\frac{2}{4} - \frac{7}{4} =$

Subtract the numerators: $(2 - 7) = -5$.

Retain the denominator in your final answer: $-\frac{5}{4}$.

When subtracting fractions, the order of the fractions is important. Write the numerator that you are subtracting *from* first. Then subtract as you would any two numbers.

Fractions that have different denominators are called **unlike fractions**. Before you can add or subtract unlike fractions, you first need to change them into like fractions so that they have the same number in the denominator. This is called *finding a common denominator*.

There are two main ways to find a common denominator. One way is to multiply the denominators together. The other way is to multiply each denominator by 2, 3, 4, 5, and so on. Then compare the lists of multiples of each denominator. The numbers that are the same, or that are in common, are common denominators.

Follow these steps when adding or subtracting unlike fractions.

Step 1 Find a common denominator.

Step 2 Change each fraction so that it has the common denominator.

Step 3 Add or subtract the fractions as indicated.

Step 4 Reduce your answer to lowest terms.

Examples

1. $\frac{3}{4} + \frac{3}{24} =$

Find a common denominator. The LCD of 4 and 24 is 24.

Convert the first fraction to have a denominator of 24: $\frac{3}{4} \times \frac{6}{6} = \frac{18}{24}$.

Perform the addition: $\frac{18}{24} + \frac{3}{24} = \frac{21}{24}$.

Finally, simplify: $\frac{7}{8}$.

2. Find a common denominator for $\frac{1}{4}$ and $\frac{1}{6}$.

List the multiples for each denominator.

Multiples of 4: 4, 8, 12, 16, . . .

Multiples of 6: 6, 12, 18, 24, . . .

The numbers 4 and 6 share the multiple 12. So, 12 is a common denominator for $\frac{1}{4}$ and $\frac{1}{6}$. In fact, it is the LCD.

3. Find a common denominator for $\frac{1}{4}$ and $\frac{1}{6}$.

Multiply the denominators together: $4 \times 6 = 24$. So, 24 is a common denominator for $\frac{1}{4}$ and $\frac{1}{6}$. However, it can be reduced to 12, which is the LCD.

▶ Multiplying and Dividing Fractions

You do not need to find a common denominator when multiplying or dividing fractions. In this sense, multiplying and dividing fractions is easier than adding and subtracting them. If you know how to multiply, then you basically already know how to multiply and divide fractions.

To multiply fractions, multiply the numerators and then multiply the denominators. Finally, simplify if needed.

Example

$\frac{5}{3} \times \frac{4}{8} =$

Multiply the numerators and denominators:

$\frac{5 \times 4}{3 \times 8} = \frac{20}{24}$

Simplify your result: $\frac{5}{6}$.

You can simplify your multiplication by *canceling* before multiplying. Like reducing a fraction, canceling involves dividing. If you can see a number that will divide evenly into one of the numerators and one of the denominators of each fraction you are multiplying, then do so. This is canceling.

Example

$\frac{3}{4} \times \frac{2}{3}$

There is a 3 in the numerator of the first fraction and in the denominator of the second fraction. You can cancel by dividing by 3:

$\frac{3\!\!\!/^1}{4} \times \frac{2}{3\!\!\!/_1}$

You have simplified your problem to $\frac{1}{4} \times \frac{2}{1}$. Do you see a way to further simply this problem with canceling? Both 4 and 2 can be divided by 2:

$\frac{1}{4\!\!\!/_2} \times \frac{2\!\!\!/^1}{1}$

So now your multiplication is very easy:

$\frac{1}{2} \times \frac{1}{1} = \frac{1}{2}$.

Dividing fractions is very similar to multiplying fractions. To divide a fraction by another fraction, follow these steps.

Step 1 Invert the second fraction. That is, write the numerator on the bottom and the denominator on the top. The new fraction is the reciprocal of the original fraction.

Step 2 Multiply the two fractions.

Step 3 Write the answer in lowest terms.

Example

$\frac{5}{8} \div \frac{1}{2} =$

Find the reciprocal of $\frac{1}{2}$: $\frac{2}{1}$.

Multiply the first fraction by the reciprocal of the second: $\frac{5}{8} \times \frac{2}{1}$.

Multiply the numerators and denominators: $\frac{5 \times 2}{8 \times 1} = \frac{10}{8}$

Simplify your result: $\frac{5}{4}$.

▶ Improper Fractions

So far, the fractions you have been working with have all been proper fractions. A **proper fraction** is one in which the numerator is smaller than the denominator. These are examples of proper fractions: $\frac{1}{2}$, $\frac{2}{3}$, $\frac{5}{6}$, $\frac{34}{91}$, and so on. Proper fractions are always equal to or less than 1. They represent a part of whole.

The numerator of an **improper fraction** is the same as or greater than its denominator. Here are some examples of improper fractions: $\frac{4}{2}$, $\frac{25}{5}$, $\frac{12}{4}$, $\frac{10}{3}$, and so on. Remember that the bar in a fraction means to divide the top number by the bottom number. Now, look again at the examples of improper fractions.

Let's try dividing the first one: $\frac{4}{2}$. What is $4 \div 2$? Yes, it's 2. So the improper fraction $\frac{4}{2} = 2$. Now you try $\frac{25}{5}$. Do you see that $\frac{25}{5} = 5$? Notice the pattern here. Improper fractions are all equal to or greater than 1.

▶ Mixed Numbers

Many improper fractions are equal to whole numbers. For example, $\frac{4}{2} = 2$ and $\frac{25}{5} = 5$. But some improper fractions are not equal to a whole number. They represent a whole number plus a proper fraction. A whole number plus a proper fraction is called a **mixed number**. Examples of mixed numbers are $1\frac{2}{3}$, $3\frac{1}{2}$, $25\frac{7}{8}$, and so on.

When working with mixed numbers, it is usually easiest to change the mixed number to an improper fraction and then perform the given operations. To convert a mixed number to an improper fraction, multiply the whole number part by the denominator. Add this product to the numerator. This sum is the numerator of the improper fraction. The denominator stays the same.

Example

Convert $5\frac{2}{3}$ to an improper fraction.

Multiply the whole number part by the denominator: $5 \times 3 = 15$.

Add this product to the numerator: $15 + 2 = 17$.

The improper fraction is $\frac{17}{3}$.

To convert an improper fraction to a mixed number, divide the numerator by the denominator. Find the whole number part, and the remainder becomes the numerator of the fractional part of the mixed number. The denominator stays the same.

Example

Convert $\frac{62}{8}$ to a mixed number.

Find how many times 8 divides into 62:

$$\begin{array}{r} 7 \\ 8\overline{)62} \\ 56 \\ \hline 6R \end{array}$$

Find the whole number part: 7.

Find the remainder: 6.

The mixed number is $7\frac{6}{8}$ or $7\frac{3}{4}$.

To perform mixed-number operations, convert to improper fractions.

Example

$2\frac{3}{8} - 5\frac{3}{4} =$

Change to improper fractions: $2\frac{3}{8} - 5\frac{3}{4} = \frac{19}{8} - \frac{23}{4}$.

Find the common denominator: $\frac{19}{8} - \frac{46}{8}$.

Perform the subtraction:

$\frac{19 - 46}{8} = \frac{-27}{8}$

Change the improper fraction to a mixed number (if needed): $\frac{-27}{8} = -3\frac{3}{8}$.

▶ Writing and Recognizing Decimals

If you've ever gone shopping, then you are familiar with decimals, because decimals are often used to represent amounts of money. Like fractions, decimals represent parts of whole numbers. For example, you know that $1.50 is neither one whole dollar nor two whole dollars. It's one dollar and one-half of another dollar, or 1.5 dollars. Another way to write 1.5 is $1\frac{1}{2}$.

▶ How to Read a Decimal

Notice that **decimals** are numbers written with a dot or period either to the far left or somewhere in the middle. The dot is called a **decimal point**. The numbers to the left of the decimal point are whole numbers. Those to the right of the decimal point are fractions, or parts, of whole numbers.

You already know that each digit in the number 1,234 represents a place value, or a position in the number. So, for example, the 1 in 1,234 stands for one thousand. The 2 stands for two hundreds. The 3 stands for three tens. And the 4 stands for four ones. These are the place values that occur to the *left* of a decimal point. Each digit to the *right* of a decimal point also has a place value.

When you see a decimal, here's how to read it.

Step 1   Begin reading from left to right. Read the part of the number that is to the left of the decimal point as you would any other whole number.

Step 2   Read the decimal point as the word *and*.

Step 3   Read the number to the right of the decimal point as you would any other number. But then follow it with the name of the decimal place. You can determine the name of the decimal place by counting the number of digits to the right of the decimal point.

Example

Write out the following decimal in words: 12.304

Begin reading from left to right. Read the part of the number that is to the left of the decimal point as you would any other

whole number. The number to the left of the decimal point is 12. So you would write (or say if you were reading aloud) "twelve."

Read the decimal point as the word *and*. So you would next write "and."

Read the numbers to the right of the decimal point as you would any other similar group of numbers. But then follow with the name of the last decimal place. There are three numbers to the right of the decimal point, so the last place value is called thousandths. You would write "three hundred four thousandths."

So, the decimal 12.304 can be written in the following words: "twelve and three hundred four thousandths."

Decimal numbers are easy to compare and order, when you remember that the place value has meaning. However, trailing zeros to the right of the decimal point are disregarded. In math, 2.4 is the same number as 2.400 because both numbers represent 2 and 4 tenths. A whole number is understood to have a decimal point to the right of the number. For example, 21 = 21. = 21.0 = 21.000. Each expression represents 21 with no remainder.

Notice that the decimal in the example has a zero in the middle: 12.304. This zero happens to be in the hundredths place. It tells you that there are no hundredths in the number. However, there are tenths and thousandths, so the zero serves as a **placeholder** between the 3 and the 4. When a zero falls in between two numbers, it serves as a placeholder, and it affects the value of the number.

To compare decimals, it is best to change each decimal into an equivalent decimal with the same number of decimal places. Try ordering the numbers from least to greatest: .016, 0.7, .203, .75. Because some of the numbers have three places to the right of the decimal point, change each decimal to an equivalent decimal with three decimal places to the right of the decimal point. One of the numbers shows a leading zero; also include this leading zero in all of the numbers:

0.016, 0.700, 0.203, 0.750

Now the decimals can be compared in the same manner as whole numbers, and $16 < 203 < 700 < 750$, so the answer is .016, .203, 0.7, .75.

▶ Adding and Subtracting Decimals

To add decimal numbers, follow these steps:

Step 1 Write the numbers so that the decimal points are lined up.

Step 2 Make all the decimals have the same number of digits to the right of the decimal point by adding trailing zeros to the ends of shorter decimals.

Step 3 Write the decimal point in the answer so that it lines up with the decimal points in the problem.

Step 4 Add the decimals just as you would if you were adding whole numbers.

GED Tip

The position of the decimal point in a number makes a big difference in its value. Always line up the decimal points before adding or subtracting decimals. This will help you put the decimal point in the correct place and get the correct answer.

Example

$9.23 + 6.02 + 1.1 =$

Write the numbers so that the decimal points are lined up:

```
  9.23
  6.02
+ 1.1
```

Make all the decimals have the same number of digits to the right of the decimal point by adding a trailing zero to the end of the shorter decimal:

```
  9.23
  6.02
+ 1.10
```

Write the decimal point in the answer so that it lines up with the decimal points in the problem:

```
  9.23
  6.02
+ 1.10
    .
```

Add the decimals just as you would if you were adding whole numbers to find your answer:

```
  9.23
  6.02
+ 1.10
 16.35
```

To add a whole number and a decimal together, you would follow the same steps.

Example

$12 + 5.013 =$

Write the numbers so that the decimal points are lined up. Insert a decimal point to the right of the whole number:

```
 12.
+ 5.013
```

Make all the decimals have the same number of digits to the right of the decimal point by adding trailing zeros to the end of the shorter decimal:

```
 12.000
+ 5.013
```

Write the decimal point in the answer so that it lines up with the decimal points in the problem:

```
 12.000
+ 5.013
```

.

Add the decimals just as you would if you were adding whole numbers to find your solution:

```
 12.000
+ 5.013
 17.013
```

Setting decimals up for subtraction is very similar to the setup when adding them. To subtract decimals, use the following steps:

Step 1   Write the numbers so that the decimal points are lined up. Insert a decimal point to the right of any whole number.

Step 2   Make all the decimals have the same number of digits to the right of the decimal point by adding trailing zeros to the ends of shorter decimals.

Step 3   Write the decimal point in the answer so that it lines up with the decimal points in the problem.

Step 4   Subtract the decimals just as you would if you were subtracting whole numbers.

Example

$11 - 5.2 =$

Write the numbers so that the decimal points are lined up:

```
 11.
- 5.2
```

Make all the decimals have the same number of digits to the right of the decimal point by adding a trailing zero to the end of the shorter decimal:

```
 11.0
- 5.2
```

Write the decimal point in the answer so that it lines up with the decimal points in the problem:

```
 11.0
- 5.2
```

.

Subtract the decimals, and don't forget to borrow to arrive at the final answer:

```
10 1
1̸1.0
- 5.2
  5.8
```

▶ Multiplying Decimals

If you can multiply whole numbers, then you can multiply decimals. The main thing to watch out for is the placement of the decimal point. Placing the decimal point in your answer is just a matter of counting place values.

When multiplying with decimals, multiply as you would for whole numbers, and ignore the decimal points until after the product is found. After performing the multiplication, count the number of digits after the decimal points (to the right of the decimal point) in both factors being multiplied. This count is the number of decimal places (to the right of the decimal point) that will be in the answer. Start at the rightmost side of the product (the answer) and count to the left the number of digits (the number of digits to the right of the decimal point in both terms) in order to place the decimal point.

Example

$2.48 \times 1.7 =$

Multiply, ignoring the decimal points:

$248 \times 17 = 4,216.$

Determine the digits to the right of the decimal points in the factors: 4, 8, and 7. Starting to the right of the 6 in the answer, move three digits to the left: 4.216.

▶ Dividing Decimals

To divide with decimal numbers, first change the problem to division by a whole number. It may be necessary to move the decimal point in the divisor (the number you are dividing *by*) to make it a whole number. Move the decimal in the dividend (the number you are dividing *into*) the same number of places, and copy the new decimal placeholder straight up into the quotient (the *answer* to the division problem). Once the decimal point is placed, divide as you normally would with long division.

Example

$3.26 \div 0.02 =$

Solve using long division. First move the decimal point two places to the right in each number:

$0.02.\overline{)3.26.}$

GED Tip

Remember, when you add or subtract decimals, you must line up the decimal points in a straight line. You can use the following memory aid to help you remember that often decimal points must be moved when mutiplying or dividing decimals:

Multiply, Divide = Move Decimal

▶ Decimal Operations: Multiplying or Dividing by the Powers of 10

The decimal number system is based on the powers of 10. This makes multiplication and division by 10, 100, 1,000, . . . a matter of moving the decimal point the number of places dictated by the number of zeros in 10, 100, or 1,000. This is because once you add or remove the zeros, you are essentially multiplying or dividing by 1.

To *multiply* a number by 10, move the decimal point one place to the *right*.

To *multiply* a number by 100, move the decimal point two places to the *right*.

To *multiply* a number by 1,000, move the decimal point three places to the *right*.

To *divide* a number by 10, move the decimal point one place to the *left*.

To *divide* a number by 100, move the decimal point two places to the *left*.

To *divide* a number by 1,000, move the decimal point three places to the *left*.

▶ Converting between Fractions and Decimals

To convert a fraction to a decimal, recall that $\frac{1}{4}$ means 1 divided by 4. Divide 1 by 4 to get the decimal equivalent of 0.25. To convert a decimal to a fraction, use the place value names for decimals. Rewrite the decimal as the named fraction, and then simplify the fraction. For example, 0.018 is read as "eighteen thousandths," which is $\frac{18}{1,000}$. Now simplify: $\frac{18}{1,000} \div \frac{2}{2} = \frac{9}{500}$.

▶ Common Fraction and Decimal Equivalents

Although you can always convert a fraction to a decimal by dividing the numerator by the denominator, it's a good idea to know common decimal and fraction equivalents for the GED. Here are some common decimals and fractions you might want to learn.

Decimal and Fraction Equivalents to Know

FRACTION	DECIMAL
$\frac{1}{100}$	0.01
$\frac{1}{10}$	0.1
$\frac{1}{5}$	0.2
$\frac{1}{4}$	0.25
$\frac{1}{3}$	0.33 (rounded)
$\frac{1}{2}$	0.5
$\frac{2}{3}$	0.67 (rounded)
$\frac{3}{4}$	0.75
$\frac{4}{5}$	0.80
$\frac{9}{10}$	0.90

► Fractions and Decimals Posttest

1. $\frac{9}{11} \div \frac{7}{22} =$
   a. $4\frac{1}{2}$
   b. $\frac{9}{2}$
   c. $2\frac{4}{7}$
   d. $2\frac{11}{7}$
   e. $\frac{2}{11}$

2. $1\frac{1}{5} \div \frac{1}{3} =$
   a. $\frac{18}{5}$
   b. $\frac{6}{15}$
   c. $\frac{15}{6}$
   d. $2\frac{1}{2}$
   e. $\frac{2}{5}$

3. $\frac{2}{3} \div \frac{5}{6} =$
   a. $\frac{10}{18}$
   b. $\frac{18}{10}$
   c. $\frac{15}{18}$
   d. $\frac{20}{36}$
   e. $\frac{4}{5}$

4. Which is greatest?
   a. $\frac{5}{8}$
   b. $\frac{17}{20}$
   c. $\frac{1}{2}$
   d. $\frac{7}{10}$
   e. $\frac{4}{5}$

5. Which is smallest?
   a. $\frac{1}{3}$
   b. $\frac{2}{6}$
   c. $\frac{5}{12}$
   d. $\frac{1}{2}$
   e. $\frac{1}{4}$

6. $34.7 + 4.1 + 0.03 =$
   a. 391
   b. 3.91
   c. 38.83
   d. 39.1
   e. 41.8

7. $125.05 - 11.4 =$
   a. 123.91
   b. 123.01
   c. 113.01
   d. 113.65
   e. 114.65

8. $16.8 \times 0.2 =$
  a. 3.36
  b. 336
  c. 0.336
  d. 33.6
  e. 3.28

10. $42.19 \times 0.4 =$
  a. 168.19
  b. 16.876
  c. 168.19
  d. 16876
  e. 1.6876

9. $5.34 \times 10 =$
  a. 50.34
  b. 15.34
  c. 5.44
  d. 53.4
  e. 534

Now, check your answers on page 148.

3 ▶ Measurement

THE GED MATHEMATICS Exam emphasizes real-life applications of math concepts, and this is especially true of questions about measurement. This chapter reviews the basics of measurement systems used in the United States and other countries, performing mathematical operations with units of measurement, and the process of converting between different units.

▶ Measurement Pretest

1. 6 feet = _____ yard(s)
   a. 0.5
   b. 2
   c. 3
   d. 9
   e. 18

2. A recipe calls for 3 ounces of olive oil. Convert this measurement into cups.
   a. 0.3 cups
   b. 0.5 cups
   c. 0.375 cups
   d. 24 cups
   e. $2\frac{2}{3}$ cups

3. 48 inches = _____ yard(s)
   a. $0.\overline{33}$
   b. 1
   c. $1.\overline{33}$
   d. 2
   e. 84

4. A 2-liter bottle of soda contains approximately how many fluid ounces?
   a. 0.06 fluid ounces
   b. 968.96 fluid ounces
   c. 128.53 fluid ounces
   d. 256 fluid ounces
   e. 67.6 fluid ounces

5. The perimeter of a room (the measure around a room) is measured and found to be 652 inches. Trim for the room is sold by the foot. How many feet of trim must be purchased so that the room can be trimmed?
   a. 50 feet
   b. 54 feet
   c. 55 feet
   d. 60 feet
   e. 18 feet

6. Thomas is 6 feet 1 inch in height. His son is 3 feet 3 inches tall. What is the difference in their heights, in inches?
   a. 30 inches
   b. 32 inches
   c. 34 inches
   d. 36 inches
   e. 38 inches

7. Martha walks to school, a distance of 0.85 miles. What is the distance she walks to school in feet?
   a. 4,488 feet
   b. 6,212 feet
   c. 1,496 feet
   d. 5,280 feet
   e. 1,760 feet

8. A road race is 33,000 feet long. How many miles long is the race?
   a. 18.75 miles
   b. 6.25 miles
   c. 11,000 miles
   d. 38,280 miles
   e. 5 miles

9. A child's sandbox is being constructed in Tony's backyard. The sandbox is 6 feet wide and 5 feet long. Tony wants the sand to be at least 1.5 feet deep. The volume of sand in the box is 6 feet × 5 feet × 1.5 feet = 45 cubic feet. Convert the volume into cubic yards.
   a. 72 cubic yards
   b. 15 cubic yards
   c. 0.6 cubic yards
   d. $1.\overline{66}$ cubic yards
   e. 5 cubic yards

10. Which of the following represents a method by which one could convert inches into miles?

    a. Multiply by 12 and then multiply by 5,280.

    b. Divide by 12 and then divide by 5,280.

    c. Add 12 and then multiply by 5,280.

    d. Multiply by 12 and then divide by 5,280.

    e. Divide by 12 and then multiply by 5,280.

11. Which of the following statements is false?

    a. 32 centimeters = 320 millimeters

    b. 3.2 meters = 3,200 millimeters

    c. 84 millimeters = 840 centimeters

    d. 84 millimeters = 0.084 meters

    e. 8.4 kilometers = 8,400 meters

12. It took Kaitlyn two hours to finish her homework. How many minutes did it take her to finish her homework?

    a. 90 minutes

    b. 60 minutes

    c. 100 minutes

    d. 120 minutes

    e. 150 minutes

13. Michael takes four minutes to shave each morning. How many seconds does Michael spend shaving each morning?

    a. 240 seconds

    b. 64 seconds

    c. 200 seconds

    d. 120 seconds

    e. 400 seconds

14. It is a commonly known fact that 0° C = 32° F, the freezing point of water. However, the conversion from 0° F to degrees Celsius is not as commonly known. Find the equivalent Celsius temperature for zero degrees Fahrenheit.

    a. 17.8° C

    b. −17.8° C

    c. −32° C

    d. 32° C

    e. −57.6° C

15. On the beach, the ratio of boogie boards to surfboards is 12 to 3. If there are 84 boogie boards, how many surfboards are there on the beach?

    a. 24

    b. 21

    c. 3

    d. 36

    e. 15

16. There are 48 people on a camping trip. Sixteen are females. What is the ratio of males to females?

    a. 3 to 1

    b. 16 to 48

    c. 1 to 3

    d. 32 to 48

    e. 2 to 1

17. Two numbers are in the ratio of 5 to 8. If the larger number is 72, what is the smaller number?

    a. 5

    b. 13

    c. 45

    d. 117

    e. 9

18. The ratio of lunch buyers to lunch packers is 7 to 2. How many people pack their lunches if 35 people buy their lunches?

   a. 123

   b. 42

   c. 10

   d. 119

   e. 7

19. A map has a scale that specifies $\frac{1}{4}$ inch = 1 mile. How wide is an island that measures 6.2 inches on the map?

   a. 24.8 miles

   b. 1.55 miles

   c. 4.43 miles

   d. 6.45 miles

   e. 7.6 miles

20. Sonia puts $700 in a savings account that pays 5% simple interest each year. Which expression tells how much Sonia will have in 18 months?

   a. $700 + (\$700 \times \frac{1}{5} \times \frac{3}{2})$

   b. $700 + (\$700 \times \frac{1}{20} \times \frac{2}{3})$

   c. $700 + (\$700 \times \frac{1}{20} \times \frac{3}{2})$

   d. $700 \times \frac{1}{20} \times \frac{3}{2}$

   e. $700 - (\$700 \times \frac{1}{20} \times \frac{3}{2})$

Now, check your answers on page 149.

▶ Types of Measurements

Units tell us two important things about the object being measured—what is being measured and its size. Are you measuring capacity, weight, length, or temperature? And how big, heavy, long, or hot is the object? For each type of measurement, you must use an appropriate unit of measurement. For example, you might use grams to measure weight, liters to measure capacity, degrees to measure temperature, feet to measure height, and so on.

Today, there are two major systems of measurement. The **U.S. customary system** is used in everyday life in the United States. The following are the types of measurements used most frequently in the United States:

Units of Length

1 foot (ft.) = 12 inches (in.)

1 yard (yd.) = 3 feet = 36 inches

1 mile (mi.) = 1,760 yards = 5,280 feet

1 square foot (ft.^{2}) = 144 square inches (in.^{2})

1 square yard (yd.^{2}) = 9 square feet

1 square mile (mi.^{2}) = 640 acres = 3,097,600 square yards

1 acre (A) = 4,840 square yards = 43,560 square feet

1 cubic foot (ft.^{3}) = 1,728 cubic inches (in.^{3}) ≈* 7.48 gallons

1 cubic yard (yd.^{3}) = 27 cubic feet

Units of Volume

1 tablespoon (tbs.) = 0.5 fluid ounce (fl. oz.)**

1 tablespoon = 3 teaspoons (tsp.)

1 cup (c.) = 8 fluid ounces

1 pint (pt.) = 2 cups = 16 fluid ounces

1 quart (qt.) = 2 pints = 32 fluid ounces

1 gallon (gal.) = 4 quarts = 128 fluid ounces

1 gallon ≈* 231 cubic inches ≈* 0.1337 cubic foot

Units of Weight

1 pound (lb.) = 16 ounces (oz.)**

1 ton (T) = 2,000 pounds

Units of Time

1 minute (min.) = 60 seconds (sec.)

1 hour (hr.) = 60 minutes

1 day = 24 hours

1 week = 7 days

1 year (yr.) = 52 weeks

1 year = 12 months

1 year = 365 days

*The symbol ≈ means about equal to.

**Notice that ounces are used to measure the dimensions of both volume and weight.

The other major system of measurement is the **metric system.** This system is used in most other industrialized countries outside of the United States. It is also used by doctors and scientists in the United States. The basic units of the metric system are the meter, gram, and liter.

Converting units in the metric system is much easier than converting units in the U.S. customary system of measurement. However, making conversions between the two systems is much more difficult. Luckily, the GED test will provide you with the appropriate conversion factor when needed. Here is a general idea of how the two systems compare:

Conversions between U.S. Customary and Metric Units

1 inch ≈ 25.4 millimeters ≈ 2.54 centimeters

1 foot ≈ 0.3048 meter ≈ 30.480 centimeters

1 yard ≈ 0.9144 meter

1 mile ≈ 1,609.34 meters ≈ 1.6093 kilometers

1 kilometer ≈ 0.6214 mile

1 meter ≈ 3.281 feet ≈ 39.37 inches

1 centimeter ≈ 0.3937 inch

1 square inch ≈ 645.16 square millimeters ≈ 6.4516 square centimeters

1 square foot ≈ 0.0929 square meter

1 square yard ≈ 0.8361 square meter

1 square mile ≈ 2,590,000 square meters ≈ 2.59 square kilometers

1 acre ≈ 4,046.8564 square meters ≈ 0.004047 square kilometer

1 cubic inch ≈ 16,387.064 cubic millimeters ≈ 16.3871 cubic centimeters

1 cubic foot ≈ 0.0283 cubic meter

1 cubic yard ≈ 0.7646 cubic meter

1 teaspoon ≈ 5 milliliters

1 tablespoon ≈ 15 milliliters

1 fluid ounce ≈ 29.57 milliliters ≈ 2.957 centiliters

1 fluid ounce ≈ 0.00002957 cubic meter

1 gallon ≈ 3.785 liters

1 liter ≈ 1.057 quarts ≈ 0.264 gallon

1 quart ≈ 0.946 liter

Prefixes are attached to the basic metric units to indicate the amount of each unit.

For example, the prefix *deci* means one-tenth $(\frac{1}{10})$; therefore, one decigram is one-tenth of a gram, and one decimeter is one-tenth of a meter. The following six prefixes can be used with every metric unit:

KILO (k)	HECTO (h)	DEKA (dk)	DECI (d)	CENTI (c)	MILLI (m)
1,000	100	10	$\frac{1}{10}$	$\frac{1}{100}$	$\frac{1}{1,000}$

1 hectometer = 1 hm = 100 meters

1 millimeter = 1 mm = $\frac{1}{1,000}$ meter = .001 meter

1 dekagram = 1 dkg = 10 grams

1 centiliter = 1 cL* = $\frac{1}{100}$ liter = 0.01 liter

1 kilogram = 1 kg = 1,000 grams

1 deciliter = 1 dL* = $\frac{1}{10}$ liter = 0.1 liter

*Notice that liter is abbreviated with a capital letter—L.

The following are some common relationships used in the metric system:

Units of Length

1 centimeter (cm) = 10 millimeters (mm)

1 meter (m) = 100 centimeters = 1,000 millimeters

1 kilometer (km) = 1,000 meters

1 square centimeter (cm^2) = 100 square millimeters (mm^2)

1 square meter (m^2) = 10,000 square centimeters = 1,000,000 square millimeters

1 square kilometer (km^2) = 1,000,000 square meters

1 cubic centimeter (cm³) = 1,000 cubic millimeters (mm³)

1 cubic meter (m³) = 1,000,000 cubic centimeters

Units of Volume

1 liter (L) = 1,000 milliliters (mL) = 100 centiliters (cL)

1 kiloliter (kL) = 1,000 liters = 1,000,000 milliliters

Units of Weight

1 kilogram (kg) = 1,000 grams (g)

1 gram (g) = 0.001 kilogram (kg) = 100 centigrams (cg)

1 centigram (cg) = 0.01 gram (g)

1 gram = 1,000 milligrams (mg)

1 milligram (mg) = 0.001 gram (g)

► Converting Units

Units of measure are converted by using either multiplication or division. To change from one unit to another, you need to determine whether more or fewer of the new units are needed. If more are needed, multiply. If fewer are needed, divide. Multiplying ends up with the smaller unit of measurement; dividing ends up with the larger unit.

To change a larger unit to a smaller unit, multiply the specific number of larger units by the number of smaller units in only one of the larger units.

Examples

1. 5 feet = ? inches

There are 12 inches in one foot. To find how many inches are in 5 feet, multiply 5 by 12: 5 feet × 12 inches = 60 inches.

2. Change 3.5 tons to pounds.

There are 2,000 pounds in a ton. To find how many pounds are in 3.5 tons, multiply 3.5 by 2,000: 3.5 tons × 2,000 pounds = 7,000 pounds.

To change a smaller unit to a larger unit, divide the specific number of smaller units by the number of smaller units in only one of the larger units.

Example

Find the number of pints in 64 ounces.

Remember, there are 16 ounces in 1 pint. So, divide 64 by 16 to determine the number of pints: 64 ounces ÷ 16 ounces = 4 pints.

GED Tip

After solving a time problem, be sure to use common sense and ask yourself if the answer you arrive at is reasonable. If a question asks how many seconds are in two hours, for example, you have the common sense to know that the answer will be a number much larger than 2.

Also, many of the time problems will require you to make more than one conversion to arrive at a solution, as in the seconds-to-hours example; hours would be first converted to minutes and then minutes to seconds.

► Conversions within the Metric System

An easy way to do conversions with the metric system is to move the decimal point either to the right or left, because the conversion factor is always ten or a power of ten. As you learned previously, when you change from a large unit to a smaller unit you multiply, and when you change from a small unit to a larger unit you divide.

When you multiply by a power of ten, you move the decimal point to the right. When you divide by a power of ten, you move the decimal point to the left. To change from a large unit to a smaller unit, move the decimal point to the right.

$$\xrightarrow{\text{kilo hecto deka UNIT deci centi milli}}$$
$$\xleftarrow{\phantom{\text{kilo hecto deka UNIT deci centi milli}}}$$

To change from a small unit to a larger unit, move the decimal point to the left.

Suppose you are packing your bicycle for a trip from New York City to Detroit. The rack on the back of your bike can hold 20 kilograms. If you exceed that limit, you must buy stabilizers for the rack that cost $2.80 each. Each stabilizer can hold an additional kilogram. If you want to pack 23,000 grams of supplies, how much money will you have to spend on the stabilizers?

Step 1 First, change 23,000 grams to kilograms.
kg   hg   dkg   g   dg   cg   mg

Step 2 Move the decimal point three places to the left: 23,000 g = 23.000 kg = 23 kg.

Step 3 Subtract to find the amount over the limit. 23 kg – 20 kg = 3 kg.

Step 4 Because each stabilizer holds one kilogram and your supplies exceed the weight limit of the rack by three kilograms, you must purchase three stabilizers from the bike store.

Step 5 Each stabilizer costs $2.80, so multiply $2.80 by 3: $2.80 × 3 = $8.40.

▶ Addition with Measurements

To add measurements, follow these two steps:

1. Add like units.
2. Simplify the answer.

Example

Add 4 pounds 5 ounces to 20 ounces.

Be sure to add ounces to ounces.

```
   4 lb. 5 oz.
+       20 oz.
  4 lb. 25 oz.
```

Because 25 ounces is more than 16 ounces (1 pound), simplify by dividing by 16. The result is 1 pound 9 ounces.

```
      1 lb.
16)25
   –16
     9 oz.
```

Thus, 4 pounds 25 ounces = 4 pounds + 1 pound 9 ounces = 5 pounds 9 ounces.

▶ Subtraction with Measurements

To subtract measurements, follow these three steps:

1. Subtract like units.
2. Regroup units when necessary.
3. Write the answer in simplest form.

For example, to subtract 6 pounds 2 ounces from 9 pounds 10 ounces, first subtract ounces from ounces. Then subtract pounds from pounds.

```
   9 lb. 10 oz.
– 6 lb.  2 oz.
  3 lb.  8 oz.
```

Sometimes, it is necessary to regroup units when subtracting.

Example

Subtract 3 yards 2 feet from 5 yards 1 foot.

$$\begin{array}{r} \overset{4}{\cancel{5}} \text{ yd. } \overset{4}{\cancel{1}} \text{ ft.} \\ - 3 \text{ yd. 2 ft.} \\ \hline 1 \text{ yd. 2 ft.} \end{array}$$

From 5 yards, regroup 1 yard to become 3 feet. Add 3 feet to 1 foot. Then subtract feet from feet and yards from yards.

▶ Multiplication with Measurements

To multiply measurements, follow these two steps:

1. Multiply like units if units are involved.
2. Simplify the answer.

Examples

1. Multiply 5 feet 7 inches by 3.

First multiply 7 inches by 3; then multiply 5 feet by 3. Keep the units separate.

$$\begin{array}{r} 5 \text{ ft. } 7 \text{ in.} \\ \times \qquad 3 \\ \hline 15 \text{ ft. 21 in.} \end{array}$$

Because 12 inches = 1 foot, simplify 21 inches: 15 ft. 21 in. = 15 ft. + 1 ft. + 9 in. = 16 feet 9 inches.

2. Multiply 9 feet by 4 yards.

First, change yards to feet by multiplying the number of feet in a yard (3) by the number of yards in this problem (4).

3 feet in a yard × 4 yards = 12 feet

Then multiply 9 feet by 12 feet = 108 square feet.

(Note: feet × feet = square feet)

▶ Division with Measurements

To divide measurements, follow these five steps:

1. Divide into the larger units first.
2. Convert the remainder to the smaller unit.
3. Add the converted remainder to the existing smaller unit, if any.
4. Then divide into smaller units.
5. Write the answer in simplest form.

Example

Divide 5 quarts 4 ounces by 4.

First, divide 5 ounces by 4, for a result of 1 quart and a remainder of 1.

$$\begin{array}{r} 1 \text{ qt. R1} \\ 4\overline{)5} \\ -4 \\ \hline 1 \end{array}$$

Convert the remainder to the smaller unit (ounces): R1 = 32 oz.

Add the converted remainder to the existing smaller unit: 32 oz. + 4 oz. = 36 oz.

Now, divide the smaller units by 4.

$$\begin{array}{r} 9 \text{ oz.} \\ 4\overline{)36} \\ -36 \\ \hline 0 \end{array}$$

The answer is 1 quart 9 ounces.

▶ Temperature

Much of the world measures temperature in **degrees Celsius**. The Celsius unit of temperature is based on 0° C as the freezing point and at 100° C as the boiling point of water at sea level. In the United States, temperature is measured in **degrees Fahrenheit**, which is based on 32° F as the freezing point and 212° F as the boiling point.

Thermometers are used to measure temperature. They show measurements as points on a scale. Positive temperatures are shown as numbers greater than 0. Negative numbers are shown as numbers less than 0.

To find the difference between two temperatures, subtract the lower temperature from the higher temperature. Think of a thermometer as a number line: The difference between two points on a number line is equal to the distance between the points.

Find the difference between 60° F and −15° F. Remember, subtracting a negative number is the same as adding a positive number.

$$60° \text{ F} - (-15° \text{ F}) = 60° \text{ F} + 15° \text{ F} = 75° \text{ F}$$

GED Tip

When working with negative numbers on Part I of the GED Mathematics Exam, your calculator can be a useful friend. To enter a negative number, press the change sign key (+/−) after you enter the number.

To convert from degrees Celsius (° C) to degrees Fahrenheit (° F), use the formula:

$$F = \tfrac{9}{5}(C) + 32$$

Substitute the given number of Celsius degrees in the formula for C.

Multiply by $\tfrac{9}{5}$ and then add 32.

Example

Convert 40° C into Fahrenheit.

$$F = \tfrac{9}{5}(40) + 32 = \tfrac{360}{5} + 32 = 72 + 32 = 104°$$

Therefore, 40° C = 104° F.

To convert from degrees Fahrenheit (° F) to degrees Celsius (° C), use the formula:

$$C = \tfrac{5}{9}(F - 32)$$

Substitute the given number of Fahrenheit degrees in the formula for F.

Subtract 32, then multiply by $\tfrac{5}{9}$.

Example

Convert 50° F into Celsius.

$$C = \tfrac{5}{9}(50 - 32) = \tfrac{5}{9}(18) = \tfrac{90}{9} = 10°$$

Therefore, 50° F = 10° C.

▶ Ratios

Ratios are numbers that are used to compare things. Ratios play an important role in mathematics because they quantify all of the items that you compare on a day-to-day basis. There are several different ways to write ratios. Here are some examples of ways to write ratios.

- with the word *to*: 1 to 2
- using a colon (:) to separate the numbers: 1:2
- using the phrase *for every*: 1 for every 2
- separated by a division sign or fraction bar: 1/2 or $\tfrac{1}{2}$

Let's look at an example. In the community gardening group, there are 24 women and 16 men. If you want to compare the number of women to the number of men, you can show this comparison in several different ways:

24:16

24 to 16

24/16

$\tfrac{24}{16}$

Regardless of which form is used, the meaning is the same: "There were 24 women for every 16 men." Notice that $\frac{24}{16}$ is a fractional form of a ratio. The fractional form of a ratio is often a convenient way to represent a ratio when solving problems.

In addition to comparing women to men, a comparison could also be made between women and total members. The total membership is 24 + 16 = 40 people. This ratio is $\frac{24}{40}$, or 24 to 40, or 24:40.

> **GED Tip**
>
> Keep the terms of a ratio in the order that the problem compares them. Because the preceding example compared women to total members, your answer should give the number of women to the number of total members.

Ratios are usually shown in lowest terms and can be simplified in the same way that fractions are simplified. For example, in the gardening group, there are 24 women and 16 men. This ratio can be expressed as 3:2, because $\frac{24}{16} \div \frac{8}{8} = \frac{3}{2}$. In this group there are three women for every two men. You can also express the ratio of men to total group members. This ratio is 2:5, because $\frac{16}{16+24} = \frac{16}{40} = \frac{2}{5}$.

Example

Write the following ratio as a fraction: 10 wins to 5 losses.

This ratio is $\frac{10}{5}$.

Even though $\frac{10}{5}$ looks like an improper fraction, it's not, here—it's a ratio comparing the number of wins to the number of losses. You can, however, reduce the ratio to lowest terms: $\frac{10}{5} = \frac{2}{1}$.

▶ Solving Ratio Problems

There are several kinds of ratio problems. The examples that follow show how to solve different kinds of ratio problems.

Examples

1. A painter mixes two quarts of red paint to three quarts of white paint. What is the ratio of red paint to white paint?

There are several ways you could write this ratio:

2 quarts of red paint to 3 quarts of white paint, or 2 to 3

2 quarts red paint : 3 quarts white paint, or 2:3

2 quarts red paint/3 quarts white paint, or $\frac{2}{3}$

2. Last season, the Tigers won 30 games. They lost only 6 games. There were no tied games last season.

What is the ratio of games won to games lost, and what is the ratio of games won to games played?

Write your answers as fractions.

The first part of the question asks for the ratio of games won to games lost. So, you would write $\frac{30}{6}$. You could reduce the ratio to $\frac{5}{1}$.

The second part of the question asks for the ratio of games won to games played. First, you need to calculate the total number of games played. Because the Tigers won 30 games, lost 6 games, and tied no games, they must have played a total of 36 games. The ratio of games won to games played is 30 games won to 36 total games, or $\frac{30}{36}$. You could reduce $\frac{30}{36}$ to $\frac{5}{6}$.

▶ Proportions

A **proportion** is an equation that states that two ratios are equal. Often, in addition to comparing items, it is natural to want to compare ratios.

For example, if you want to choose an amusement park, you might want to compare the number of gift shops to the number of rides. Park A has 10 gift shops and 50 rides. Park B has 17 gift shops and 85 rides. For park A, the ratio is 1 to 5: shops/rides $= \frac{10}{50} \div \frac{10}{10} = \frac{1}{5}$. For park B, the ratio is also 1 to 5: shops/rides $= \frac{17}{85} \div \frac{17}{17} = \frac{1}{5}$. For both parks, the ratios are exactly the same. By using a proportion, you can compare these parks on this issue. The proportion is $\frac{10}{50} = \frac{17}{85}$, because both ratios equal $\frac{1}{5}$.

A proportion is a way of relating two ratios to one another. Let's say that 8 out of 10 students in your study group are expected to take the GED this year. If there are 100 people in your study group, then 80 people are expected to take the test this year. This is an example of a proportion. Proportions can be written as equations. For example, this proportion can be written as $\frac{8}{10} = \frac{80}{100}$.

Proportions show equivalent fractions. Both $\frac{8}{10}$ and $\frac{80}{100}$ reduce to the same fraction: $\frac{4}{5}$.

For a proportion to work, the terms in both ratios have to be written in the same order. Notice that the numerator in each ratio in the study group proportion example refers to the number of students expected to take the exam. The denominator refers to the total number of students.

Let's say you didn't see immediately that $\frac{8}{10}$ would be equal to $\frac{80}{100}$. How could you have figured out the equivalent ratio? Remember in Chapter 2 when you were working with fractions? You learned the following steps to raise a fraction to higher terms.

Step 1 Divide the denominator of the fraction into the new denominator.

Step 2 Multiply the quotient, or the answer to step 1, by the numerator.

Step 3 Write the product, or the answer to step 2, over the new denominator.

Example

$\frac{8}{10} = \frac{?}{100}$

Divide the denominator into the new denominator, which is 100: $100 \div 10 = 10$. Multiply 10 by the numerator: $8 \times 10 = 80$. Write 80 over the new denominator: $\frac{80}{100}$.

There's another way to solve for the missing term. It's called **cross multiplying** or finding the **cross products**. Here's how cross multiplying works.

Step 1 Multiply the numerator of the first ratio by the denominator in the second ratio.

Step 2 Divide the product (the answer to step 1) by the denominator in the first ratio. The answer is the missing numerator in the second ratio.

You can also use cross multiplication to check that two ratios are equal. When a proportion is set up properly, the results of cross multiplication should be equal.

Example

Use cross multiplication to check that the two ratios in this proportion are equal: $\frac{8}{10} = \frac{80}{100}$.

Multiply the numerator of the first ratio by the denominator in the second ratio: $8 \times 100 = 800$.

Multiply the denominator of the first ratio by the numerator in the second ratio: $10 \times 80 = 800$.

The answers are equal, so your proportion is valid: $800 = 800$.

▶ Solving Proportion Word Problems

Proportions are common in word problems. Let's look at some examples of proportion word problems.

Examples

1. Margaret drove 220 miles in five hours. If she maintained the same speed, how far could she drive in seven hours?

Set up a proportion: 220 miles/5 hours = ? miles/7 hours, or $\frac{220}{5} = \frac{?}{7}$.

Solve for the missing number in the second ratio:
$220 \times 7 \div 5 = 308$, so $\frac{220}{5} = \frac{308}{7}$.

Check your work by cross multiplying:
$220 \times 7 = 5 \times 308$
$1{,}540 = 1{,}540$

Keeping the same speed, Margaret could drive 308 miles in seven hours.

2. Harry earns $6 per hour at his job. If he works nine hours this week, how much will Harry earn?

Set up a proportion: $6/1 hour = $?/9 hours, or $\frac{6}{1} = \frac{?}{9}$.

Solve for the missing number in the second ratio: $6 \times 9 \div 1 = \$54$. Therefore, $\frac{6}{1} = \frac{54}{9}$.

Check your work by cross multiplying:
$6 \times 9 = 54$ and $1 \times 54 = 54$.

Working seven hours, Harry will make $54.

▶ Scale

Scale is a special ratio used for models of real-life items, such as model railroads and model airplanes, or scale drawings such as blueprints and maps. On model airplanes, you will often find the scale ratio printed on the model as model:real. For example, a toy car may have the ratio 1:62 printed on the bottom. This is the ratio of all of the dimensions of the toy to the corresponding dimensions of the real car. This scale ratio says that the real car is 62 times larger than the toy, since the ratio is 1:62.

Example

A model locomotive measures 8.7 inches in length. If the scale given is 1:16, how long is the real locomotive?

Because the real train engine is 16 times as big as the model, the real train engine will be 8.7 times 16, which is 139.2 inches, or 11.6 feet.

On scale drawings, the scale will be a comparison of a small distance unit, like inches, to a large distance unit, like feet or even miles. So a scale on a map could read "3 inches = 10 miles." This means for every 3 inches on the map, the actual distance is 10 miles. This ratio is $\frac{3}{10}$, but care should be taken to remember that the units do not agree. If a scale drawing reads "1 inch = 10 feet," this does not mean that the real item is only 10 times bigger, even though the ratio would be 1:10. Solve scale drawing problems as you would any type of ratio problem, keeping the units consistent and clear in your answer.

▶ Rates

A **rate** is a ratio that compares two different units of measurement. It is usually written as a fraction with a denominator of 1. Sometimes, the word *per* is used to indicate a rate. *Per* means for each (for 1). For example, a rate of $0.99 per minute is written $0.99/1 minute. (Notice that the units for this rate are dollars and minutes.)

Some common rates include the following:

calories per serving	feet per yard
cents per pound	heartbeats per minute
dollars per hour	inches per foot
dollars per pound	miles per gallon
dollars per year	miles per hour
feet per mile	words per minute

Rate problems can be solved by writing a proportion. Suppose the price of five pounds of grapes is $3.50. What is the price of three pounds of grapes?

price/pound = $3.50/5 pounds = ?/3 pounds

Solve for ? by cross multiplying:

$$5 \times ? = \$3.50 \times 3$$
$$5 \times ? = \$10.50$$

Divide each side of the equation by 5.
$$\frac{5 \times ?}{5} = \frac{\$10.50}{5}$$
$$? = \$2.10$$

GED Tip

You cannot add or subtract a number from a ratio unless you know the exact numbers that make up a ratio. However, you can always multiply or divide *both sides* of a ratio by a given number, especially if you need to simplify the ratio.

▶ Calculating Simple Interest

Interest is the amount of money that is paid for using someone else's money. For example, a bank pays you interest for money you have placed in a savings account. Or, you pay a bank interest for money that you borrow.

Here is the interest formula:

$$\text{interest} = \text{principal} \times \text{rate} \times \text{time}$$

Suppose you put $500 in a savings account that pays 5% simple interest each year. How much interest will you have earned in 18 months?

$$\text{interest} = \$500 \times 5\% \times 18 \text{ months}$$

The rate (5%) can be written as a decimal or a fraction: 0.05 or $\frac{5}{100}$, which reduces to $\frac{1}{20}$.

$$\text{interest} = \$500 \times \tfrac{1}{20} \times 18 \text{ months}$$

Because the rate is a yearly rate, write 18 months as a number of years: 18 months = $\frac{18}{12}$ years, which reduces to $\frac{3}{2}$ years.

$$\text{interest} = \$500 \times \tfrac{1}{20} \times \tfrac{3}{2}$$
$$= \$37.50$$

► Measurement Posttest

1. 4.5 miles = _____ feet
   a. 13.5
   b. 5,275.5
   c. 5,284.5
   d. 7,920
   e. 23,760

2. What is the sum of 2 pints 6 ounces + 1 cup 7 ounces?
   a. 1 quart
   b. 3 pints 1 cup 13 ounces
   c. 2 pints 5 ounces
   d. 3 pints 5 ounces
   e. 3 pints 1 cup

3. 35 mm = _____ cm
   a. 0.35
   b. 3.5
   c. 35
   d. 350
   e. 3,500

4. Susan wishes to create bows from 12 yards of ribbon. Each bow requires 6 inches of ribbon to make. How many inches of ribbon does Susan have?
   a. 18 inches
   b. 432 inches
   c. 48 inches
   d. 144 inches
   e. 24 inches

5. The living room in Donna's home is 182 square feet. How many square yards of carpet should she purchase to carpet the room?
   a. 9 square yards
   b. 1,638 square yards
   c. 61 square yards
   d. 21 square yards
   e. 546 square yards

6. Sofie needs to take $\frac{3}{4}$ teaspoon of cough syrup three times a day. Convert $\frac{3}{4}$ teaspoon into milliliters.
   a. 0.375 milliliter
   b. 3.75 milliliters
   c. 2.25 milliliters
   d. 22.5 milliliters
   e. 0.15 milliliter

7. 3.9 kiloliters = _____ milliliters
   a. 0.00000039
   b. 0.0000039
   c. 0.0039
   d. 3,900,000
   e. 39,000,000

8. The 1,500-meter race is a popular distance running event at track meets. How far is this distance in miles?
   a. 0.6214 mile
   b. 0.5 mile
   c. 0.9321 mile
   d. 2.4139 miles
   e. 0.4143 mile

9. 58.24 mm^3 = _____ cm^3
   a. 0.05824
   b. 5.824
   c. 58,240
   d. 582.4
   e. 5,824

10. Abigail is 5.5 feet tall. Which of the following is closest to this height?
a. 17 meters
b. 170 centimeters
c. 1.7 kilometers
d. 170 millimeters
e. 0.17 kilometers

11. 62.4 meters ≈ _____ feet
a. 1.58
b. 2,456.7
c. 65.7
d. 19.01
e. 205

12. Bill worked for a steel manufacturer for three decades. How many years did Bill work for the steel manufacturer?
a. 15 years
b. 60 years
c. 30 years
d. 6 years
e. 12 years

13. How many minutes are there in 12 hours?
a. 24 minutes
b. 1,440 minutes
c. 36 minutes
d. 1,200 minutes
e. 720 minutes

14. If the temperature is 10 degrees below zero Fahrenheit, what is the temperature in degrees Celsius?
a. 12.2° C
b. −37.6° C
c. 26.4° C
d. −23.3° C
e. 14° C

15. A family drove 390 miles at a constant speed. It took 6 hours of driving time. What was the speed of their car?
a. 55 miles per hour
b. 60 miles per hour
c. 234 miles per hour
d. 65 miles per hour
e. 35 miles per hour

16. Strawberries are 3 quarts for $4.98. How much will 10 quarts of strawberries cost?
a. $14.98
b. $16.60
c. $25
d. $49.80
e. $4.98

17. Driving 60 miles per hour, it takes one-half hour to drive to work. How much *additional* time will it take to drive to work if the speed is now 40 miles per hour?
a. 1 hour
b. 2 hours
c. 15 minutes
d. one-half hour
e. 45 minutes

18. The height of the Eiffel Tower is 986 feet. A replica of the tower made to scale is 4 inches tall. What is the scale of the replica to the real tower?
a. 1 to 246.5
b. 1 to 3,944
c. 246.5 to 1
d. 1 to 2,958
e. 2,958 to 1

19. An 8" × 10" photograph is blown up to a billboard size that is in proportion to the original photograph. If 8" is considered the height of the photo, what would be the length of the billboard if its height is 5.6 feet?

a. 7 feet
b. 400 feet
c. 56 feet
d. 9 feet
e. 156 inches

20. Kim put $5,000 into a savings account that pays 8% simple interest each year. What will her total be in 18 months?

a. $600
b. $4,600
c. $5,000
d. $5,600
e. $420,000

Now, check your answers on page 150.

  Percentages

NOW THAT YOU KNOW all about fractions and decimals and ratios and proportions, it's time to learn about percentages. **Percentages** are just *hundredths*. In this chapter, you will review how to express given percentages as both fractions and decimals. You'll find that you come into contact with percentages every day with sales tax, tips, and discounts.

▶ Percentages Pretest

1. What is 57% of 350?
  a. 614
  b. 16.29
  c. 182
  d. 199.5
  e. 19.95

2. What percent of 200 is 68?
  a. 68%
  b. 2.94%
  c. 34%
  d. 136%
  e. 0.34%

3. Nineteen is 76% of what number?
  a. 76
  b. 25
  c. 14.44
  d. 400
  e. 250

4. Two out of every five members of the town board are male. What percentage of the board members is male?
  a. 25%
  b. 40%
  c. 20%
  d. 4%
  e. 15%

5. Hockey sticks that normally sell for $89 are on sale for 35% off the regular price. There is also a 6% sales tax. How much will the stick cost after the sale and the sales tax?
  a. $57.85
  b. $33.02
  c. $54.38
  d. $29.28
  e. $61.32

6. The book club attendance rose from 25 members to 30 members. What is the percentage increase in membership, to the nearest whole percent?
  a. 20%
  b. 83%
  c. 17%
  d. 2%
  e. 5%

7. Out of the 28 selections on the menu, four are desserts. What percentage, to the nearest tenth, of the menu are NOT desserts?
  a. 14.3%
  b. 12.5%
  c. 85.7%
  d. 75.0%
  e. 7.0%

8. Twenty-five percent of the voters voted for the incumbent. How many voted for the incumbent if there were 1,032 voters?
  a. 258
  b. 4,128
  c. 25
  d. 1,007
  e. 2,422

9. How much will be paid for a $28 dinner, assuming a 15% tip?
  a. $4.20
  b. $43
  c. $23.80
  d. $30.80
  e. $32.20

10. Ninety-one percent of what number is 200.2?
  a. 2.2
  b. 220
  c. 45.45
  d. 454.5
  e. 182.182

Now, check your answers on page 152.

▶ Percents

Percents are everywhere you look. Go to the mall, and you'll see plenty of signs announcing "20% off" or "Take an additional 30% off." Packages at the supermarket regularly claim to include "30% more free." Even your grades for schoolwork are probably percents.

Percent is another way to represent the parts of a whole. Notice that percents are written with the **percent sign** after a number: 10%, 25%, 30%, 50%, 99%, and so on. The percent sign represents the words *out of 100 parts* or *per 100 parts.*

Recall that fractions represent the parts of a whole that is divided into any number of equal parts. So, you can find fractions with any whole number in the denominator: $\frac{1}{2}, \frac{2}{3}, \frac{4}{5}, \frac{6}{10}, \frac{15}{212}$, and so on. Decimals represent the parts of a whole that is divided into either 10, 100, 1,000, or another multiple of ten equal parts. Percents, by contrast, always represent a whole that is divided into 100 equal parts. That means that percents can be written as fractions with 100 in the denominator and as decimals written to the hundredths place.

▶ Converting Percents to Decimals

Changing percents to decimals is as simple as moving the decimal point two digits to the left after removing the percent sign. Follow these basic steps:

Step 1 Drop the percent sign.
Step 2 Add a decimal point if there isn't already one. Remember that even when it's not written in, whole numbers are followed by a decimal point.
Step 3 Move the decimal point two places to the left. Add zeros if needed.

Examples

1. Convert 25% to a decimal.
Drop the percent sign (25% becomes 25).
Add a decimal point: 25.
Move the decimal point two places to the left and add a leading zero: 0.25
25% = 0.25

2. Convert 2.5% to a decimal.
Drop the percent sign (2.5% becomes 2.5).
There is already a decimal point, so move the decimal point two digits to the left. Doing this requires a zero as a placeholder in the tenths place. Also add a leading zero to the left of the decimal point: 0.025.
2.5% = 0.025

▶ Converting Decimals to Percents

Changing decimals to percents is the opposite of what you've just done. When you change a decimal to a percent, you move the decimal point two digits to the right.

Examples

1. Convert 0.15 to a percent.
Move the decimal point two places to the right: 0.15 becomes 15.
Add a percent sign after the number: 15%.
Therefore, 0.15 = 15%.

2. Convert 7.9 to a percent.
Move the decimal point two places to the right. Add zeros as needed: 7.9 becomes 790.
Add a percent sign after the number: 790%.
Therefore, 7.9 = 790%.

► Converting Percents to Fractions

To change a percent to a fraction, you write the percent over 100. Don't forget to reduce the fraction to lowest terms as you would any other fraction. Here are the steps to follow.

Step 1   Drop the percent sign.
Step 2   Write the number as a numerator over 100.
Step 3   Write improper fractions as mixed numbers. Reduce the fraction to lowest terms.

Examples

1. Convert 15% to a fraction.

Drop the percent sign: 15% becomes 15.

Write the number as a numerator over 100: $\frac{15}{100}$.

Reduce the fraction to lowest terms. Both 15 and 100 can be divided by 5: $\frac{15 \div 5}{100 \div 5} = \frac{3}{20}$.

Therefore, $15\% = \frac{3}{20}$.

2. Convert 150% to a fraction.

Drop the percent sign: 150% becomes 150.

Write the number as a numerator over 100: $\frac{150}{100}$.

Write the improper fraction as a mixed number, and reduce the fraction to lowest terms:

$\frac{150 \div 50}{100 \div 50} = \frac{3}{2} = 1\frac{1}{2}$.

Therefore, $150\% = 1\frac{1}{2}$.

► Converting Fractions to Percents

There are two basic ways to convert fractions to percents. You should try both ways, and see which one works better for you.

Method 1

Step 1   Divide the numerator by the denominator.
Step 2   Multiply by 100. (This is the same as moving the decimal point two digits to the right.)
Step 3   Add a percent sign.

Method 2

Step 1   Multiply the fraction by $\frac{100}{1}$.
Step 2   Write the product as either a whole or a mixed number.
Step 3   Add a percent sign.

Example
Change $\frac{2}{5}$ to a percent.

Method 1
Divide the numerator by the denominator.

$$5\overline{)2.0} \quad 0.4$$
$$\underline{20}$$

Multiply by 100: $0.4 \times 100 = 40$.
Add a percent sign: 40%.

Method 2
Multiply the fraction by $\frac{100}{1}$: $\frac{2}{5} \times \frac{100}{1} = \frac{200}{5} = \frac{40}{1}$.
Write the product as either a whole number or a mixed number: 40.
Add a percent sign: 40%.

Although you can always convert between percents, decimals, and fractions using the described methods, it's a good idea to know common percent, decimal, and fraction equivalents for standardized tests. Knowing them in advance can save you valuable time on a timed test. Besides, working with a value in one form is often easier than working with it in another form. Knowing the equivalents can help you see the easier route faster. Here are some common equivalents you might want to learn.

Equivalents to Know

PERCENT	DECIMAL	FRACTION
1%	0.01	$\frac{1}{100}$
5%	0.05	$\frac{5}{100}$
10%	0.1	$\frac{1}{10}$
12.5%	0.125	$\frac{1}{8}$
20%	0.2	$\frac{1}{5}$
25%	0.25	$\frac{1}{4}$
$33\frac{1}{3}$%	0.33 (rounded)	$\frac{1}{3}$
40%	0.40	$\frac{2}{5}$
50%	0.5	$\frac{1}{2}$
$66\frac{2}{3}$%	0.67 (rounded)	$\frac{2}{3}$
75%	0.75	$\frac{3}{4}$
80%	0.80	$\frac{4}{5}$
90%	0.90	$\frac{9}{10}$
100%	1.00	$1 = \frac{1}{1}$

▶ Solving Percent Problems

Percent problems ask you to find one of three things: the part, the whole, or the percent. Here's how these three elements are related to one another.

$$\text{whole} \times \text{percent} = \text{part}$$

This is called an **equation**, or a kind of math sentence. It tells how different elements are related to one another. You can use this equation to find any one of the elements that might be missing.

▶ Finding a Part of a Whole

Often you will be asked to find a part of a whole. In these problems, you are given a whole and a percent and asked to find the part represented by the percent of the whole. Let's go through an example.

Example

What is 30% of 60?

Begin by figuring out what you know from the problem and what you're looking for. You have the percent: 30%. You have the whole: 60. You are looking for the part.

Then, use the equation to solve the problem: whole × percent = part.

Plug in the pieces of the equation that you know: 60 × 30% = part.

Convert the percent to a decimal to make your multiplication easier: 60 × 0.30 = part.

Solve: 60 × 0.30 = 18.

So, 30% of 60 is 18.

▶ Finding a Percent

In the following types of problems, you will be given the part and the whole. Your task is to determine what percent the part is of the whole. Remember that a percent is just a fraction written over 100. You can solve these types of problems by writing the part over the whole and converting the fraction to a percent.

Examples

1. 10 is what percent of 200?

Begin by figuring out what you know from the problem and what you're looking for. You have the part: 10.

You have the whole: 200.

You are looking for the percent.

Write a fraction of the part over the whole: $\frac{10}{200}$.

Convert the fraction to a percent. Remember there are two methods for converting fractions to percents. Use either method. Method 1 is shown: $10 \div 200 = 0.05$; $0.05 \times 100 = 5$.

Therefore, 10 is 5% of 200.

2. There are 500 people in Sandra's travel club. Fifty people were chosen to go to Washington, D.C., for a trip. What percent of Sandra's travel club was chosen to go on the trip?

Begin by figuring out what you know from the problem and what you're looking for.
You have the part: 50.
You have the whole: 500.
You are looking for the percent.

Write a fraction of the part over the whole: $\frac{50}{500}$.

Convert the fraction to a percent. Remember there are two methods for converting fractions to percents. Use either method. Method 1 is shown:

$50 \div 500 = 0.1$

$0.1 \times 100 = 10$ or 10%

Therefore, 50 is 10% of 500; 10% of Sandra's travel club was chosen to go on the trip.

Sometimes problems will ask you to find a percentage change. The problem will give you one part of the whole. Your task is to calculate the part of the whole represented by the percentage *difference* between the whole and the part given.

Example

Last year, Sasha could run one mile in 12 minutes. This year, he can run a mile in 8 minutes. By what percentage did his timing improve?

Begin by figuring out what you know from the problem and what you're looking for.

You have the part: 10 minutes − 8 minutes = 2 minutes.

You also have the whole: 10 minutes.

You are looking for the percent.

Write a fraction of the part over the whole:

$$\frac{2 \text{ minutes}}{10 \text{ minutes}}$$

Convert the fraction to a percent:

$2 \div 10 = 0.2$

$0.2 \times 100 = 20$ or 20%

Therefore, 2 minutes is 20% of 10 minutes. Sasha's running time improved by 20% since last year.

When you see the following types of phrases, you are probably being asked to calculate the part of the whole represented by the *difference* between the whole and the part given.

- Find the percent change.
- Find the percent increase.
- Find the percent decrease.
- By what percent did it improve?
- By what percent did it go down?
- By what percent did it go up?

Sometimes the problem will not directly tell you the whole amount. Instead, you will be given enough information to calculate the whole on your own. Here's an example.

Example

Priyanka made a beaded bracelet using 10 red beads, 5 turquoise beads, 8 yellow beads, and 2 white beads. What percent of the bracelet do the red beads make up?

Begin by figuring out what you know from the problem and what you're looking for.

You have the parts:

10 red beads

5 turquoise beads

8 yellow beads

2 white beads

You also have the whole: $10 + 5 + 8 + 2 = 25$ beads.

You are looking for the percent.

Write a fraction of the part over the whole:

$$\frac{10 \text{ red beads}}{25 \text{ total beads}}$$

Convert the fraction to a percent:

$10 \div 25 = 0.4$

$0.4 \times 100 = 40$ or 40%

Therefore, 40% of the beads are red.

▶ Finding the Whole

In the following types of problems, you will be given the part and the percent. Your task is to determine the whole. You can solve these types of problems by writing the part over the percent and dividing.

$$\text{whole} = \frac{\text{part}}{\text{percent}}$$

Examples

1. 45 is 75% of what number?

Begin by figuring out what you know from the problem and what you're looking for.

You have the part: 45.

You also have the percent: 75%.

You are looking for the whole.

Write the part over the percent: $\frac{45}{75\%}$.

Convert the percent to a fraction to make your division easier: $45 \div \frac{75}{100} = \text{whole}$.

Solve:

$45 \div \frac{75}{100} = \frac{45}{1} \times \frac{100}{75} = 60$

Therefore, 45 is 75% of 60.

2. Five people on a track team qualified to go to the state competition. This represents 20% of the track team. How many people are on the track team?

Begin by figuring out what you know from the problem and what you're looking for.

You have the part: 5 people.

You also have the percent: 20%.

You are looking for the whole.

Write the part over the percent: $\frac{5}{20\%}$.

Convert the percent to a fraction to make your division easier: $5 \div \frac{20}{100} = \text{whole}$.

Solve:

$5 \div \frac{20}{100} = \frac{5}{1} \times \frac{100}{20} = 25$

So, there are 25 people on the track team.

▶ Percentages Posttest

1. Change $\frac{15}{16}$ to a percent.

  a. 0.9375%

  b. 93.75%

  c. 15.16%

  d. 15%

  e. 85%

2. Change 23.5% to a decimal.

  a. 2.35

  b. 23.5

  c. 0.235

  d. 235.00

  e. 23,500.00

3. Change 1.8 to a percent.
   a. 18%
   b. 80%
   c. 1.8%
   d. 180%
   e. 20%

4. What is 12.8% of 405, to the nearest hundredth?
   a. 51.84
   b. 0.03
   c. 31.64
   d. 0.52
   e. 518.40

5. 272 is what percent of 400?
   a. 1.47%
   b. 147%
   c. 0.68%
   d. 10.88%
   e. 68%

6. 533 is 82% of what number?
   a. 15.38
   b. 6.5
   c. 149.24
   d. 650
   e. 437.06

7. 49% of 3,000 is
   a. 6,122.45
   b. 14.70
   c. 1,470
   d. 1,530
   e. 612.25

8. 4.25 is what percent of 25?
   a. 5.88%
   b. 0.17%
   c. 106.25%
   d. 1.06%
   e. 17%

9. The number of customers in the ABC department store rose from 1,200 on Saturday to 1,350 on Sunday. What is the percent increase?
   a. 11.11%
   b. 88.9%
   c. 150%
   d. 12.5%
   e. 112.5%

10. The population of West Elm fell from 25,670 in 1990 to 24,500 in 2000. What was the percent decrease during this time frame, to the nearest tenth?
   a. 4.6%
   b. 8%
   c. 46%
   d. 4.8%
   e. 95.44%

Now, check your answers on page 153.

5 ▶ Exponents and Roots

RECALL THAT A FACTOR of a number is a whole number that divides evenly, without a remainder, into the given number. Frequently, you multiply the same factor times itself several times. In math, there is a special notation for this idea: exponents and the inverse operation, roots. This chapter explores powers and exponents, negative exponents, square roots, fractional exponents, scientific notation, laws of exponents, and exponents and the order of operations.

▶ **Exponents and Roots Pretest**

1. Simplify 7^2.
   a. 14
   b. 7.2
   c. 3.5
   d. $\frac{1}{49}$
   e. 49

2. Simplify 2^{-3}.
   a. 6
   b. −8
   c. −6
   d. $\frac{1}{8}$
   e. $\frac{1}{6}$

3. Simplify $\sqrt[3]{27}$.
   a. 5
   b. 3
   c. 9
   d. $\frac{27}{3}$
   e. $\frac{1}{3}$

4. $25^{1/2} =$
   a. 12.5
   b. 625
   c. −625
   d. $\frac{1}{5}$
   e. 5

5. $2^2 \times 2^3 =$
   a. 2^5
   b. 10
   c. 4^5
   d. 64
   e. 2

6. What is 7.206×10^{-4} written in standard form?
   a. 72,060
   b. 0.00007206
   c. 0.0007206
   d. 7,206
   e. 72,060,000

7. What is 567,090,000 written in scientific notation?
   a. $567,090 \times 10^3$
   b. 5.6709×10^3
   c. 5.679×10
   d. 567×10^9
   e. 0.56709×10^9

8. $(5.4 \times 10^{16}) \div (9 \times 10^{14}) =$
   a. 600
   b. 0.6
   c. 60
   d. 6
   e. 0.006

9. $-5^2 =$
   a. −10
   b. $\frac{1}{25}$
   c. 25
   d. −25
   e. 10

10. $700 + 25 - 5^2 \times 2 =$
   a. 725
   b. 1,036,800
   c. 675
   d. 1,400
   e. 705

Now, check your answers on page 153.

► Powers and Exponents Review

Recall that when whole numbers are multiplied together, each of these numbers is a factor of the result. When all of the factors are identical, the result is called a **power** of that factor. For example, because $6 \times 6 \times 6 \times 6 \times 6 = 7,776$, the number 7,776 is called the "fifth power of 6."

There is a shorthand notation used to indicate repeated multiplication by the same factor. This is called **exponential form**. In exponential form, 7,776 can be written as 6^5, and it is said that "six to the fifth power is 7,776." In the expression 6^5, the 6 is called the base and the 5 is called the exponent.

The base is the number that is used as a repeated factor in an exponential expression. It is the bottom number in an exponential expression. For example, in the expression 5^3, 5 is the base number.

The exponent indicates the number of times that a repeated factor is multiplied together to form a power; it is the superscript in an exponential expression. In the expression 5^3, the 3 is the exponent and indicates that 5 is multiplied by itself twice.

The power is a product that is formed from repeated factors multiplied together. For example, 27 is the third power of 3, because $3 \times 3 \times 3 = 27$.

► Finding Squares

Anytime a number is written with a 2 raised after it, it means to multiply the number by itself, or to **square** the number. A *square* of a number is just the number multiplied by itself. For example, 4^2 is called "four squared." Because $4^2 = 4 \times 4$, which is 16, 16 is called a **perfect square**.

Examples
1. What is the square of 30?
To find the square of a number, multiply it by itself. The square of 30 is 30×30, or 900.

2. Find 9^2.
When a number is followed by a raised 2, you should square it: $9^2 = 9 \times 9 = 81$.

Although you can always calculate the square of a number by multiplying, it's a good idea to know some of the perfect squares, both for raising to an exponent and for taking roots (discussed on page 80).

Here are some common squares you might want to learn.

Squares to Know

NUMBER	SQUARE	CALCULATION
1	1	1×1
2	4	2×2
3	9	3×3
4	16	4×4
5	25	5×5
6	36	6×6
7	49	7×7
8	64	8×8
9	81	9×9
10	100	10×10
11	121	11×11
12	144	12×12
13	169	13×13
14	196	14×14
15	225	15×15
16	256	16×16
17	289	17×17
18	324	18×18
19	361	19×19
20	400	20×20
21	441	21×21
22	484	22×22
23	529	23×23
24	576	24×24
25	625	25×25

▶ Negative Exponents

Observe the following pattern for the base of 3:

EXPONENT	EXPONENTIAL FORM	STANDARD FORM
1	3^1	3
2	3^2	9
3	3^3	27
4	3^4	81
5	3^5	243

Look at the last column, standard form. As you go down this column, each time the entry is multiplied by 3 to obtain the next entry below, such as $81 \times 3 = 243$. Notice that as you go *up* this column, each time you would divide the entry by 3 to get the entry above. Now extend this pattern to include an exponent of zero and some negative exponents:

EXPONENT	EXPONENTIAL FORM	STANDARD FORM
−3	3^{-3}	$\frac{1}{9} \div 3 = \frac{1}{27} = \frac{1}{3^3}$
−2	3^{-2}	$\frac{1}{3} \div 3 = \frac{1}{9} = \frac{1}{3^2}$
−1	3^{-1}	$1 \div 3 = \frac{1}{3} = \frac{1}{3^1}$
0	3^0	$3 \div 3 = 1$
1	3^1	3
2	3^2	9
3	3^3	27

From the patterns noted, the rules for zero exponents and negative exponents follow:

- Any number (except zero) to the zero power is 1. $x^0 = 1$, where x is any number not equal to zero. For example, $7^0 = 1$, $29^0 = 1$, and $2,159^0 = 1$.
- A negative exponent is equivalent to the reciprocal of the base, raised to that positive exponent. $x^{-a} = \frac{1}{x^a}$, where x is not equal to zero. Recall that the reciprocal of 4 is $\frac{1}{4}$. So, for example, $4^{-2} = \frac{1}{4^2} = \frac{1}{16}$, and $2^{-3} = \frac{1}{2^3} = \frac{1}{8}$, and $(\frac{1}{3})^{-3} = \frac{3^3}{1^3} = 27$.

▶ Square Roots

You may have seen this symbol before: $\sqrt{\ }$. This is the symbol for a square root. When a number is written after it, you are being asked to find the square root of that number. In an expression such as $\sqrt{25}$, 25 is called the **radicand**, and the expression is the **radical**.

The **square root** of a number is one of the two identical factors whose product is the given number. For example, 64 is a perfect square because 8×8, or 8^2, equals 64. This factor, 8, is called the square root of 64.

The number 64 has another square root, −8, because $-8 \times -8 = (-8)^2 = 64$. If we want to indicate the positive square root, use the $\sqrt{n}$ radical symbol to denote square root. So $\sqrt{64} = 8$, and $-\sqrt{64} = -8$.

▶ Working with Square Roots

You can simplify square roots by expressing the radicand (the number after the radical symbol) as the product of other numbers, where one of the factors is a perfect square. For example, $\sqrt{288} = \sqrt{144 \times 2} = \sqrt{144} \times \sqrt{2} = 12\sqrt{2}$, which means 12 times the square root of 2.

Likewise, when you are given a problem of two radicals multiplied together, you can combine by multiplying the radicands: $\sqrt{3} \times \sqrt{27} = \sqrt{3 \times 27} = \sqrt{81} = 9$.

The same rule holds for division: $\sqrt{192} \div \sqrt{3} = \sqrt{192 \div 3} = \sqrt{64} = 8$, and $\sqrt{3 \div 9} = \sqrt{3} \div \sqrt{9} = \sqrt{3} \div 3$.

You can add or subtract radicals only if they have the same radicand. $5\sqrt{3} + 7\sqrt{3} = 12\sqrt{3}$, and $7\sqrt{2} - 10\sqrt{2} = -3\sqrt{2}$, but $6\sqrt{2} + 7\sqrt{3}$ cannot be combined because the radicands are different.

Examples

1. What is $\sqrt{25}$?

The problem is asking you to calculate the square root of 25. Ask yourself what number multiplied by itself equals 25. If you have memorized the list of common squares, this problem is not very hard. Even if you haven't learned the list of common squares yet, though, you can figure this problem out: $5 \times 5 = 25$. So the square root of 25 is 5.

2. What is $\sqrt{45}$?

The problem is asking you what number equals 45 when multiplied by itself. You know that $6^2 = 36$ and $7^2 = 49$. Thus, the square root of 45 is a number between 6 and 7. You can find a more precise answer using a calculator.

GED Tip

If you aren't sure what the square root of a given number is, make a guess and multiply the likely number by itself. If it's not the correct square root, at least now you can make a better guess the second time!

▶ Fractional Exponents

When an exponent is a fraction, the denominator of this fractional exponent means the root of the base number, and the numerator means a raise of the base to that power.

numerator—the power to which the base is raised
denominator—the root of the base number

For example, $8^{1/3}$ is the same as $\sqrt[3]{8^1} = 2$. Another example is $8^{2/3}$ means $\sqrt[3]{8^2}$, which is $\sqrt[3]{64} = 4$, or alternatively, $\left(\sqrt[3]{8}\right)^2$, which is $2^2 = 4$.

▶ Scientific Notation

Scientists measure very large numbers, such as the distance from the earth to the sun, or very small numbers, such as the diameter of an electron. Because these numbers involve a lot of digits as placeholders, a special notation was invented as a shorthand for these numbers. This **scientific notation** is very specific in the way it is expressed:

$$n \times 10^e$$

where n = a number greater than 1 and less than 10
e = the exponent of 10

To find the scientific notation of a number greater than 10, locate the decimal point and move it either right or left so that there is only one non-zero digit to its left. The result will produce the n part of the standard scientific notational expression. Count the number of places that you had to move the decimal point. If it is moved to the left, as it will be for numbers greater than 10, that number of positions will equal the e part.

Example

What is 23,419 in scientific notation?

Position the decimal point so that there is only one non-zero digit to its left: 2.3419

Count the number of positions you had to move the decimal point to the left, and that will be e: 4.

In scientific notation, 23,419 is written as 2.3419×10^4.

For numbers less than 1, follow the same steps except in order to position the decimal point with only one non-zero decimal to its left, you will have to move it to the right. The number of positions that you move it to the right will be equal to $-e$. In other words, there will be a negative exponent.

Example

What is 0.000436 in scientific notation?

First, move the decimal point to the right in order to satisfy the condition of having one non-zero digit to the left of the decimal point: 4.36

Then, count the number of positions that you had to move it: 4.

That will equal $-e$, so $-e = -4$, and 0.000436 $= 4.36 \times 10^{-4}$.

For numbers already between 1 and 10, you do not need to move the decimal point, so the exponent will be zero.

▶ Laws of Exponents

When working with exponents, there are three rules that can be helpful.

1. When you multiply powers with the same base, keep the base and add the exponents: $4^2 \times 4^3 = 4^{2+3} = 4^5$.
2. When you divide powers with the same base, keep the base and subtract the exponents: $3^7 \div 3^4 = 3^{7-4} = 3^3$.
3. When you raise a power to a power, you keep the base and multiply the exponents: $(7^3)^2 = 7^{3 \times 2} = 7^6$.

If two powers are being multiplied together and the bases are not the same, check to see if you can convert the numbers to have the same base to use the preceding laws. For example, to simplify $27^2 \times 3^2$, recognize that 27 can be written as 3^3. Change the problem to $(3^3)^2 \times 3^2$. Use law number 3 to get $3^{3 \times 2} \times 3^2 = 3^6 \times 3^2$. Now, you can use law number 1 to get $3^{6+2} = 3^8$.

▶ Exponents and the Order of Operations

Be aware of some distinctions when working with the order of operations and exponents. Exponents are done after parentheses and before any other operations, including the negative sign. For example, $-3^2 = -(3 \times 3) = -9$ because you first take the second power of 3 and then the answer is negative. However, $(-3)^2 = -3 \times -3 = 9$, because -3 is enclosed in parentheses.

Example

$-20 + (-2 + 5)^3 \div (10 - 7) \times 2 =$

Evaluate the parentheses, left to right:
$-20 + 3^3 \div 3 \times 2$.
Now, evaluate the exponent: $-20 + 27 \div 3 \times 2$.
Division will be done next: $-20 + 9 \times 2$.
Evaluate multiplication: $-20 + 18$.
Finally, perform addition to arrive at the answer: -2.

► Exponents and Roots Posttest

1. $-11^2 =$
   a. -22
   b. -121
   c. 121
   d. 22
   e. 101

2. $81^{1/4} =$
   a. 20.25
   b. 3
   c. 324
   d. $\frac{1}{3}$
   e. $\frac{1}{324}$

3. $\sqrt[3]{64} =$
   a. 4
   b. 192
   c. $21\frac{1}{3}$
   d. $\frac{1}{192}$
   e. $\frac{1}{3}$

4. $\sqrt{169} =$
   a. 13
   b. 16
   c. 16.9
   d. 84.5
   e. -16

5. $\sqrt{48} \times \sqrt{3} =$
   a. $\sqrt[4]{144}$
   b. -16
   c. 12
   d. $\frac{1}{12}$
   e. $3\sqrt{48}$

6. $\sqrt{\frac{3}{9}}$
   a. $\frac{1}{3}$
   b. $\sqrt{3}$
   c. $\frac{3}{9}$
   d. $-3\sqrt{3}$
   e. $\frac{\sqrt{3}}{3}$

7. Write 2.701×10^7 in standard form.
   a. 27×10^6
   b. $27,010,000$
   c. $27,010,000,000$
   d. 0.0002701
   e. 0.0000002701

8. Write 4.09×10^{-5} in standard form.
   a. $409,000$
   b. 0.00000409
   c. 0.0000409
   d. $40,900,000$
   e. 409×10^{-7}

9. $(2.5 \times 10^{-4}) \times (3.0 \times 10^8) =$
   a. 0.00075
   b. 7.5
   c. $75,000$
   d. $7,500,000,000,000$
   e. 750

10. $5 - (-17 + 7)^2 \times 3 =$
   a. -135
   b. 315
   c. -295
   d. -45
   e. 75

Now, check your answers on page 154.

CHAPTER

6 ▶ Algebra and Functions

ALGEBRA IS THE BRANCH of mathematics that denotes quantities with letters and uses negative numbers as well as ordinary numbers. You often use algebra to translate everyday situations into a math sentence so that you can then solve problems. This is the reason why the GED Mathematics Exam will test your knowledge of algebra skills and concepts.

▶ Algebra and Functions Pretest

1. $9a + 12a^2 - 5a =$
   a. $16a$
   b. $16a^2$
   c. $12a^2 - 4a$
   d. $12a^2 + 4a$
   e. $26a^2$

2. $\frac{(3a)(4a)}{6(6a^2)} =$
   a. $\frac{1}{3}$
   b. $\frac{2}{a}$
   c. $\frac{1}{3a}$
   d. $\frac{1}{3a^2}$
   e. 2

3. What is the product of $(x - 3)(x + 7)$?
   a. $x^2 - 21$
   b. $x^2 - 3x - 21$
   c. $x^2 + 4x - 21$
   d. $x^2 + 7x - 21$
   e. $x^2 - 21x - 21$

4. What is the product of $(x - 6)(x - 6)$?
   a. $x^2 + 36$
   b. $x^2 - 36$
   c. $x^2 - 12x - 36$
   d. $x^2 - 12x + 36$
   e. $x^2 - 36x + 36$

5. What are the factors of $x^2 - x - 6$?
   a. $(x - 3)(x - 2)$
   b. $(x - 3)(x + 2)$
   c. $(x + 3)(x - 2)$
   d. $(x - 6)(x + 1)$
   e. $(x - 1)(x + 6)$

6. If $9a + 5 = -22$, what is the value of a?
   a. -27
   b. -9
   c. -3
   d. -2
   e. $-\frac{17}{9}$

7. If $f(x) = 2x - 1$ and $g(x) = x^2$, what is the value of $f[g(-3)]$?
   a. -7
   b. 2
   c. 9
   d. 17
   e. 49

8. If $f(x) = 3x + 2$ and $g(x) = 2x - 3$, what is the value of $g[f(-2)]$?
   a. -19
   b. -11
   c. -7
   d. -4
   e. -3

9. Which of the following is true of $f(x) = \frac{-x^2}{2}$?
   a. The range of the function is all real numbers less than or equal to 0.
   b. The range of the function is all real numbers less than 0.
   c. The range of the function is all real numbers greater than or equal to 0.
   d. The domain of the function is all real numbers greater than or equal to 0.
   e. The domain of the function is all real numbers less than or equal to $\sqrt{2}$.

10. Which of the following is true of $f(x) = \sqrt{4x-1}$?

    a. The domain of the function is all real numbers greater than $\frac{1}{4}$ and the range is all real numbers greater than 0.

    b. The domain of the function is all real numbers greater than or equal to $\frac{1}{4}$ and the range is all real numbers greater than 0.

    c. The domain of the function is all real numbers greater than or equal to $\frac{1}{4}$ and the range is all real numbers greater than or equal to 0.

    d. The domain of the function is all real numbers greater than 0 and the range is all real numbers greater than or equal to $\frac{1}{4}$.

    e. The domain of the function is all real numbers greater than or equal to 0 and the range is all real numbers greater than or equal to $\frac{1}{4}$.

Now, check your answers on page 155.

► What Are Algebraic Expressions?

An **algebraic expression** is a group of numbers, variables (letters), and operation signs $(+, -, \times, \div)$. Variables are usually written in italics. For example, the x in the following algebraic expressions is the variable:

$$5x + 2$$
$$3x - 8$$
$$\frac{4x}{9}$$

Any letter can be used to represent a number in an algebraic expression. The letters $x, y,$ and z are commonly used.

Algebraic expressions translate the relationship between numbers into math symbols.

MATH RELATIONSHIP: IN WORDS	TRANSLATED INTO AN ALGEBRAIC EXPRESSION
a number plus six	$x + 6$
five times a number	$5x$
three less than a number	$x - 3$
the product of seven and a number	$7x$
a number divided by eight	$x \div 8$ or $\frac{x}{8}$
a number squared	x^2

When multiplying a number and a variable, you just have to write them side by side. You don't need to use a multiplication symbol.

Example

Translate the following math relationship into an algebraic expression: the quotient of 3 divided by a number plus the difference between 3 and 2.

You know that the word *quotient* indicates division, so write "$3 \div$."

The word *number* represents your variable, so write "$3 \div x$."

The word *plus* means to add, so write "$3 \div x +$."

The word *difference* means to subtract, so write: "$3 \div x + (3 - 2)$."

(Remember that parentheses are used to indicate an operation that should be performed first.)

So, the answer is $3 \div x + (3 - 2)$.

When translating a math relationship into an algebraic expression, keep these key words in mind.

Translating Math Relationships into Algebraic Expressions

THESE WORDS . . .	. . . OFTEN TRANSLATE INTO THESE MATH SYMBOLS
added to sum plus increased by combine all together	+
subtracted from difference decreased by minus take away less	–
multiplied by product times	×, · ( ) Parentheses can also indicate multiplication. 3(5) is the same as 3 × 5 or 3 · 5.
divided by quotient per	÷, ≠
equals is are	=
a number	x, y, n

Remember that the order of the numbers and the exact wording are very important when dividing and subtracting. For example:

- The difference between 3 and 2 means 3 – 2 (which equals 1).
- Three less 2 means 3 – 2 (which equals 1).

- Three less than 2 means 2 – 3 (which equals –1).
- Four divided by 2 means 4 ÷ 2 (which equals 2).
- Two divided by 4 means 2 ÷ 4 (which equals $\frac{1}{2}$).
- Two divided into 4 means 4 ÷ 2 (which equals 2).

It's the same when variables are used:

- The difference between 3 and a number means $3 - x$.
- Three less than a number means $x - 3$.
- Four divided by a number means $4 \div x$.
- A number divided by 4 means $x \div 4$.

Example

Translate the following math relationship into an algebraic expression: one-fourth of a number is decreased by nine.

You know that the word *one-fourth* is a fraction, so write "$\frac{1}{4}$."
The word *number* represents your variable, and when you are talking about fractions, the word *of* indicates that you should multiply, so write "$\frac{1}{4}x$."
The words *decreased by* mean to subtract, so write "$\frac{1}{4}x - 9$."
The answer is $\frac{1}{4}x - 9$.

▶ Evaluating Algebraic Expressions

Algebraic expressions have specific values only when the variables have values. Finding the value of an algebraic expression by plugging in the known values of its variables is called **evaluating** an expression.

Examples

1. Evaluate $5 \div (x + y)$, when $x = 2$ and $y = 3$.

Plug the numbers into the algebraic expression: $5 \div (2 + 3)$.

Solve by following the order of operations. Add the numbers in parenthesis:
$5 + (2 + 3) = 5 + 5$.
Divide to find the final answer: $5 \div 5 = 1$.

2. Find the value of $5 + x$, when $x = -2$.
Plug the numbers into the algebraic expression:
$5 + (-2)$.
Solve: $5 - 2 = 3$.

▶ Simplifying Algebraic Expressions

The parts of an algebraic expression are called **terms**. A term is a number, or a number and the variables associated with it. For example, the following algebraic expression has three terms:

algebraic expression: $5x^2 - 5x + 1$
terms: $+5x^2, -5x, +1$

As you can see, the terms in an algebraic expression are separated by + and – signs. Notice that the sign in front of each term is included as part of that term—the sign is *always* part of the term. If no sign is given, it is positive (+).

Simplifying an algebraic expression means to combine like terms. **Like terms** are terms that use the same variable and are raised to the same power. Here are some examples of like terms.

LIKE TERMS	WHAT BOTH TERMS CONTAIN
$5x$ and $9x$	x
$3x^2$ and $8x^2$	x^2
xy and $-5xy$	xy

When you combine like terms, you group all the terms that are alike together. This makes it easier to evaluate the expression later on.

Examples

1. Simplify the following algebraic expression: $5x + 3y + 9x$.

Write the like terms next to each other. You know that $5x$ and $9x$ are like terms because they both have x. So write them next to each other: $5x + 9x + 3y$.

Combine the like terms. In this case, add them: $5x + 9x + 3y = 14x + 3y$.

You can't simplify the $3y$ because there are no other terms in the expression with the variable y. So you leave it alone. The simplified expression is $14x + 3y$.

2. Simplify the following algebraic expression: $2x^2 + 3y + 9xy + 3y^2$.

You cannot write the like terms next to each other, because there are no like terms in this expression. It is already simplified.

3. Simplify the following algebraic expression: $5x(2x - 1) + 9x$.

Write the like terms next to each other. Begin by distributing the $5x$ so that you can remove the parentheses. Multiply $5x(2x - 1)$: $10x^2 - 5x$.

So now the expression is $10x^2 - 5x + 9x$.

Now you can see that $-5x$ and $9x$ are like terms because each contains the x term.

Combine the like terms. Add the like terms: $-5x + 9x = 4x$.

Now your expression is simplified to $10x^2 - 4x$.

You can't simplify further because there are no other terms in the expression with the same variable. Therefore, the simplified expression is $10x^2 - 4x$.

When combining like terms, begin by solving to remove the parentheses. If a negative sign is in front of a set of parentheses, it affects every term inside the parentheses. Here's an example.

Example

$-2(x - 3y + 2)$

When you multiply each term inside the parentheses by -2, the result is $-2x + 6y - 4$.

Notice that the negative sign $(-)$ affects each term inside the parentheses.

▶ Equations

An **algebraic equation** is a math sentence. It always has an equal $(=)$ sign. Algebraic equations say one quantity is equal to another quantity. Here are a few examples of algebraic equations:

$$5 + x = 25$$
$$x - 5 = 25$$
$$5x = 25$$

An equation is solved by finding a number that is equal to an unknown variable. To solve for the value of the variable, you first need to get it alone on one side of the equal sign. This is sometimes called **isolating the variable**.

You want to get the variable alone on one side of the equal sign, so you perform mathematical operations to both sides of the equation to isolate the variable. With every step you take to solve the equation, you should ask yourself, "What operations can I use to get the x alone on one side of the equal sign?" But remember, whatever you do to one side of the equation, you have to do to the other.

Examples

1. Solve the following algebraic equation:
$x + 5 = 10$.

What operation is used in the equation? Addition. In order to get the x alone, you will need to get rid of the 5. So, you should use the **inverse operation** and subtract. Remember, you have to perform the operation to both sides of the equation:

$$x + 5 = 10$$
$$\underline{-5 \quad -5} \quad \rightarrow \quad \text{Subtract 5 from both sides of the equation.}$$

Combine like terms on both sides of the equal sign:

$$x + 5 = 10$$
$$\underline{-5 \quad -5}$$
$$x + 0 = 5 \quad \rightarrow \quad \text{All like terms have been combined.}$$

Therefore, $x = 5$.

You can check your answer by going back to the original equation and plugging in your answer for x. If your answer makes the algebraic equation true, then it's correct. Let's try it out: $x + 5 = 10$, and $x = 5$, so $5 + 5 = 10$.

You know that $10 = 10$, so your answer, $x = 5$, is correct.

2. Solve the following algebraic equation:
$z - 3 = 8$.

Ask yourself: What operation is used in the equation? Subtraction. What is the inverse operation of subtraction? Addition. So, add 3 to each side of the equation in order to isolate the variable:

$$z - 3 = 8$$
$$\underline{+3 \quad +3} \quad \rightarrow \quad \text{Add 3 to each side of the equation.}$$

Combine like terms on both sides of the equal sign:

$$z - 3 = 8$$
$$\underline{+3 \quad +3}$$
$$z + 0 = 11 \quad \rightarrow \quad \text{All like terms have been combined.}$$

Therefore, $z = 11$.

Again, check your answer by going back to the original equation and plugging in your answer: $z - 3 = 8$, and $z = 11$, so $11 - 3 = 8$. You know that $8 = 8$, so your answer, $z = 11$, is correct.

3. Solve the following algebraic equation: $5r = -25$.

Ask yourself: What operation is used in the equation? Multiplication. What is the inverse operation of this multiplication? Division. So, divide each side of the equation by 5 in order to isolate the variable: $\frac{5r}{5} = -\frac{25}{5}$.

Combine like terms on both sides of the equal sign: $\frac{5r}{5} = r$ and $-\frac{25}{5} = -5$.

So, $r = -5$.

4. Solve the following algebraic equation: $\frac{x}{2} = 12$.

What operation is used in the equation? Division. What is the inverse operation of this division? Multiplication. So, multiply each side of the equation by 2 in order to isolate the variable.

$2 \times \left(\frac{x}{2}\right) = 12 \times 2$

Combine like terms on both sides of the equal sign: $\frac{2x}{2} = x$ and $12 \times 2 = 24$.

Therefore, $x = 24$.

▶ Solving Multiple-Step Algebraic Equations

The algebraic equations you've solved so far in this lesson have mostly required only one inverse operation. But some algebraic equations require more than one inverse operation to isolate the variable and then solve the equation.

When solving multiple-step algebraic equations, you should first add or subtract. Then, multiply or divide. In other words, you follow the order of operations in inverse order. Another way to look at it is to solve for the number attached to the variable last. Let's look at some examples.

Examples

1. Solve the following algebraic expression: $2m + 5 = 13$.

First, look for numbers that are being added or subtracted to the term with the variable. In this equation, 5 is added to the $2m$. To simplify, subtract 5 from both sides of the equation.

$$2m + 5 = 13$$
$$\underline{\quad -5 \quad -5 \quad} \rightarrow \quad \text{Subtract 5 from each side of}$$
$$2m \quad = \quad 8 \qquad \text{the equation.}$$

Perform the inverse operation for any multiplication or division. The variable in this equation is multiplied by 2, so you must divide each side of the equation by 2 in order to isolate the variable.

$$\frac{2m}{2} = \frac{8}{2} \rightarrow \quad \begin{array}{l}\text{Divide both sides of the equation} \\ \text{by 2 to isolate the variable.}\end{array}$$

The answer is $m = 4$.

2. Solve the following algebraic equation: $5p + 24 = 3p - 4$.

This equation has a variable on each side of the equal sign. So, you first need to get the variable terms on one side of the equation. You can do this by subtracting the smaller of the two variables from each side, because they have like terms.

$$5p + 24 = 3p - 4$$
$$\underline{-3p \qquad -3p \qquad} \rightarrow \quad \text{Subtract } 3p \text{ from both}$$
$$2p + 24 = \qquad -4 \qquad \text{sides of the equation.}$$

Look for numbers that are being added to or subtracted from the term with the variable. In this equation, 24 is added to the $2p$. So you subtract 24 from both sides of the equation.

$$2p + 24 = -4$$
$$\underline{\quad -24 \quad -24 \quad} \rightarrow \quad \text{Subtract 24 from both}$$
$$2p \quad = -28 \qquad \text{sides to isolate the term}$$
$$\text{with the variable.}$$

Perform the inverse operation for any multiplication or division. The variable in this equation is multiplied by 2, so you divide each side of the equation by 2 to isolate the variable.

$$\frac{2p}{2} = \frac{-28}{2} \rightarrow$$ Divide both sides of the equation by 2 to isolate the variable.

The answer is $p = -14$.

3. Solve the following algebraic equation: $4(b + 1) = 20$.

This equation has parentheses, so you need to remove the parentheses by distributing the 4. $4(b + 1) = 4b + 4$

So, your equation becomes $4b + 4 = 20$.

Look for numbers that are being added to or subtracted from the term with the variable. Subtract 4 from both sides of the equation. $4b + 4 = 20$

$$\frac{-4\ -4}{4b\ \ = 16} \rightarrow$$ Subtract 4 from both sides of the equation.

Perform the inverse operation for any multiplication or division. Divide each side of the equation by 4.

$$\frac{4b}{4} = \frac{16}{4} \rightarrow$$ Divide both sides of the equation by 4.

The answer is $b = 4$.

▶ Polynomials

A **polynomial** is the sum or difference of two or more unlike terms. For example, look at $2x + 3y - z$. This expression represents the sum of three unlike terms: $2x$, $3y$, and $-z$. There are three kinds of polynomials:

1. A **monomial** is a polynomial with one term, as in $2b^3$.
2. A **binomial** is a polynomial with two unlike terms, as in $5x + 3y$ or $5x3y$.
3. A **trinomial** is a polynomial with three unlike terms, as in $y^2 + 2z - 6$.

▶ Operations with Polynomials

To add polynomials, be sure to change all subtraction to addition and change the sign of the number that was being subtracted to its opposite. Then, combine like terms.

Example

$(3y^3 - 5y + 10) + (y^3 + 10y - 9)$

Change all subtraction to addition and change the sign of the number being subtracted: $3y^3 + -5y + 10 + y^3 + 10y + -9$.

Combine like terms: $3y^3 + y^3 + -5y + 10y + 10 + -9 = 4y^3 + 5y + 1$.

If an entire polynomial is being subtracted, change all of the subtraction to addition within the parentheses and then add the opposite of each term in the polynomial.

Example

$(8x - 7y + 9z) - (15x + 10y - 8z) =$

Change all subtraction within the parentheses first: $(8x + -7y + 9z) - (15x + 10y + -8z)$. Then, change the subtraction sign outside of the parentheses to addition and change the sign of each term in the polynomial being subtracted: $(8x + -7y + 9z) + (-15x + -10y + 8z)$. Note that the sign of the term $8z$ changes twice because it is being subtracted twice.

All that is left to do is combine like terms: $8x + -15x + -7y + -10y + 9z + 8z$ $= -7x + -17y + 17z$.

To multiply two polynomials, multiply every term of the first polynomial by every term of the second polynomial. Then, add the products and combine like terms.

Example

$(-5x^3y)(2x^2y^3) = (-5)(2)(x^3)(x^2)(y)(y^3) = -10x^5y^4$

To multiply a polynomial by a monomial, multiply each term of the polynomial by the monomial and add the products.

Example

$6x(10x - 5y + 7) =$

Change subtraction to addition:
$6x(10x + -5y + 7)$.
Multiply: $(6x)(10x) + (6x)(-5y) + (6x)(7)$.
Combine like terms: $60x^2 + -30xy + 42x$.

▶ FOIL

To multiply binomials, you must multiply each term by every other term and add the products. The acronym **FOIL** can help you remember how to multiply binomials. FOIL stands for first, outside, inside, and last.

Example

$(3x + 1)(7x + 10) =$

$3x$ and $7x$ are the first pair of terms, $3x$ and 10 are the outermost pair of terms, 1 and $7x$ are the innermost pair of terms, and 1 and 10 are the last pair of terms.

Therefore, $(3x)(7x) + (3x)(10) + (1)(7x) + (1)(10) = 21x^2 + 30x + 7x + 10$.

After you combine like terms, you are left with the answer: $21x^2 + 37x + 10$.

▶ Factoring

Multiplying the binomials $(x + 1)$ and $(x + 2)$ creates the quadratic expression $x^2 + 3x + 2$. That expression can be broken back down into $(x + 1)(x + 2)$ by factoring.

A quadratic trinomial (a trinomial is an expression with three terms) that begins with the term x^2 can be factored into $(x + a)(x + b)$. **Factoring** is the reverse of FOIL. Find two numbers, a and b, that multiply to the third value of the trinomial (the constant) and that add to the coefficient of the second value of the trinomial (the x term).

Given the quadratic $x^2 + 6x + 8$, you can find its factors by finding two numbers whose product is 8 and whose sum is 6. The numbers 1 and 8 and the numbers 4 and 2 multiply to 8, but only 4 and 2 add to 6. The factors of $x^2 + 6x + 8$ are $(x + 2)$ and $(x + 4)$. You can check your factoring by using FOIL: $(x + 2)(x + 4) = x^2 + 4x + 2x + 8 = x^2 + 6x + 8$.

What are the factors of $2x^2 + 9x + 9$?

This quadratic will be factored into $(2x + a)(x + b)$. Find two numbers that multiply to 9. Two times one of those numbers plus the other must equal 9, the coefficient of the second term of the quadratic trinomial. The numbers 1 and 9 and the numbers 3 and 3 multiply to 9. Two times 3 plus 3 is equal to 9, so the factors of $2x^2 + 9x + 9$ are $(2x + 3)$ and $(x + 3)$.

GED Tip

Remember, factoring is the reverse of multiplication:

Multiplication: $2(x + y) = 2x + 2y$

Factoring: $2x + 2y = 2(x + y)$

▶ Removing a Common Factor

If a polynomial contains terms that have common factors, the polynomial can be factored by using the reverse of the distributive law.

Look at the binomial $49x^3 + 21x$. The greatest common factor of both terms is $7x$.

Therefore, you can divide $49x^3 + 21x$ by $7x$ to get the other factor.

$$\frac{49x^3 + 21x}{7x} = \frac{49x^3}{7x} + \frac{21x}{7x} = 7x^2 + 3$$

Factoring $49x^3 + 21x$ results in $7x(7x^2 + 3)$.

▶ Quadratic Equations

A **quadratic expression** is an expression that contains an x^2 term. The expressions $x^2 - 4$ and $x^2 + 3x + 2$ are two examples of quadratic expressions. A **quadratic equation** is a quadratic expression set equal to a value. The equation $x^2 + 3x + 2 = 0$ is a quadratic equation.

Quadratic equations have two solutions. To solve a quadratic equation, combine like terms and place all terms on one side of the equal sign, so that the quadratic is equal to 0. Then, factor the quadratic and find the values of x that make each factor equal to 0. The values that solve a quadratic are the roots of the quadratic.

Example

Solve $x^2 + 5x + 2x + 10 = 0$.

Combine like terms: $x^2 + 7x + 10 = 0$.
Factor: $(x + 5)(x + 2) = 0$, so $x + 5 = 0$ and/or $x + 2 = 0$.
$x = -5$ and/or $x = -2$.

Now check the answers.
$-5 + 5 = 0$ and $-2 + 2 = 0$
Therefore, x is equal to both -5 and -2.

▶ Inequalities

Linear inequalities are solved in much the same way as simple equations. The most important difference

is that when an inequality is multiplied or divided by a negative number, the inequality symbol changes direction.

Example

$10 > 5$; but if you multiply by -3, $-30 < -15$.

▶ Solving Linear Inequalities

To solve a linear inequality, isolate the letter and solve the same as you would in a first-degree equation (an equation in which x is raised only to the first power). Remember to reverse the direction of the inequality sign if you divide or multiply both sides of the equation by a negative number.

Example

If $7 - 2x > 21$, find x.

Isolate the variable:
$7 - 2x > 21$
$7 - 2x - 7 > 21 - 7$
$-2x > 14$

Then divide both sides by -2. Because you are dividing by a negative number, the inequality symbol changes direction: $\frac{-2x}{-2} > \frac{14}{-2}$ becomes $x < -7$, so the answer consists of all real numbers less than -7.

▶ Functions

A **function** is an equation with one input (variable) in which each unique input value yields no more than one output. The set of elements that make up the possible inputs of a function is the domain of the function. The set of elements that make up the possible outputs of a function is the range of the function.

A function commonly takes the form $f(x) = x + c$, where x is a variable and c is a constant. The values for x are the domain of this function. The values of $f(x)$ are the range of the function.

If $f(x) = 5x + 2$, what is $f(3)$?

To find the value of a function given an input, substitute the given input for the variable: $f(3) = 5(3) + 2 = 15 + 2 = 17$.

▶ Domain

The function $f(x) = 3x$ has a domain of all real numbers. Any real number can be substituted for x in the equation, and the value of the function will be a real number.

The function $f(x) = \frac{2}{x} - 4$ has a domain of all real numbers excluding 4. If $x = 4$, the value of the function would be $\frac{2}{0}$, which is undefined. In a function, the values that make a part of the function undefined are the values that are NOT in the domain of the function.

What is the domain of the function $f(x) = \sqrt{x}$?

The square root of a negative number is an imaginary number, so the value of x must not be less than 0. Therefore, the domain of the function is $x \geq 0$.

▶ Range

As you just saw, the function $f(x) = 3x$ has a domain of all real numbers. If any real number can be substituted for x, $3x$ can yield any real number. The range of this function is also all real numbers.

Although the domain of the function $f(x) = \frac{2}{x} - 4$ is all real numbers excluding 4, the range of the function is all real numbers excluding 0, because no value for x can make $f(x) = 0$.

What is the range of the function $f(x) = \sqrt{x}$?

You already found the domain of the function to be $x \geq 0$. For all values of x greater than or equal to 0, the function will return values greater than or equal to 0.

▶ Nested Functions

Given the definitions of two functions, you can find the result of one function (given a value) and place it directly into another function. For example, if $f(x) = 5x + 2$ and $g(x) = -2x$, what is $f[g(x)]$ when $x = 3$?

Begin with the innermost function: find $g(x)$ when $x = 3$. In other words, find $g(3)$. Then, substitute the result of that function for x in $f(x)$: $g(3) = -2(3) = -6$, $f(-6) = 5(-6) + 2 = -30 + 2 = -28$. Therefore, $f[g(x)] = -28$ when $x = 3$.

What is the value of $g[f(x)]$ when $x = 3$?

Start with the innermost function; this time, it is $f(x)$: $f(3) = 5(3) + 2 = 15 + 2 = 17$. Now, substitute 17 for x in $g(x)$: $g(17) = -2(17) = -34$. When $x = 3$, $f[g(x)] = -28$ and $g[f(x)] = -34$.

▶ Algebra and Functions Posttest

1. $\frac{(5a + 7b)b}{b + 2b} =$

    a. $4a$

    b. $4ab$

    c. $2a + 4b$

    d. $\frac{5a + 7b}{3}$

    e. $5a + 5b$

2. $(2x^2)(4y^2) + 6x^2y^2 =$

    a. $12x^2y^2$

    b. $14x^2y^2$

    c. $2x^2 + 4y^2 + 6x^2y^2$

    d. $8x^2 + y^2 + 6x^2y^2$

    e. $8x^4y^4 + 6x^2y^2$

3. The inequality $3x - 6 \leq 4(x + 2)$ is equivalent to which of the following?

a. $x \geq -14$

b. $x \leq -14$

c. $x \leq -8$

d. $x \geq -8$

e. $x \leq 2$

4. What is the product of $(x - 1)(x + 1)$?

a. $x^2 - 1$

b. $x^2 + 1$

c. $x^2 - x - 1$

d. $x^2 - x + 1$

e. $x^2 - 2x - 1$

5. What is the value of $(x + c)^2$?

a. $x^2 + c^2$

b. $x^2 + cx + c^2$

c. $x^2 + c^2x^2 + c^2$

d. $x^2 + cx^2 + c^2x + c^2$

e. $x^2 + 2cx + c^2$

6. What is one factor of $x^2 - 4$?

a. x^2

b. -4

c. $(x - 1)$

d. $(x + 2)$

e. $(x - 4)$

7. If $f(x) = 2x + 1$ and $g(x) = x - 2$, what is the value of $f\{g[f(3)]\}$?

a. 1

b. 3

c. 5

d. 7

e. 11

8. If $f(x) = 6x + 4$ and $g(x) = x^2 - 1$, what is the value of $g[f(x)]$?

a. $6x^2 - 2$

b. $36x^2 + 16$

c. $36x^2 + 48x + 15$

d. $36x^2 + 48x + 16$

e. $6x^3 + 4x^2 - 6x - 4$

9. What is the domain of the function $f(x) = \frac{1}{x^2 - 9}$?

a. all real numbers excluding 0

b. all real numbers excluding 3 and −3

c. all real numbers greater than 9

d. all real numbers greater than or equal to 9

e. all real numbers greater than 3 and less than −3

10. What is the range of the function $f(x) = x^2 - 4$?

a. all real numbers excluding 0

b. all real numbers excluding 2 and −2

c. all real numbers greater than or equal to 0

d. all real numbers greater than or equal to 4

e. all real numbers greater than or equal to −4

Now, check your answers on page 156.

7 ▶ Geometry

GEOMETRY IS THE STUDY of shapes and the relationships among them. The geometry that you are required to know for the GED Mathematics Exam is fundamental and practical. You should become familiar with the properties of angles, lines, polygons, triangles, and circles, as well as the formulas for area, volume, and perimeter. A grasp of coordinate geometry will also be important when you take the GED.

▶ Geometry Pretest

Use the following diagram to answer questions 1 to 5. The diagram is not to scale.

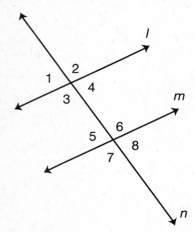

1. If the measure of angle 2 is equal to $12x + 10$ and the measure of angle 8 is equal to $7x - 1$, what is the measure of angle 2?
a. 9 degrees
b. 62 degrees
c. 108 degrees
d. 118 degrees
e. The measure cannot be determined.

2. If the measure of angle 5 is five times the measure of angle 6, what is the measure of angle 5?
a. 30 degrees
b. 36 degrees
c. 120 degrees
d. 130 degrees
e. 150 degrees

3. If the measure of angle 4 is $6x + 20$ and the measure of angle 7 is $10x - 40$, what is the measure of angle 6?
a. 60 degrees
b. 70 degrees
c. 110 degrees
d. 116 degrees
e. 120 degrees

4. Which of the following is NOT true if the measure of angle 3 is 90 degrees?
a. Angles 1 and 2 are complementary.
b. Angles 3 and 6 are supplementary.
c. Angles 5 and 7 are adjacent.
d. Angles 5 and 7 are congruent.
e. Angles 4 and 8 are supplementary and congruent.

5. If the measure of angle 2 is $8x + 10$ and the measure of angle 6 is $x^2 - 38$, what is the measure of angle 8?
a. 42 degrees
b. 74 degrees
c. 84 degrees
d. 108 degrees
e. 138 degrees

6. The length of a rectangle is four less than twice its width. If x is the width of the rectangle, what is the perimeter of the rectangle?
a. $2x^2 - 4x$
b. $3x - 4$
c. $6x - 4$
d. $6x + 4$
e. $6x - 8$

7. The area of one face of a cube is $9x$ square units. What is the volume of the cube?
a. $27\sqrt{x}$ cubic units
b. $27x$ cubic units
c. $27x\sqrt{x}$ cubic units
d. $27x^2$ cubic units
e. $27x^3$ cubic units

8. If the diameter of a circle is doubled, the circumference of the new circle is
 a. one-fourth of the circumference of the original circle.
 b. one-half of the circumference of the original circle.
 c. the same as the circumference of the original circle.
 d. two times the circumference of the original circle.
 e. four times the circumference of the original circle.

9. If the height of a triangle is half its base, b, what is the area of the triangle?
 a. $\frac{1}{4}b$
 b. $\frac{1}{4}b^2$
 c. $\frac{1}{2} \div 2b$
 d. $\frac{1}{2}b^2$
 e. b

10. The bases of a right triangle measure $x - 3$ and $x + 4$. If the hypotenuse of the triangle is $2x - 3$, what is the length of the hypotenuse?
 a. 4
 b. 5
 c. 8
 d. 12
 e. 13

11. The endpoints of a line segment are $(-3,6)$ and $(7,4)$. What is the slope of this line?
 a. -5
 b. $-\frac{1}{5}$
 c. $\frac{1}{5}$
 d. 5
 e. 10

12. What is the midpoint of a line segment with endpoints at $(0,-8)$ and $(-8,0)$?
 a. $(-8,-8)$
 b. $(-4,-4)$
 c. $(-1,-1)$
 d. $(4,4)$
 e. $(8,8)$

13. What is the distance from the point $(-6,2)$ to the point $(2,17)$?
 a. $3\sqrt{41}$ units
 b. $\sqrt{229}$ units
 c. 17 units
 d. $\sqrt{365}$ units
 e. $5\sqrt{17}$ units

Now, check your answers on page 157.

▶ What Are Angles?

Now you are ready to learn about angles. An **angle** is formed by two rays that share a common endpoint. One ray forms each side of the angle, and the common endpoint is called the **vertex**. Here is an example of an angle.

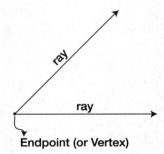

Endpoint (or Vertex)

There is more than one way to name an angle. The symbol for an angle is ∠. Here are some ways to name an angle.

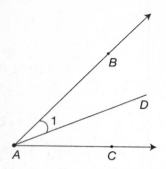

- **You can use three letters to name an angle.** The middle letter represents the vertex. For example, the largest angle (bisected by ray *AD*) could be named ∠*BAC* or ∠*CAB*. In both cases, the *A* is in the middle because it represents the vertex, or the endpoint, of the two rays that make up the angle.
- **You can use only one letter to name an angle** if the angle you are naming does not share its vertex point with another angle. For example, the vertex illustration shows an angle that is alone. It does not share its vertex point with any other angle. So, you could name it ∠*A*.
- **You can use a number.** Look at the second angle diagram again. Notice that a number is written inside the angle. Sometimes angles will be numbered in this way. When this number does not represent the measurement of the angle, you can use the number to name the angle: ∠1.

▶ Measuring Angles

Angles are measured in a unit called the **degree**. The symbol for a degree is °. You can use an instrument called a **protractor** to measure an angle.

Here's how to use a protractor to measure an angle.

Step 1 Place the cross mark or hole in the middle of the straight edge of the protractor on the vertex of the angle you wish to measure.

Step 2 Line up one of the angle's rays with one of the zero marks on the protractor. (Note that there are two zero marks on the protractor. It doesn't matter which one you use.)

Step 3 Keeping the protractor in place, trace the length of the angle's other ray out to the curved part of the protractor.

Step 4 Read the number closest to the ray. (Notice that there are two rows of numbers on the protractor. Make sure you are measuring from zero.) This is the measure of the angle in degrees.

Naming Angles

Rule	How to Use the Rule	Example
Use the angle symbol with three letters.	The middle letter should represent the vertex.	∠ABC ∠CBA
Use the angle symbol with the vertex letter.	Use only if the angle you are naming does not share its vertex point with another angle.	∠B
Use the angle symbol with a number.	Use only if the number isn't the measurement of the angle.	∠1

▶ Classifying Angles

Angles are classified by their measures. They can be **acute** (less than 90 degrees), **right** (90 degrees), **obtuse** (more than 90 degrees), or **straight** (180 degrees). Here are some examples these different kinds of angles.

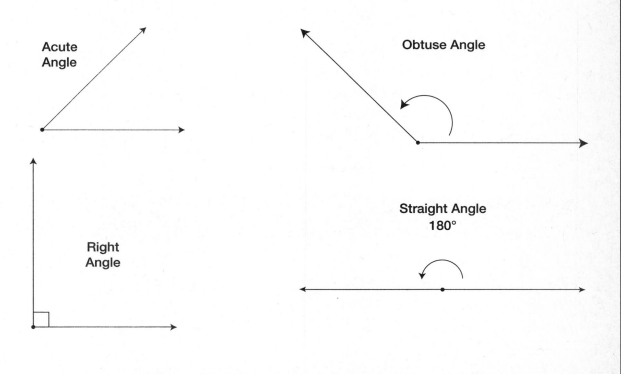

Acute Angle

Obtuse Angle

Right Angle

Straight Angle
180°

Line Relationships

Name	Definition	Example
parallel lines	two lines on a flat surface (also called a **plane** in geometry) that never intersect (the symbol ‖ indicates that two lines are parallel)	
perpendicular lines	two lines that intersect and form right angles (the symbol ⊥ indicates that two lines are perpendicular)	
transversal	a line that cuts across two or more lines at different points	

▶ Relationships between Lines and Angles

Lines have different relationships with one another depending on whether and how they intersect to form angles. Here are some examples of different relationships lines can have with one another.

When a **transversal** intersects two parallel lines, eight angles form. These angles have different names, depending on their relationships both to each other and to the parallel lines. For example, some pairs of angles formed by a transversal and two parallel lines are said to be **congruent**. Congruent angles are equal in measure. Some pairs of angles formed by a transversal and two parallel lines are said to be **supplementary**. The measures of supplementary angles add up to 180°.

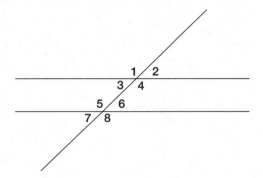

Angles Formed by Parallel Lines and a Transversal

Name	Definition	Relationship	Example
vertical angles	angles directly across from or opposite each other	congruent	angles 1 and 3 angles 2 and 4 angles 5 and 7 angles 6 and 8
corresponding angles	angles on the same side of the transversal and either both above or both below the parallel lines	congruent	angles 1 and 5 angles 2 and 6 angles 3 and 7 angles 4 and 8
alternate interior angles	angles inside the parallel lines and on opposite sides of the transversal	congruent	angles 3 and 5 angles 4 and 6
alternate exterior angles	angles outside the parallel lines and on opposite sides of the transversal	congruent	angles 1 and 7 angles 2 and 8
same-side interior angles	angles inside the parallel lines and on the same side of the transversal	supplementary	angles 3 and 6 angles 4 and 5
same-side exterior angles	angles outside the parallel lines and on the same side of the transversal	supplementary	angles 1 and 8 angles 2 and 7

▶ Polygons

Plane figures are two-dimensional objects that reside on a plane. You can think of a plane like a sheet of paper that extends forever in all directions. Special figures are called **polygons**.

A good grasp of geometry requires a knowledge of the basic polygon shapes. Study the following geometry vocabulary.

A **polygon** is a closed plane figure made up of line segments.
A **triangle** is a polygon with three sides.
A **quadrilateral** is a polygon with four sides.
A **pentagon** is a polygon with five sides.
A **hexagon** is a polygon with six sides.
A **heptagon** or a **septagon** is a polygon with seven sides.
An **octagon** is a polygon with eight sides.

▶ Quadrilaterals

Four-sided polygons are called **quadrilaterals**, and there are classifications for quadrilaterals.

A quadrilateral with one pair of parallel sides (bases) is called a **trapezoid**. In an isosceles trapezoid, the sides that are not bases are congruent (equal in measure). Because the parallel bases are not the same length in a trapezoid, we call these bases b_1 and b_2.

A quadrilateral with two pairs of parallel sides is called a **parallelogram**. The two sets of opposite sides that are parallel are equal and congruent in a parallelogram, as shown in the diagram:

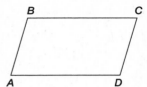

Parallelograms are broken down into further subgroups.

■ A **rectangle** is a parallelogram with four right angles.

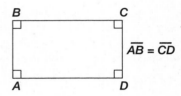

$$\overline{AB} = \overline{CD}$$

■ A **rhombus** is a parallelogram with four equal and congruent sides.

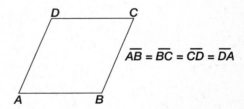

$$\overline{AB} = \overline{BC} = \overline{CD} = \overline{DA}$$

■ A **square** is a parallelogram with both four right angles and four equal and congruent sides. A square is a rhombus, a rectangle, a parallelogram, and a quadrilateral.

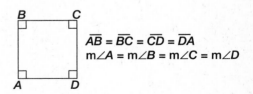

$$\overline{AB} = \overline{BC} = \overline{CD} = \overline{DA}$$
$$m\angle A = m\angle B = m\angle C = m\angle D$$

▶ Finding Perimeter and Circumference

The GED provides you with several geometrical formulas. One of these is for the perimeter. **Perimeter** is the distance around a figure. You can calculate the perimeter of a figure by adding up the lengths of all the sides.

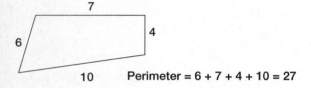

Perimeter = 6 + 7 + 4 + 10 = 27

Example

Find the perimeter of a square whose side is 5 cm.

You know that each side of a square is equal. So, if you know that one side of a square is 5 cm, then you know that each side of the square is 5 cm. To calculate the perimeter, add up the lengths of all four sides.

5 + 5 + 5 + 5 = 20

So, the perimeter of a square whose side measures 5 cm is 20 cm.

> **GED Tip**
> A quick way to calculate the perimeter of a square is $4 \times s$, where s = the length of one side of the square. So, the perimeter of a square whose side measures 5 cm would be $4 \times 5 = 20$ cm.

The perimeter of a circle is called its **circumference**. You can calculate a circle's circumference using either its radius or its diameter.

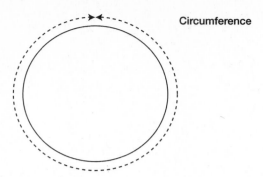

Circumference

The **diameter** is a line segment that goes through the center of a circle. The endpoints of the diameter are on the curve of the circle. Any line that begins at the center of a circle and ends on a point on the circle is called a **radius**. A circle's diameter is twice as long as its radius. So, if you know either the radius or the diameter, you can easily find the other.

To calculate circumference, use either of these formulas, where $\pi = 3.14$ (π is a Greek symbol, spelled *pi*, and pronounced "pie"), d is the circle's diameter, and r is the circle's radius:

$$C = \pi d$$
$$C = 2\pi r$$

Example

Find the circumference of a circle with a diameter of 5 inches.

Because you know the diameter, use the formula that includes the diameter:
$C = \pi d$.
$$C = \pi(5)$$
$$= (3.14)(5)$$
$$= 15.7$$

The final answer is 15.7 inches.

▶ Finding Area

Area is a measure of the surface of a two-dimensional figure. The following table shows how to calculate the area of different figures.

☐ = Area

Calculating Area

FIGURE	AREA CALCULATION	AREA FORMULA
square	side × side or base × height	$A = s^2$ or $A = bh$
rectangle	base × height	$A = bh$
parallelogram	base × height	$A = bh$
triangle	$\frac{1}{2}$ × base × height	$A = \frac{1}{2}bh$
trapezoid	$\frac{1}{2}$ × base$_1$ × height + $\frac{1}{2}$ × base$_2$ × height	$A = \frac{1}{2}h(b_1 + b_2)$
circle	π × radius squared	$A = \pi r^2$

▶ Finding Volume

Volume is a measure of the amount of space inside a three-dimensional shape. Three-dimensional shapes are sometimes called **solids**.

The formula for calculating the volume of a rectangular solid is:

$$V = Ah$$

where V = the volume

   A = the area of the base

   h = the height

Examples

1. Find the volume of a cube that is 3 inches long on each edge.

Choose the correct formula. The problem tells you that you are measuring the volume of a cube. The formula for the volume of a cube is $V = Ah$ or $V = s^3$.

Plug in the known measures and solve:

$V = 3^3$

   $= 3 \times 3 \times 3$

   $= 27$

So the final answer is 27 square inches.

2. Find the volume of a cylinder that has a height of 10 cm and a radius of 5 cm.

Choose the correct formula. The problem tells you that you are measuring the volume of a cylinder. The formula for the volume of a cylinder is $V = Ah$ or $V = \pi r^2 h$.

Plug in the known measures and solve:

$V = \pi r^2 h$

   $= \pi(5)^2(10)$

   $= \pi(25)(10)$

   $= \pi(250)$

   $= 785$

So the final answer is 785 cubic centimeters. (Cubic centimeters can also be written as cm^3.)

▶ Surface Area

The surface area of a three-dimensional object measures the area of each of its faces and adds them together. The total surface area of a rectangular solid is double the sum of the areas of the three different faces. For a cube, simply multiply the surface area of one of its sides by 6.

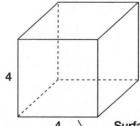

4

4

Surface area of front side = 16
Therefore, the surface area
of the cube = 16 × 6 = 96.

▶ Triangles

Triangles are three-sided polygons. The three **interior angles** of a triangle add up to 180 degrees. Triangles are named by their vertices. The triangle pictured is named *ABC* because of the vertices *A*, *B*, and *C*, but it could also be named *ACB*, *BCA*, *BAC*, *CBA*, or *CAB*. The vertices must be named in order, but can start from any one of the vertices.

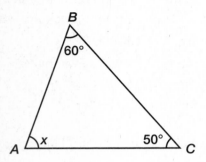

If you know the measure of two angles of a triangle, you can find the measure of the third angle by adding the measures of the first two angles and subtracting that sum from 180. The third angle of triangle *ABC* at left is equal to 180 − (50 + 60) = 180 − 110 = 70 degrees.

The **exterior angles** of a triangle are the angles that are formed outside the triangle.

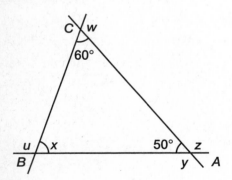

Adjacent interior and exterior angles are supplementary. Angle *y* and the angle that measures 50 degrees are supplementary. Angle *z* is also supplementary to the angle that measures 50 degrees, because these angles form a line. The measure of angle *y* is equal to 180 − 50 = 130. Because angle *z* is also supple-

mentary to the 50-degree angle, angle *z* also measures 130 degrees. Notice that angles *y* and *z* are vertical angles—another reason why these two angles are equal in measure.

The measure of an exterior angle is equal to the sum of the two interior angles to which the exterior angle is not adjacent. You already know angle *y* measures 130 degrees, because it and angle *BAC* are supplementary. However, you could also find the measure of angle *y* by adding the measures of the other two interior angles. Angle *ABC*, 70, plus angle *ACB*, 60, is equal to the measure of the exterior angle of *BAC*: 70 + 60 = 130, the measure of angles *y* and *z*.

If you find the measure of one exterior angle at each vertex, the sum of these three exterior angles is 360 degrees. The measure of angle *y* is 130 degrees. The measure of angle *u* is 110 degrees, because it is supplementary to the 70-degree angle (180 − 70 = 110) and because the sum of the other interior angles is 110 degrees (50 + 60 = 110). The measure of angle *w* is 120 degrees, because it is supplementary to the 60-degree angle (180 − 60 = 120) and because the sum of the other interior angles is 120 degrees (70 + 50 = 120). The sum of angles *y*, *u*, and *w* is 130 + 110 + 120 = 360 degrees.

▶ Types of Triangles

If the measure of the largest angle of a triangle is less than 90 degrees, the triangle is an **acute triangle**. The largest angle in this triangle measures 70 degrees; therefore, it is an acute triangle.

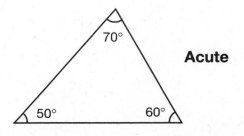

If the measure of the largest angle of a triangle is equal to 90 degrees, the triangle is a **right triangle**. The largest angle this triangle measures 90 degrees; therefore, it is a right triangle.

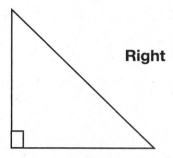

Right

If the measure of the largest angle of a triangle is greater than 90 degrees, the triangle is an **obtuse triangle**. The largest angle in this triangle measures 150 degrees; therefore, it is an obtuse triangle.

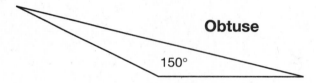

Obtuse

150°

There are three other types of triangles. If no two sides or angles of a triangle are equal, the triangle is **scalene**. If exactly two sides (and therefore, two angles) of a triangle are equal, the triangle is **isosceles**. If all three sides (and therefore, all three angles) of a triangle are equal, the triangle is **equilateral**.

In a triangle, the side opposite the largest angle of the triangle is the longest side, and the side opposite the smallest angle is the shortest side. You can see this in the scalene triangle pictured. In an isosceles triangle, the sides opposite the equal angles are the equal sides. In a right triangle, the angle opposite the right angle is the hypotenuse, which is always the longest side of the triangle.

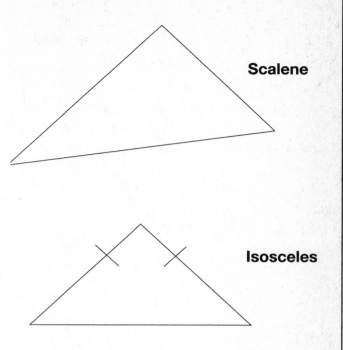

Scalene

Isosceles

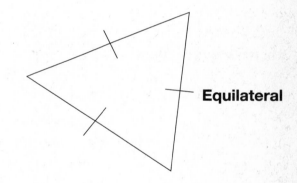

Equilateral

▶ Congruent Triangles

Triangles are **congruent** if they are exactly the same size and the same shape. You might look at two triangles and guess whether they are the same—you're probably a pretty good judge as to whether two triangles are the same size and shape. Or, you could cut out one of the triangles and see if it fits exactly on top of the other one. If so, they are congruent. However, geometry is largely about *proving* things, not guessing about them. So, you need to be able to use basic geometry rules, such as **theorems** (formulas or statements in mathematics that can be proved true) to show that two triangles are congruent.

Though geometry rules come in different forms, they can be generally understood as statements that all mathematicians have agreed to accept as true or that can be proved true. **Postulates** are statements that are accepted without proof. **Theorems** are statements that can be proved true. You will learn more about these principles when you take a geometry course (if you have not already taken one). For now, you just need to know that you must follow certain steps to prove that two triangles are congruent.

In fact, there are three rules for proving that two triangles are congruent to one another. Notice that the symbol ≅ means congruent to. When you see this symbol, say the word *congruent*.

Proving That Triangles Are Congruent

RULE NAME	WHAT IT SAYS
side-side-side (SSS)	If three sides of one triangle are congruent to three sides of another triangle, then the two triangles are congruent.
side-angle-side (SAS)	If two sides and the angle they form are congruent to the corresponding parts of another triangle, then the two triangles are congruent.
angle-side-angle (ASA)	If two angles and the side in between them of one triangle are congruent to the corresponding parts of another triangle, then the two triangles are congruent.

▶ Similar Triangles

Triangles are **similar** if they have the same shape and their sizes are proportional to one another. You can prove that two triangles are similar using one of the following three rules. Notice that the symbol ~ means similar to.

Proving That Triangles Are Similar

RULE NAME	WHAT IT SAYS
angle-angle (AA)	If two angles of one triangle are congruent to two angles of another triangle, then the two triangles are similar.
side-side-side (SSS)	If the lengths of all three corresponding sides of two triangles are proportional, then the two triangles are similar.
side-angle-side (SAS)	If the lengths of two pairs of corresponding sides of two triangles are proportional and the corresponding angles in between those two sides are congruent, then the two triangles are similar.

▶ Parts of a Right Triangle

A triangle that has a right angle is called a **right triangle**. The sides and angles of right triangles have special relationships.

As you know, a right triangle has three sides. Two of the sides come together to form the right angle.

These two sides are called **legs**. The third side of the triangle is called the **hypotenuse**. The hypotenuse is always the longest side of a right triangle. It is directly across from the right angle.

▶ The Pythagorean Theorem

Right triangles are special triangles used for measuring. In a right triangle, the base and one side are perpendicular.

In right triangles, there is a special relationship between the hypotenuse and the legs of the triangle. This relationship is always true and it is known as the Pythagorean theorem. The following equation summarizes the Pythagorean theorem.

$$a^2 + b^2 = c^2$$

In the equation, a and b are the legs of the right triangle, and c is the hypotenuse.

In words, the Pythagorean theorem states that in a right triangle, the sum of the squares of the lengths of the legs is equal to the square of the length of the hypotenuse.

▶ Coordinate Geometry

The **coordinate plane** is the grid of boxes on which the x-axis and y-axis are placed and coordinate points called **ordered pairs** can be plotted. The points and figures that can be plotted on the plane and the operations that can be performed on them fall under the heading **coordinate geometry**.

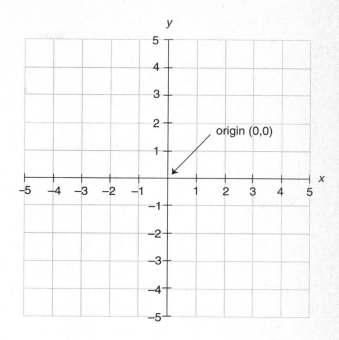

The graph is an example of the coordinate plane. The **x-axis** and the **y-axis** meet at the origin, a point with the coordinates (0,0). The **origin** is zero units from the x-axis and zero units from the y-axis.

Look at the point labeled A, with the coordinates (2,3). The x-coordinate is listed first in the coordinate pair. The x value of a point is the distance from the y-axis to that point. Point A is two units from the y-axis, so its x value is 2. The y-coordinate is listed second in the coordinate pair. The y value of a point is the distance from the x-axis to that point. Point A is three units from the x-axis, so its y value is 3.

What are the coordinates of point B? Point B is minus four units from the y-axis and four units from the x-axis. The coordinates of point B are (−4,4).

The coordinate plane is divided into four sections, or quadrants. The points in quadrant I, the top right corner of the plane, have positive values for both x and y. Point A is in quadrant I and its x and y values are both positive. The points in quadrant II, the top left corner of the plane, have negative values for x and positive values for y. Point B is in quadrant II and its x value is negative, while its y value is positive. The points in quadrant III, the bottom left corner of the plane, have negative values for both x and y, and the points in quadrant IV, the bottom right corner of the plane, have positive values for x and negative values for y.

▶ Slope

When two points on the coordinate plane are connected, a line is formed. The **slope** of a line is the difference between the y values of two points divided by the difference between the x values of those two points. When the equation of a line is written in the form $y = mx + b$, the value of m is the slope of the line.

If both the y value and the x value increase from one point to another, or if both the y value and the x value decrease from one point to another, the slope of the line is positive. If the y value increases and the x value decreases from one point to another, or if the y value decreases and the x value increases from one point to another, the slope of the line is negative.

A horizontal line has a slope of 0. Lines such as $y = 3$, $y = -2$, or $y = c$, where c is any constant, are lines with slopes of 0.

A vertical line has no slope. Lines such as $x = 3$, $x = -2$, or $x = c$ are lines with no slopes.

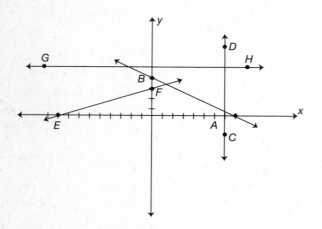

The slope of the line AB at left is equal to $[5 - (-3)] \div [2 - (-2)] = \frac{8}{4} = 2$. The slope of line AB is 2. The slope of line EF is equal to $[(-5) - 4] \div (9 - 6) = \frac{-9}{3} = -3$. Line GH is a horizontal line; there is no change in the y values from point G to point H. This line has a slope of 0. Line CD is a vertical line; there is no change in the x values from point C to point D. This line has no slope.

Parallel lines have the same slope. Perpendicular lines have slopes that are negative reciprocals of each other. Lines given by the equations $y = 3x + 5$ and $y = 3x - 2$ are parallel, while the line given by the equation $y = -\frac{1}{3}x + 1$ is perpendicular to those lines.

▶ Midpoint

The **midpoint** of a line segment is the coordinates of the point that falls exactly in the middle of the line segment. If (a,c) is one endpoint of a line segment and (b,d) is the other endpoint, the midpoint of the line segment is equal to $(\frac{a+b}{2}, \frac{c+d}{2})$. In other words, the midpoint of a line segment is equal to the average of the x values of the endpoints and the average of the y values of the endpoints.

Example

What is the midpoint of a line segment with endpoints at $(1,5)$ and $(-3,3)$?

Using the midpoint formula, the midpoint of this line is equal to

$$\left(\frac{1+(-3)}{2}, \frac{5+3}{2}\right) = \left(\frac{-2}{2}, \frac{8}{2}\right) = (-1,4).$$

▶ Distance

To find the **distance** between two points, use the following formula. The variable x_1 represents the x-coordinate of the first point, x_2 represents the x-coordinate of the second point, y_1 represents the y-coordinate of the first point, and y_2 represents the y-coordinate of the second point:

$$D = \sqrt{(x_2 - x_1)^2 + (y_2 - y_1)^2}$$

Example

What is the distance between the points $(-2, 8)$ and $(4, -2)$?

Substitute these values into the formula:

$$\begin{aligned} D &= \sqrt{[4 - (-2)]^2 + [(-2) - 8]^2} \\ &= \sqrt{(4 + 2)^2 + (-2 - 8)^2} \\ &= \sqrt{(6)^2 + (-10)^2} \\ &= \sqrt{36 + 100} \\ &= \sqrt{136} \end{aligned}$$

▶ Geometry Posttest

Use the following diagram to answer questions 1 to 5.

Lines AE, BF, GD, and ray OC all intersect at point O (not labeled), and AE is perpendicular to OC.

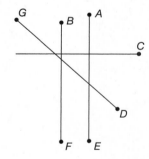

1. Which of the following pairs of angles are complementary?
   a. angles 1 and 2
   b. angles 2 and 3
   c. angles 1 and 4
   d. angles 1, 2, and 3
   e. angles 1, 6, and 7

2. Which of the following number sentences is NOT true?
   a. angle 1 + angle 2 = angle 3 + angle 4
   b. angle 1 + angle 2 + angle 3 + angle 7 = angle 4 + angle 5 + angle 6
   c. angle 2 + angle 3 = angle 6
   d. angle 1 + angle 7 = angle 2 + angle 3
   e. angle 2 + angle 3 + angle 4 + angle 5 = 180 degrees

3. If the measure of angle 3 is $2x + 2$ and the measure of angle 4 is $5x - 10$, what is the measure of angle 7?
   a. 14 degrees
   b. 30 degrees
   c. 60 degrees
   d. 90 degrees
   e. 115 degrees

4. If angle 1 measures 62 degrees and angle 4 measures 57 degrees, what is the measure of angle 6?
   a. 33 degrees
   b. 61 degrees
   c. 72 degrees
   d. 95 degrees
   e. 119 degrees

5. If the measure of angle 3 is $5x + 3$ and the measure of angle 4 is $15x + 7$, what is the sum of angles 5 and 6?
   a. 67 degrees
   b. 113 degrees
   c. 134 degrees
   d. 157 degrees
   e. The sum cannot be determined.

6. The length of a rectangle is 4 times the length of a square. If the rectangle and the square share a side, and the perimeter of the square is 2 units, what is the perimeter of the rectangle?
a. 5 units
b. 6 units
c. 8 units
d. 10 units
e. 20 units

7. The area of a rectangle is $x^2 + 7x + 10$ square units. If the length of the rectangle is $x + 2$ units, what is the width of the rectangle?
a. $x + 2$ units
b. $x + 4$ units
c. $x + 5$ units
d. $2x + 4$ units
e. $x^2 + 6x + 8$ units

8. The length of a rectangular solid is twice the sum of the width and height of the rectangular solid. If the width is equal to the height and the volume of the solid is 108 cubic inches, what is the length of the solid?
a. 3 inches
b. 6 inches
c. 8 inches
d. 9 inches
e. 12 inches

9. If the length of the base of right triangle *DEF* is 8 units and the hypotenuse of *DEF* is $8\sqrt{5}$ units, what is the length of the other base?
a. 4 units
b. 8 units
c. $8\sqrt{2}$ units
d. 16 units
e. 32 units

10. If the measure of angle *A* of triangle *ABC* is $3x$, the measure of angle *B* is $5x$, and the measure of angle *C* is $4x$, what is the value of x?
a. 12
b. 15
c. 20
d. 30
e. 45

11. What is the distance from the point $(0,-4)$ to the point $(4,4)$?
a. $5\sqrt{2}$ units
b. 4 units
c. $4\sqrt{2}$ units
d. $4\sqrt{3}$ units
e. $4\sqrt{5}$ units

12. What is the midpoint of a line segment with endpoints at $(6,-4)$ and $(15,8)$?
a. $(9,4)$
b. $(9,12)$
c. $(10.5,2)$
d. $(12,2)$
e. $(12,9)$

13. The endpoints of a line segment are $(5,-5)$ and $(-5,-5)$. What is the slope of this line?
a. -10
b. -5
c. 0
d. 5
e. This line has no slope.

Now, check your answers on page 158.

Data Analysis, Statistics, and Probability

MANY QUESTIONS ON THE GED will test your ability to analyze data. Analyzing data can be in the form of statistical analysis (as in using measures of central location), finding probability, or reading charts and graphs. All of these topics are covered in this chapter.

▶ Data Analysis, Statistics, and Probability Pretest

1. Find the mean for the set of data:
{96, 90, 78, 90, 92}.
a. 18
b. 89.2
c. 90
d. 89.5
e. 71.2

2. The fuel efficiency for a truck varies, depending on whether the truck is traveling uphill or downhill. The following efficiencies were recorded for one hour at ten-minute intervals, in miles per gallon: 16, 22, 14, 28, 16, 12. What is the mean fuel efficiency for the truck in this hour?
a. 16 miles per gallon
b. 12 miles per gallon
c. 18 miles per gallon
d. 6 miles per gallon
e. 20 miles per gallon

3. Given the set of numbers {26, 27, 29, 27, 29, 27, 30, 30}, which of the following is true?
a. The mean equals the median.
b. There are three modes.
c. The median is greater than the mode.
d. The median is 27.
e. The median equals the mode.

4. In the set of data {15, 12, 13, 11, 14, 10, 8}, what is the mode?
a. 0
b. There is no mode.
c. 11
d. 7
e. 12

5. On a standard die, what is the probability of rolling a 3?
a. $\frac{1}{6}$
b. $\frac{3}{6}$
c. $\frac{3}{8}$
d. $\frac{1}{3}$
e. $\frac{5}{6}$

Questions 6 and 7 refer to the following information.

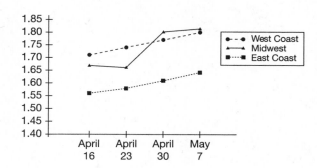

6. On what date and in what location was there the greatest jump in the price of gasoline from one week to the next?
a. April 23 on the West Coast
b. April 30 in the Midwest
c. April 30 on the West Coast
d. May 7 on the East Coast
e. May 7 in the Midwest

7. Based on the information in the graph, which of the following is the best prediction of the price per gallon of gasoline on the West Coast for the week following May 7?
a. $2.64
b. $2.71
c. $2.76
d. $2.82
e. $2.86

Please use the following to answer questions 8 and 9.

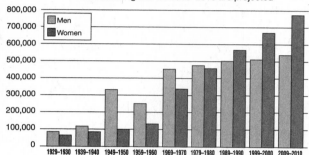

U.S. Higher Education Trends: Bachelor's Degrees Conferred
Source: National Center for Education Statistics, U.S. Dept. of Education Figures for 2009–2010 are projected

8. In which academic year did the number of women receiving bachelor's degrees exceed the number of men receiving bachelor's degrees for the first time?
   a. 1929–1930
   b. 1939–1940
   c. 1969–1970
   d. 1979–1980
   e. 1989–1990

9. Approximately how many more women received a bachelor's degree in 1989–1990 than men?
   a. 150,000
   b. 120,000
   c. 60,000
   d. 35,000
   e. 15,000

Now, check your answers on page 160.

▶ Measures of Central Tendency

Statistics are everywhere—in news reports, in sports, and on your favorite websites. Mean, median, and mode are three common statistics that give information on a group of numbers. They are called **measures of central tendency** because they are different ways of finding the central trend in a group of numbers.

▶ Finding the Mean

Mean is just another word for *average*. The **mean**, or average, is one of the most useful and common statistics. You probably already average your grades at school regularly, so you may already know the basic steps to finding the mean of a set of numbers.

Step 1 Add all the numbers in the list.
Step 2 Count how many numbers are in the list.
Step 3 Divide the sum (the result of step 1) by the number of numbers (the result of step 2).

Another way to think about the mean is in the form of this equation:

$$\text{mean} = \frac{\text{sum of the numbers}}{\text{the number of numbers}}$$

Example
Find the mean of the following set of numbers: 5, 7, 19, 12, 4, 11, 15.

Step 1 Add all the numbers in the list: $5 + 7 + 19 + 12 + 4 + 11 + 15 = 73$.
Step 2 Count how many numbers are in the list: There are seven numbers in the list.
Step 3 Divide the sum (the result of step 1) by the number of numbers (the result of step 2): $73 \div 7 = 10.4$.

So, the mean is 10.4.

Example

Jason has four grades of equal weight in his history class. They are 82, 90, 88, and 85. What is Jason's mean (average) in history?

Add all the numbers in the list:
82 + 90 + 88 + 85 = 345.

Count how many numbers are in the list: There are four numbers in the list.

Divide the sum (the result of step 1) by the number (the result of step 2): 345 ÷ 4 = 86.25.

The mean is 86.25.

▶ Finding the Median

The **median** is the middle number in a group of numbers arranged in sequential order. In a set of numbers, about half will be greater than the median and the same number will be less than the median.

Step 1 Put the numbers in sequential order.
Step 2 The middle number is the median.

Example

Find the median of the following set of numbers: 5, 7, 19, 12, 4, 11, 15.

Put the numbers in sequential order:
4, 5, 7, 11, 12, 15, 19.

The middle number is the median: The middle number is 11.

The median is 11.

In the last example, there was an odd number of numbers, so the middle number was easy to find. But what if you are given an even number of numbers? Let's see how it works.

Example

Find the median of the following set of numbers: 5, 7, 19, 12, 4, 11, 15, 13.

Put the numbers in sequential order:
4, 5, 7, 11, 12, 13, 15, 19.

The middle number is the median. But there are two middle numbers: 11 and 12. In this case, you find the *mean* (or average) of the two middle numbers. That value is your *median*. Remember, to find the mean of a set of numbers, you first add the numbers together (11 + 12 = 23). Then, you divide the sum by the number of numbers (23 ÷ 2 = 11.5).

The median is 11.5.

Why would you use the median instead of the mean? Let's say a teacher gives everyone above the class mean either an A or a B. Here are the grades on the most recent test.

GRADES
110
80
79
78
75
72
70
69
68
67
65
64
63
60
52

The class mean is 71, so only six students will receive an A or a B on the test. All the other students will get a C or below. How would the result be different if the teacher used the class median to determine who gets an A and a B? In that case, everyone with a test score greater than 69 would receive either an A or a B on the test—that's eight students. About half the students would get an A or a B using the median.

Notice that the mean was raised by the one person who received a 110 on the test. Often, when one number changes the mean to be higher (or lower) than the center value, the median can be used instead.

▶ Finding the Mode

The **mode** refers to the number in a set of numbers that occurs most frequently. To find the mode, you just look for numbers that occur more than once and find the one that appears *most* often.

Examples
1. Find the mode of the following set of numbers: 5, 7, 9, 12, 9, 11, 15.
The number 9 occurs twice in the list, so 9 is the mode.

2. Find the mode of the following set of numbers: 5, 7, 19, 12, 4, 11, 15.
None of the numbers occurs more than once, so there is no mode.

3. Find the mode of the following set of numbers: 5, 7, 9, 12, 9, 11, 5.
The numbers 5 and 9 both occur twice in the list, so both 5 and 9 are modes. When a set of numbers had two modes, it is called **bimodal**.

As you can see, the mode isn't always a middle number in a set of numbers. Instead, mode shows clustering. Mode is often used in stores to decide which sizes, styles, or prices are most popular. It wouldn't make sense for a clothing store to stock up on the mean size or the median size of pants. It makes more sense to buy the sizes that most people wear. There's where the mode comes in.

▶ Measures of Dispersion

Measures of dispersion, or the spread of a number set, can be in many different forms. The two forms that may appear on the GED are *range* and *standard deviation*.

▶ Range

The **range** of a data set is the greatest measurement minus the least measurement. For example, given the values 5, 9, 14, 16, and 11, the range would be $16 - 5 = 11$.

▶ Standard Deviation

As you can see, the range is affected by only the two most extreme values in the data set. **Standard deviation** is a measure of dispersion that is affected by every measurement. To find the standard deviation of n measurements, follow these six steps:

1. First, find the mean of the measurements.
2. Find the difference between the mean and each measurement.
3. Square each of the differences.
4. Sum the square values.
5. Divide the sum by n.
6. Choose the nonnegative square root of the quotient.

When you find the standard deviation of a data set, you are finding the average distance from the mean for the n measurements. It cannot be negative, and when two sets of measurements are compared, the larger the standard deviation, the larger the dispersion.

▶ Frequency Distribution

The **frequency distribution** is essentially the number of times, or how frequently, a measurement appears in a data set. It is represented by a chart like the one shown.

NUMBER OF CARS (x)	FREQUENCY (f)
0	4
1	8
2	16
3	6
4	2

To use the chart, simply list each measurement only once in the x column and then write how many times it occurs in the f column.

Example

Show the frequency distribution of the following data set that represents the number of students enrolled in 15 classes at Middleton Technical Institute:

12, 10, 15, 10, 7, 13, 15, 12, 7, 13, 10, 10, 12, 7, 12

NUMBER OF STUDENTS (x)	FREQUENCY (f)
7	3
10	4
12	4
13	2
15	2

Be sure that the total number of measurements taken is equal to the total at the bottom of the frequency distribution chart.

▶ What Is Probability?

Ratios and proportions are ways to compare statistics (see Chapter 8). Similarly, you see probabilities, or pre-

dictions, all the time. Listening to the weather report, you may hear that there is a 30% chance of rain tomorrow. At judo class, you may hear that 11 out of 20 advanced students will attain a brown belt. On television, you might hear that four out of five dentists recommend a certain toothbrush. These are all ways to express probability. In this section, you will also learn what probability is and how to calculate it.

Probability is the mathematics of chance. It is a way of calculating how likely it is that something will happen. It's expressed as the following ratio:

$$P \text{ (event)} = \frac{\text{number of favorable outcomes}}{\text{number of total outcomes}}$$

The term *favorable outcomes* refers to the events you want to occur. *Total outcomes* refers to all the possible events that could occur.

A probability of zero (0) means that the event cannot occur. A probability of 50% is said to be random or chance. A probability of 100% or 1.00 means the event is certain to occur.

Probabilities can be written in different ways:

- as a ratio: 1 out of 2 or (1:2)
- as a fraction: $\frac{1}{2}$
- as a percent: 50%
- as a decimal: 0.5

Example

Aili has four tickets to the school carnival raffle. If 150 were sold, what is the probability that one of Aili's tickets will be drawn?

Plug the numbers into the probability equation:

$$P \text{ (event)} = \frac{\text{number of favorable outcomes}}{\text{number of total outcomes}}$$

$$P \text{ (winning ticket)} = \frac{4}{150}$$

Solve the equation.

There are several ways to write your answer. Here are two of the ways. You can write the answer as a fraction: $\frac{4}{150}$, which reduces to $\frac{2}{75}$. Or you can write it as a percent: 2.7% (we rounded this answer up from 2.66666 . . .).

Now let's look at problems that involve more than one event. Sometimes, the events are **independent**. That is, the first event does not affect the probability of events that come after it.

Example

You toss a penny and a dime into the air. What is the probability that both coins will land heads up?

You could list all the possible outcomes in a table like this:

PENNY	DIME
heads	heads
heads	tails
tails	heads
tails	tails

Then, you could use this information to fill in the probability equation:

$$P\ (event) = \frac{number\ of\ favorable\ outcomes}{number\ of\ total\ outcomes}$$

From the table, you know that there are four possible outcomes. Only one of those outcomes is heads/heads.

P (heads/heads) $= \frac{1}{4}$

The probability of both coins landing heads up is $\frac{1}{4}$, or 25%.

In this problem, you had very few possible events to list. In other problems, however, you might have many possible events to account for. Another way to solve this problem is by following these steps:

Step 1 Determine the probability that each event will occur.

Step 2 Multiply the probabilities together. The product is the probability that both of the two events will occur.

Sometimes the first event does affect the probability of the next event. In this case, the events are said to be *dependent*.

Example

A sack holds three purple buttons, two orange buttons, and five green buttons. What is the probability of drawing one purple button out of the sack and then—without replacing the first button—drawing a second purple button out of the sack?

Determine the probability that each event will occur. First, notice that the first event—drawing a purple button out of the sack—affects the probability of the second event because it changes both the number of purple buttons still in the sack and the total number of buttons in the sack.

The probability of drawing the first purple button is $\frac{3}{10}$.

The probability of drawing a second purple button $\frac{2}{9}$.

Multiply the probabilities together. The product is the probability that the two events will occur together.

$\frac{3}{10} \times \frac{2}{9} = \frac{6}{90} = \frac{1}{15}$

The answer is $\frac{1}{15}$, or 6.7%.

▶ Data Representation and Interpretation

The GED exam will test your ability to analyze graphs and tables. It is important to study each graph or table very carefully before reading the question. This will help you to process the information that is presented. It is extremely important to read all of the information presented, paying special attention to headings and units of measure. Here is an overview of the types of graphs you will encounter:

Circle Graphs or Pie Charts

Circle graphs or **pie charts** show how the parts of a whole relate to one another. A pie chart is a circle divided into slices or wedges—like a pizza. Each slice represents a category.

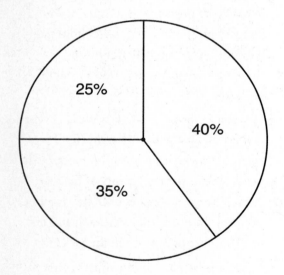

Line Graphs

Line graphs show how two categories of data or information (sometimes called **variables**) relate to one another. The data is displayed on a grid and is presented on a scale using a horizontal axis and a vertical axis for

the different categories of information the graph is comparing. Usually, the data points are connected together to form a line so that you can see trends in the data, or how the data changes over time. Therefore, often you will see line graphs with units of time or the word *time* on the horizontal axis.

Line graphs are frequently used to show the results of a scientific experiment. The variable that the scientist is measuring and tracking is often called the **dependent variable**. It is usually measured on the vertical axis of a graph. The horizontal axis is usually measuring time, so you can see how the data changes over time.

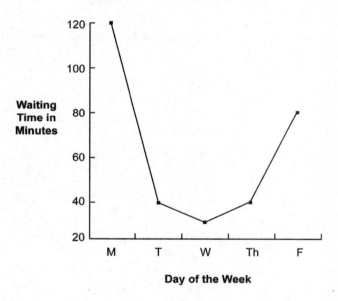

Bar Graphs

Like pie charts, **bar graphs** show how different categories of data relate to one another. A bar represents each category. The length of the bar represents the relative frequency of the category—compared to the other categories on the graph.

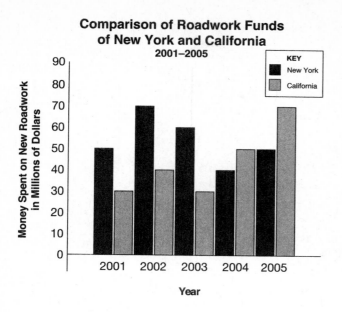

Comparison of Roadwork Funds of New York and California 2001–2005

atlases and on maps. They tell you how many miles apart different places are.

SHOE SIZE	ABSOLUTE FREQUENCY
6.0	1
6.5	4
7.0	6
7.5	11
8.0	8
8.5	6
9.0	4
9.5	3

Both pie charts and bar graphs are used to compare different categories of data. So when you have data to graph, how do you decide which kind of graph to use? Think about what your purpose is. If your purpose is to compare the absolute values of each category, then a bar chart is probably better because the amounts of each category are shown in comparison to each other. If your purpose is to show how each part relates to the whole, a pie chart is probably better.

▶ Getting Information from Tables and Charts

Tables present information in rows and columns. Rows go across, or horizontally. Columns go up and down, or vertically. The box, or cell, that is made where a row and a column meet provides specific information. When looking for information in tables, it's important to read the table title, the column headings, and the row labels on the left so you understand the information you are looking at. **Frequency tables** are used to track how often things happen. **Mileage tables** are common in

Charts present information in many different ways. You probably use charts all the time. **Flow charts** often show the steps in a process. **Time lines** are used to show the sequence of events over time. **Venn diagrams** are used to show how things are similar or different. They are often used in math when talking about sets of numbers. They can also be used to talk about the characteristics of groups.

Venn Diagram

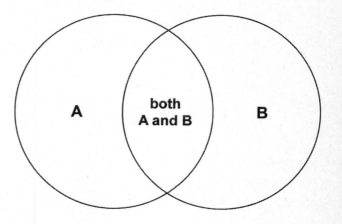

▶ Data Analysis, Statistics, and Probability Posttest

1. Find the mean of the following set of data:
{32, 34, 34, 35, 37, 38, 34, 42}.

a. 34

b. 35.75

c. 10

d. 36

e. 34.5

2. What is the mode of {71, 68, 71, 77, 65, 68, 72}?

a. 71

b. 68

c. none

d. 9

e. 71 and 68

3. The ages at the day camp were 9, 12, 9, 10, 9, 13, 11, 8, 17, 10. What is the median age?

a. 10

b. 9

c. 10.8

d. 11

e. 10.4

4. Calculate the range of these temperatures:
43°, 47°, 43°, 52°, 42°, 78°, 84°, 80°.

a. 43°

b. 42°

c. 37°

d. 47°

e. 58.625°

5. When rolling two dice, what is the probability of rolling a sum of 8?

a. $\frac{5}{12}$

b. $\frac{3}{36}$

c. $\frac{3}{12}$

d. $\frac{2}{36}$

e. $\frac{5}{36}$

Please use the following to answer questions 6 and 7.

The following table gives the annual average hourly wages of production workers in the United States in the 1990s. The data is supplied by the U.S. Department of Labor.

Average Hourly Earnings of U.S. Production Workers

YEAR	HOURLY EARNINGS
1990	$10.01
1991	$10.32
1992	$10.57
1993	$10.83
1994	$11.12
1995	$11.43
1996	$11.82
1997	$12.28
1998	$12.77

6. In which year was the increase in hourly earnings the least from the previous year?

a. 1992

b. 1994

c. 1996

d. 1997

e. 1998

7. What was the approximate percent increase to the nearest whole percent in hourly earnings from 1990 to 1996?

a. 10%

b. 15%

c. 18%

d. 20%

e. 120%

Please use the following to answer questions 8 and 9.

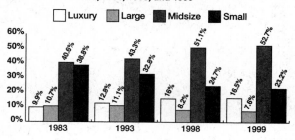

U.S. Car Sales by Vehicle Size and Type,
1983, 1993, 1998, and 1999

Year	Total U.S. Car Sales
1983	9,182,067
1993	8,517,859
1998	8,141,721
1999	8,698,284

YEAR	TOTAL U.S. CAR SALES
1983	9,182,067
1993	8,517,859
1998	8,141,721
1999	8,698,284

8. Approximately how many small cars were sold in the United States in 1998?
a. 500,000
b. 1,000,000
c. 2,000,000
d. 3,000,000
e. 4,000,000

9. In 1999, about how many times were more midsize cars sold than luxury and large cars combined?
a. eight times as many
b. five times as many
c. three times as many
d. twice as many
e. the same

Now, check your answers on page 161.

Posttest

Y OU ARE NOW FAMILIAR with the kinds of questions and answer formats you will see on the official GED. Now take this posttest to identify any areas that you may need to review in more depth before the test day. When you are finished, check the answers on page 162 carefully to assess your results. Remember to do the following:

- Work carefully.
- Use estimation to eliminate answer choices or to check your work.
- Answer every question.
- Check to make sure your answers are logical.
- Use the formula cheat sheet on page 167, when needed.

To simulate the test conditions, use the time constraints of the official GED Mathematics Test. Allow 45 minutes for Part I. You may use a calculator to answer these 25 questions. Then, give yourself 45 minutes for Part II. You should not use a calculator for these 25 questions.

Remember, on the official GED, an unanswered question is counted as incorrect, so make a good guess.

Directions: Read each of the following questions carefully and determine the best answer. Record your answers on the answer sheet for multiple-choice questions and by filling in the circles in the grids for alternative-format questions.

Note: On the GED, you are not permitted to write in the test booklet. For this pretest, practice by making any notes or calculations on a separate piece of paper.

▶ Posttest Answer Sheet

1.				
2.	ⓐ	ⓑ	ⓒ	ⓓ	ⓔ
3.	ⓐ	ⓑ	ⓒ	ⓓ	ⓔ
4.	ⓐ	ⓑ	ⓒ	ⓓ	ⓔ
5.	ⓐ	ⓑ	ⓒ	ⓓ	ⓔ
6.	ⓐ	ⓑ	ⓒ	ⓓ	ⓔ
7.	ⓐ	ⓑ	ⓒ	ⓓ	ⓔ
8.	ⓐ	ⓑ	ⓒ	ⓓ	ⓔ
9.	ⓐ	ⓑ	ⓒ	ⓓ	ⓔ
10.	ⓐ	ⓑ	ⓒ	ⓓ	ⓔ
11.				
12.	ⓐ	ⓑ	ⓒ	ⓓ	ⓔ
13.	ⓐ	ⓑ	ⓒ	ⓓ	ⓔ
14.	ⓐ	ⓑ	ⓒ	ⓓ	ⓔ
15.	ⓐ	ⓑ	ⓒ	ⓓ	ⓔ
16.	ⓐ	ⓑ	ⓒ	ⓓ	ⓔ
17.	ⓐ	ⓑ	ⓒ	ⓓ	ⓔ

18.	ⓐ	ⓑ	ⓒ	ⓓ	ⓔ
19.				
20.	ⓐ	ⓑ	ⓒ	ⓓ	ⓔ
21.	ⓐ	ⓑ	ⓒ	ⓓ	ⓔ
22.	ⓐ	ⓑ	ⓒ	ⓓ	ⓔ
23.	ⓐ	ⓑ	ⓒ	ⓓ	ⓔ
24.	ⓐ	ⓑ	ⓒ	ⓓ	ⓔ
25.	ⓐ	ⓑ	ⓒ	ⓓ	ⓔ
26.	ⓐ	ⓑ	ⓒ	ⓓ	ⓔ
27.	ⓐ	ⓑ	ⓒ	ⓓ	ⓔ
28.	ⓐ	ⓑ	ⓒ	ⓓ	ⓔ
29.				
30.	ⓐ	ⓑ	ⓒ	ⓓ	ⓔ
31.	ⓐ	ⓑ	ⓒ	ⓓ	ⓔ
32.	ⓐ	ⓑ	ⓒ	ⓓ	ⓔ
33.	ⓐ	ⓑ	ⓒ	ⓓ	ⓔ
34.	ⓐ	ⓑ	ⓒ	ⓓ	ⓔ

35.	ⓐ	ⓑ	ⓒ	ⓓ	ⓔ
36.	ⓐ	ⓑ	ⓒ	ⓓ	ⓔ
37.	ⓐ	ⓑ	ⓒ	ⓓ	ⓔ
38.	ⓐ	ⓑ	ⓒ	ⓓ	ⓔ
39.	ⓐ	ⓑ	ⓒ	ⓓ	ⓔ
40.	ⓐ	ⓑ	ⓒ	ⓓ	ⓔ
41.				
42.	ⓐ	ⓑ	ⓒ	ⓓ	ⓔ
43.	ⓐ	ⓑ	ⓒ	ⓓ	ⓔ
44.	ⓐ	ⓑ	ⓒ	ⓓ	ⓔ
45.	ⓐ	ⓑ	ⓒ	ⓓ	ⓔ
46.	ⓐ	ⓑ	ⓒ	ⓓ	ⓔ
47.	ⓐ	ⓑ	ⓒ	ⓓ	ⓔ
48.	ⓐ	ⓑ	ⓒ	ⓓ	ⓔ
49.	ⓐ	ⓑ	ⓒ	ⓓ	ⓔ
50.	ⓐ	ⓑ	ⓒ	ⓓ	ⓔ

▶ Part I

You may use a calculator for questions on this part of the test.

1. At the local bookstore, notebooks are available in two colors: white and gray. Shown are the notebooks currently in stock.

What percent of the notebooks are gray? Mark your answer in the circles in the grid.

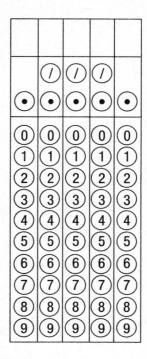

2. Estimate the average number of people who entered the Natural History Museum per day for the week shown in the following table:

DAY	PEOPLE
Monday	619
Tuesday	521
Wednesday	622
Thursday	549
Friday	704
Saturday	683

    a. 900
    b. 800
    c. 700
    d. 600
    e. 500

3. Bonnie's phone plan charges $0.1165 for each minute she uses. Her sister Blaire pays $0.095. How much more does Bonnie pay for each minute?

a. $0.0215

b. $0.107

c. $0.126

d. $0.2115

e. $1.0665

4. $5 + \dfrac{\sqrt{5^2 - 4 \times 2 \times 2}}{3} =$

a. 6

b. 7

c. 8

d. 9

e. 10

Questions 5 and 6 refer to the following table.

Shipping Charges

PURCHASE RANGE	STANDARD	RUSH	ONE-DAY
$0.01 to $15	$4.95	$11.95	$22.95
$15.01 to $30	$5.95	$12.95	$24.95
$30.01 to $45	$7.95	$14.95	$26.95
$45.01 to $100	$13.95	$20.95	$36.95

5. From an online store, Maelyn buys two CDs for $15.95 each and a poster for $5.97. What is the total cost for Maelyn's purchase if she uses standard shipping?

a. $15.97

b. $27.87

c. $29.92

d. $45.82

e. $52.82

6. Maelyn orders three DVDs from the online store for $14.50 each. How much more will her order cost if she chooses one-day shipping rather than standard shipping?

a. $19

b. $20

c. $23

d. $43.50

e. $51.45

7. Mika ran the 100-yard dash in 10.11 seconds. To the nearest hundredth of a mile, how far did Mika run?

a. 0.02 mile

b. 0.05 mile

c. 0.06 mile

d. 0.19 mile

e. 0.57 mile

8. A 1.2-ounce piece of chocolate contains about 230 calories. About how many calories does a 4-ounce piece contain?

a. 610

b. 650

c. 710

d. 770

e. 840

9. Beatriz takes a loan out for $2,000 at 12% simple interest. If she makes no payments for 18 months, how much interest will she owe?

a. $24

b. $36

c. $240

d. $360

e. $720

10. A building's blueprint has a scale that reads 1 inch = 24 inches. What is the actual length of a window that measures $1\frac{3}{4}$ inches on the blueprint?

a. 2 feet 10 inches

b. 3 feet 2 inches

c. 3 feet 4 inches

d. 3 feet 6 inches

e. 3 feet 9 inches

11. To tile a patio, Herman uses packages of tile that each cover an area of 80 square feet. If the area Herman has to cover is 3,140 square feet, how many packages will he have to purchase? Mark your answer in the circles in the grid.

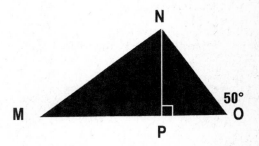

12. Valerie designed a circular garden. All of the large sections (light shaded) will be planted in roses. All the small sections (dark shaded) will be planted in lilies. What fraction of the garden will be planted in lilies?

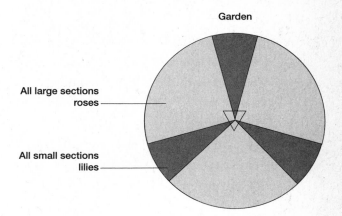

Garden

All large sections roses

All small sections lilies

a. $\frac{1}{2}$

b. $\frac{1}{3}$

c. $\frac{1}{4}$

d. $\frac{1}{5}$

e. $\frac{3}{10}$

Questions 13 and 14 refer to the following triangle.

N

M

P

O

50°

13. What is the measure of angle *PNO*?

a. 20°

b. 30°

c. 35°

d. 40°

e. 50°

14. What is the measure of angle *NMO*?
   a. 20°
   b. 30°
   c. 40°
   d. 50°
   e. Not enough information is given.

15. A swimming pool is 50 feet long and 30 feet wide. The pool is surrounded by a 5-foot-wide walkway. What is the area of this walkway?
   a. 90 square feet
   b. 350 square feet
   c. 450 square feet
   d. 900 square feet
   e. 1,200 square feet

16. A pile of dirt is in the shape of a cone. If the height of the pile is 4 feet and the diameter of the pile is 8 feet, what is the approximate volume of the pile?
   a. 70 cubic feet
   b. 110 cubic feet
   c. 160 cubic feet
   d. 200 cubic feet
   e. 220 cubic feet

Questions 17 and 18 refer to the following chart.

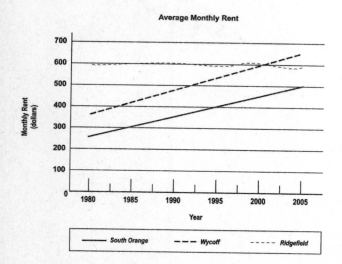

17. For the year 2000, which is the best estimate of the ratio of average rent costs in Wycoff to those in South Orange?
   a. about $\frac{12}{5}$
   b. about $\frac{2}{1}$
   c. about $\frac{4}{3}$
   d. about $\frac{2}{3}$
   e. about $\frac{5}{12}$

18. By about what percent did the rent in South Orange increase between 1980 and 2000?
   a. 10%
   b. 25%
   c. 40%
   d. 65%
   e. 80%

19. You have taken a 30-year mortgage at 6% for the amount of $100,000. Based on the following bar graph, what is the average interest paid per year?

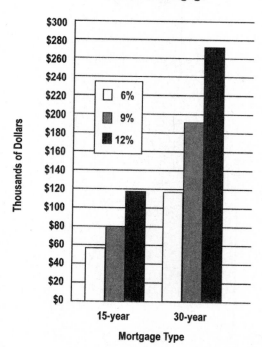

Round the average interest to the nearest thousand. Mark your answer in the circles in the grid.

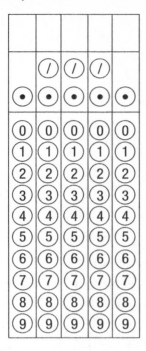

20. The profit of Two Scoops Ice-Cream Parlor by quarter is shown on the following circle graph.

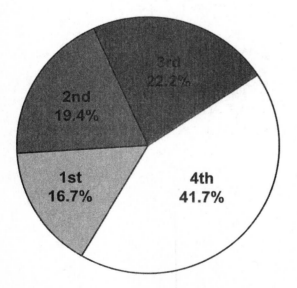

**Two Scoops
Ice-Cream Parlor**
Percent of Total Profit
by Quarter
(Total Profit = $18,000)

How much more total profits would this business need to earn during the year to increase the average profit per quarter to $5,000?
   a. $2,000
   b. $1,500
   c. $700
   d. $500
   e. $300

Questions 21 and 22 are based on the following information and table.

Sal's Pizzeria sells four types of pizzas for dinner. The table shows the pizzas ordered by customers between 8 P.M. and 9 P.M. today.

PIZZA	NUMBER ORDERED
Cheese	4
Pepperoni	8
Veggie	5
Sausage	3

21. Expressed as a percent, what is the probability that the next pizza ordered will be pepperoni?
   a. 40%
   b. 35%
   c. 30%
   d. 20%
   e. 10%

22. How many of the next 15 pizzas ordered are likely to be cheese?
   a. 1
   b. 2
   c. 3
   d. 4
   e. 5

23. Choose a rule that tells how the numbers change in the following sequence:

1, 4, −2, 10, −14, . . .

   a. Multiply by −2 and then add 6.
   b. Multiply by 2 and then add 2.
   c. Add 10 and then subtract 7.
   d. Multiply by −1 and then add 5.
   e. Add 5 and then subtract 2.

24. Lysa goes to the state fair. She must pay an admission fee and buy ticket booklets for rides. Each ticket package is good for three rides. The cost of Lysa's trip to the fair is represented by the equation $x = \$15 + \$2.25n$, where n is the number of ticket packages Lysa buys. Not counting the cost of admission, how much does each ride cost?

   a. $0.75
   b. $1.50
   c. $2.25
   d. $6.75
   e. $17.25

25. The volume of a cylinder is given by the following formula: $V = \pi \times \text{radius}^2 \times \text{height}$, or $V = \pi r^2 h$. Ms. Beacon estimated the volume of a cylindrical can to be 124 cubic inches. She used the values $r = 2$ inches and $h = 10$ inches and estimated the value of π. What value did Ms. Beacon use for π?

   a. 3
   b. 3.1
   c. 3.14
   d. 3.18
   e. Not enough information is given.

▶ Part II

You may NOT use a calculator for questions on this part of the test.

26. A new art exhibit was attended by 4,289 people. Round 4,289 to the nearest hundred.

   a. 4,000
   b. 4,200
   c. 4,300
   d. 4,500
   e. 5,000

27. Joey buys a journal for $2.25 and a pen for $0.75. He pays with a $10 bill. Which expression shows how to find the amount of his change?

   a. $\$2.25 + \$75 - \$10$
   b. $\$10 - (\$2.25 + \$75)$
   c. $(\$2.25 + \$0.75) - \$10$
   d. $\$10 - (\$2.25 + \$0.75)$
   e. $\$10 - (\$2.25 - \$0.75)$

28. A box weighing 11.3 kilograms contains two dozen cans of canned corn. When empty, the box weighs 0.5 kilograms. Which expression gives the weight, in kilograms, of one can of corn?

   a. $(11.3 + 0.5) \div (2 \times 12)$
   b. $11.3 \div (2 \times 12) - 0.5$
   c. $(11.3 \times 12) \times 2 - 0.5$
   d. $11.3 \div (12 \times 2) - 0.5$
   e. $(11.3 - 0.5) \div (2 \times 12)$

29. Before he began a workout routine, Ray weighed $147\frac{1}{2}$ pounds. After working out for one week, his weight had dropped to $146\frac{3}{4}$ pounds. What fraction of a pound did Ray lose? Mark your answer in the circles in the grid.

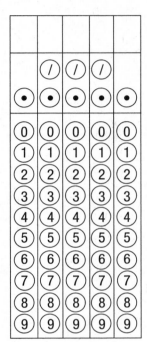

30. After being on sale for only two weeks, 63% of the television sets at Crazy Carl's were sold. Which of the following fractions is the best estimate of the fraction of the total televisions sold?

a. $\frac{1}{4}$

b. $\frac{1}{2}$

c. $\frac{3}{8}$

d. $\frac{2}{3}$

e. $\frac{5}{16}$

31. Mike needs to repair his car. Using the following graph, what is the ratio of the cost for materials to the cost for labor?

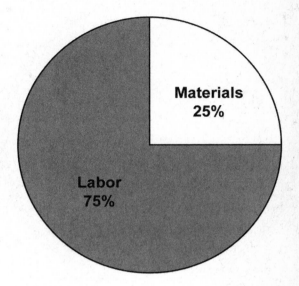

a. $\frac{1}{3}$

b. $\frac{1}{4}$

c. $\frac{2}{3}$

d. $\frac{3}{2}$

e. Not enough information is given.

32. What is the approximate length of a ladybug?

a. 1 meter

b. 1 centimeter

c. 10 centimeters

d. 1 millimeter

e. 1 liter

33. Martin arrived at the library at 10:45 A.M. He left at the time shown.

How long was Martin at the library?
a. 2 hours 45 minutes
b. 2 hours 30 minutes
c. 2 hours 15 minutes
d. 1 hour 45 minutes
e. 1 hour 30 minutes

34. Blaire earned $48 babysitting five hours on Saturday. She is scheduled to babysit three more hours on Sunday afternoon. If she is paid at the same rate, which proportion can be used to find the amount (*b*) Blaire will earn on Sunday?
a. $\frac{b}{3} = \frac{\$48}{5}$
b. $\frac{b}{5} = \frac{\$48}{3}$
c. $\frac{b}{3} = \frac{5}{\$48}$
d. $\frac{b}{3} = \frac{\$48}{8}$
e. $\frac{b}{8} = \frac{\$48}{5}$

35. Ramy needs to determine the distance between two cities, so he looks at a state map. He measures the distance between the cities on the map and sees that it is almost $2\frac{1}{2}$ inches. The map scale reads "1 inch = 15 miles." What is the distance between the cities?
a. between 25 and 30 miles
b. between 31 and 35 miles
c. between 36 and 40 miles
d. between 41 and 45 miles
e. between 46 and 50 miles

36. What is the best estimate of the angle shown here?

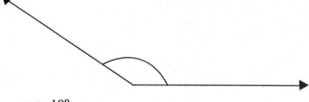

a. 10°
b. 45°
c. 85°
d. 140°
e. 185°

37. What is the area in square yards of the triangular park shown here?

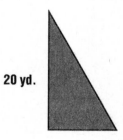

20 yd.

12 yd.

a. 120 square yards
b. 110 square yards
c. 100 square yards
d. 80 square yards
e. 60 square yards

Questions 38 and 39 refer to the following coordinate plane.

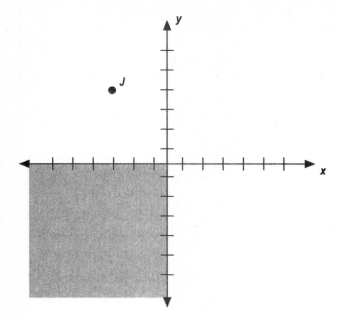

Questions 41–43 refer to the following coordinate plane.

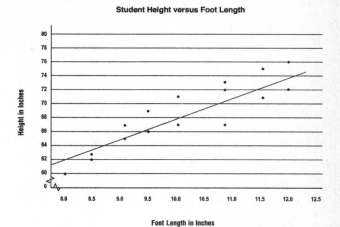

38. What are the signs of the coordinates of points in the shaded quadrant?
   a. *x* value negative, *y* value positive
   b. *x* value positive, *y* value negative
   c. *x* value negative, *y* value negative
   d. *x* value positive, *y* value positive
   e. none of the above

39. What coordinates are identified by point *J*?
   a. (–4,–3)
   b. (–4,3)
   c. (–3,–4)
   d. (3,–4)
   e. (–3,4)

40. (5,1) and (2,0) are on a graphed line. Which expression gives the slope of this line?
   a. $(5 - 1) \div (2 - 0)$
   b. $(2 - 1) \div (5 - 0)$
   c. $(5 - 2) \div (1 - 2)$
   d. $(1 - 0) \div (5 - 2)$
   e. $(1 - 0) \div (2 - 2)$

41. Use the line of best fit to estimate the average height of a student who has a foot length of 10.5 inches. Mark your answer in the circles in the grid.

42. Use the line of best fit to estimate the foot length of a person who has a height of 62 inches.
   a. about 8 inches
   b. about 8.5 inches
   c. about 9 inches
   d. about 60 inches
   e. about 62 inches

43. What is the median foot length of students in the class?
 a. 8 inches
 b. 9 inches
 c. 10 inches
 d. 11 inches
 e. 12 inches

44. Of the last 15 calls to the Rivera family, 10 have been for Mr. Rivera. Of the next 6 calls, how many of the calls most likely will be for Mr. Rivera?
 a. 2
 b. 3
 c. 4
 d. 5
 e. 6

45. In Judy's math class, there are m men in a class of n students. Which expression gives the ratio of men to women in the class?
 a. $\frac{m}{n}$
 b. $\frac{n}{m}$
 c. $\frac{m}{(m-n)}$
 d. $\frac{n}{(n-m)}$
 e. $\frac{m}{(n-m)}$

46. Cory bought 8 tennis balls and 12 golf balls. He spent a total of $32.50. Each tennis ball was $1.75. Which equation tells how to find g, the cost of each golf ball?
 a. $8g = \$32.50 + \$1.75 \times 12$
 b. $8g = \$32.50 - \$1.75 \times 12$
 c. $12g = \$32.50 \times \$1.75 - 8$
 d. $12g = \$32.50 + \$1.75 \times 8$
 e. $12g = \$32.50 - \$1.75 \times 8$

47. Jim and his family want to go to the beach. The cost of admission follows the pattern in the following table.

Beach Entry Prices by Number in Family

1	2	3	4	5
$4.50	$6.25	$8		

What will be the total cost for Jim and four other family members to go to the beach?
 a. $7
 b. $9.25
 c. $9.75
 d. $10.50
 e. $11.50

48. In the equation $y = 6p - 23$, p is a positive whole number. What is the least value of p for which y is positive?
 a. 1
 b. 2
 c. 3
 d. 4
 e. 5

49. Which of the following lines contains the point $(3,1)$?
 a. $y = 2x + 1$
 b. $y = 2x + 2$
 c. $y = (\frac{2}{3})x - 2$
 d. $y = (\frac{2}{3})x - 1$
 e. Not enough information is given.

50. At Luna Pizza, pizza pies come in two sizes. The large size has twice the diameter of the small size. About how much more cheese topping is on the large size than on the small size? Remember, the formula for the area of a circle is area = $\pi \times \text{radius}^2$.

   a. twice as much

   b. 2π times as much

   c. four times as much

   d. 4π times as much

   e. eight times as much

Now, check your answers on page 162.

GED Math Answers and Explanations ▶

▶ Pretest

1. **b.** $224.99 is greater than $220 but less than $225 (i.e., $224.99 is less than halfway between $220 and $230), so $224.99 rounded to the nearest $10 is $220.

2. **d.** Look at the numbers in the tens place: 7, 6, 0, and 8. Placing these numbers on a number line, start at zero to order them from least to greatest.

3. **b.** $589.86 − $18.12 − $50.43 + $40.11 = $561.42.

4. **d.** Add the cost of the shirts ($3 \times \$16$), the cost of the sweatshirts ($2 \times \$22$), and the shipping cost ($11).

5. **b.** $22 ÷ 4 (Chris plus his three friends) = $5.50.

6. **d.** Denise is the fastest runner because she ran the greatest distance. Rewrite the fractional distances greater than 1 mile using the greatest common denominator: 8. $1\frac{1}{2} = 1\frac{4}{8}$, $1\frac{1}{4} = 1\frac{2}{8}$, $1\frac{5}{8} = 1\frac{5}{8}$, $1\frac{3}{4} = 1\frac{6}{8}$. Now, compare numerators. The greatest numerator is 6, so $1\frac{3}{4}$ is the greatest distance.

7. **d.** Round each distance to the nearest whole number: $\frac{1}{8}$ rounds to 0; $2\frac{3}{4}$ rounds to 3; $2\frac{1}{3}$ rounds to 2. Then, add the numbers: $0 + 3 + 2 = 5$.

8.

Three pounds divided into $\frac{1}{4}$-pound pieces equals 12: $3 \div \frac{1}{4} = 3 \times 4 = 12$. You can also think about the question this way: Alexia can make four quarter-pound pieces from one pound of chocolate. With three pounds, she gets three times as much: $4 \times 3 = 12$.

9.

The grid shows the answer 42.5

$\frac{3}{8}$ = 37.5% ($\frac{3}{8}$ × 100% = 37.5%); 80% − 37.5%
= 42.5%.

10. **d.** II: The discounted price = 75% of the original price = 0.75 × $250. IV: The discounted price = (100% − 25%) of the original price = (100% − 25%) × $250 = (1 − 0.25) × $250.

11. **b.** Amount going to taxes = $300 + $100 + $124 = $524; gross earnings = $2,000; percent going to taxes = ($524 ÷ $2,000) × 100 = 26.2%, which rounds to 26%.

12. **d.** You are looking for n, and $\frac{n}{200,000} = \frac{2}{5}$ or $n = \frac{2}{5}$ × 200,000. $\frac{2}{5}$ of the 200,000 sample population bicycle to work. $\frac{2}{5}$ × 200,000 = 80,000.

13. **a.** (15.5 − 14) ÷ 14 = 0.107 = 10.7%, which rounds to 11%.

14. **d.** Only kilometers is a metric measurement used to measure distances between cities. One kilometer is a distance of about 0.6 miles. A distance of 135 kilometers is equal to a distance of about 81 miles.

15. **a.** 10:30 A.M. to 5:30 P.M. is a seven-hour period. Mike can give 13 lessons, each lasting 30 minutes, if he takes 30 minutes for lunch. $20 × 13 = $260.

16. **b.** 2 feet = 24 inches = $\frac{24}{36}$ yard = $\frac{2}{3}$ yard. You can also think that 3 feet = 1 yard, so 2 feet = $\frac{2}{3}$ yard.

17.

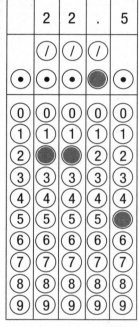

$d = r × t$; d = 4.5 mph × 5 hours = 22.5 miles.

18. **b.** Total owed = $7,000 + ($7,000 × 0.05 × 1.25) = $7,437.50. For this question, it may be easier to work using fractions, rather than decimals: total owed = $7,000 + ($7,000 × $\frac{1}{20}$ × $\frac{5}{4}$) = $7,437.50.

19. **d.** Width of copy/width of original = height of copy/height of original: $\frac{w}{8} = \frac{4}{10}$; $w = \frac{4 \times 8}{10} = \frac{32}{10}$ = 3.2.

20. **a.** $\frac{0.5}{15} = \frac{5.25}{d}$, or map distance in inches/actual distance in miles.

21. **e.** 20 seconds = $\frac{20}{60}$ minutes = $\frac{1}{3}$ minute. Now, divide the available minutes on the CD (75) by the length of one song ($2\frac{1}{3}$).

22.

	3	4	.	7
	②	②	②	
⊙	⊙	⊙	●	⊙
⓪	⓪	⓪	⓪	⓪
①	①	①	①	①
②	②	②	②	②
③	●	③	③	③
④	④	●	④	④
⑤	⑤	⑤	⑤	⑤
⑥	⑥	⑥	⑥	⑥
⑦	⑦	⑦	⑦	●
⑧	⑧	⑧	⑧	⑧
⑨	⑨	⑨	⑨	⑨

Remember that any two angles whose measures add to 90 degrees are complementary angles. $90° - 55.3° = 34.7°$.

23. c. Each of the three angles has an equal measure because each of the sides has an equal measure (4 inches). The sum of the three angles is 180 degrees.

24. c. An estimate using the Pythagorean relationship gives a length of a little more than 5 meters: $\sqrt{6^2 + 3^2} = \sqrt{36-9} = \sqrt{27} > \sqrt{25} = 5$.

25. e. Number of tiles equals area of pantry (in square feet) divided by area of a single tile (in square feet): area of pantry = 6×4 square feet; area of single tile = $\frac{2}{3} \times \frac{2}{3}$ square foot.

26. a. The volume of a rectangular solid is found by multiplying the length times the width times the height, where each dimension is in the same unit: 25 feet $\times$ 16 feet $\times$ 0.5 feet (6 inches is written as 0.5 feet).

27.

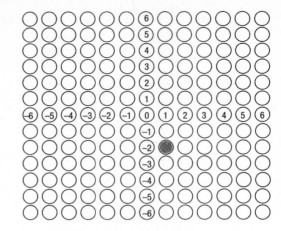

A parallelogram has two pairs of parallel sides. You can easily determine the fourth vertex by visually identifying where the lines must meet. Remember, opposite sides are parallel and have equal length.

28. d. Slope equals change in y value divided by change in x value: $(1 - 0) \div (5 - 2)$.

29. e. The mean of 80 and 100 is 90; the mean of 80, 90, and 100 is also 90. The median of 80 and 100 is 90; the median of 80, 90, and 100 is also 90. The range of 80 and 100 is 20 (100 – 80); the range of 80, 90, and 100 is also 20. Neither set has a mode.

30. b. For the lowest score Avi needs to get an A, assume his final average is 88. Average = $(90 + 80 + 85 + a) \div 4 = 88$. To find a, multiply 88 by 4. Then subtract Avi's first three scores: $88 \times 4 = 352$; $352 - (90 + 80 + 85) = 352 - 255 = 97$.

31. d. If you connect the dots, the two lines would cross at about 55° F. The number of sales of each drink at this point is about 375.

32. e. This would be about 650 servings, which is halfway between 750 (at 40° F) and 550 (at 50° F).

33. **c.** To determine the average speed, divide the miles traveled during the first 5 hours (175 miles) by the time of travel (5 hours). 175 miles ÷ 5 hours = 35 miles per hour.

34. **c.** You can determine this by finding the point on the graphed line above the 1-hour point on the horizontal axis, which is about 50 miles.

35. **d.** In 2000, 70% of women voted, and 70% of 36,200 = 0.7 × 36,200 = 25,340. In 2000, 60% of men voted, and 60% of 40,400 = 0.6 × 40,400 = 24,240. Female voters – male voters = 1,100, which is closest to 1,000.

36. **a.** Ricardo spends 11% for his car, half of the 22% he saves. (You can use % for the pie chart values without doing any additional math, since the values are out of 100 already.)

37. **a.** Savings and housing together make up 50% of Ricardo's budget: 22% + 28%.

38. **c.** Ricardo spent 6 cents more per dollar on housing than on food: 28 – 22 = 6. 6 cents is 6% of each budgeted dollar. $46,500 × 0.06 = $2,790, which is about $2,800.

39. **d.** Hillary, Mark, and Jomarie together have three chances. Probability $= \frac{3}{390} = \frac{1}{130}$.

40. **b.** Jack is likely to make $\frac{2}{5} \times 25 = 10$ of his next 25 free-throw attempts.

41.

$j = 2(4 \times 3 - 3 \times 2)^2 = 2(12 - 6)^2 = 2(6)^2 = 2(36) = 72.$

42. **a.** Percent means "out of 100 equal parts." The term $n\%$ can be written as $\frac{n}{100}$ or as $0.01n$, which is equal to $n \times 0.01$.

43. **b.** The one-time fee is $30, and the charge for working h hours is $40h$. Add $30 and $40h$ to find x: $x = \$30 + \$40h$.

44. **c.** The area of a triangle $= \frac{1}{2} \times$ base $\times$ height $= \frac{1}{2}(4x)(3x) = \frac{1}{2}(12x^2) = 6x^2$.

45. **c.** Each job will pay $21,200 after 4 years. You can see this by making a chart:

	1	2	3	4
Books R Us	$18,800	$19,600	$20,400	$21,200
Readers Galore	$17,600	$18,800	$20,000	$21,200

46. **e.** If °C = 32, then $\frac{9}{5}(32°) + 32° = 89\frac{3}{5}°$ F, not 0° F.

47. **e.** This equation matches the table. When $d = 0$, $r = \$485$: $\$485 - \$3(0) = \$485$. When $d = 1$, $r = \$482$: $r = \$485 - \$3(1) = \$482$; and so on.

48.

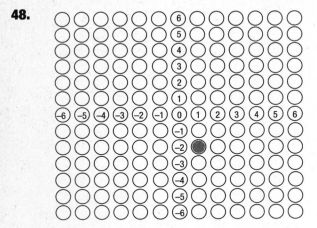

This line passes through the origin and has a slope of +1. For every point on this line, the x value is equal to the y value.

49. **c.** $I = prt$ can also be written as $r = i \div (p \times t)$. $r = \$210 \div (\$3,500 \times 1.5) = \$210 \div \$5,250 = 0.04 = 4\%$.

50. **b.** The volume of the larger box $= 1.25^3$, which is about 1.95 cubic yards. The volume of the smaller box $= 1^3$, or 1 cubic yard. 1.95 is 95% larger than 1.

▶ Numbers and Operations Pretest

1. **d.** For the order of operations, addition and subtraction are done left to right. First subtract 5 from 10, and then add 2 to get a result of 7.

2. **c.** Division is done before subtraction for the order of operations. First, divide 40 by 4, and then subtract this number from 32.

3. **c.** Using the order of operations, solve inside the parentheses first: $7 + (56) \times (7)$. Now, multiply: $7 + 392$. The answer is 399, but the question asks you to estimate the answer to the nearest 10. 399 is between 390 and 400, but it is closer to 400.

4. **e.** All of the choices show examples of factors that produce 60, but choice **e** is the only factorization showing all prime numbers.

5. **e.** $10 \times 2 = 20$, and $10 \times 3 = 30$, so the greatest common factor is 10. Also, using prime factorization, $20 = 2 \times 2 \times 5$, and $30 = 2 \times 3 \times 5$. Two and 5 are prime factors of both 20 and 30, so the greatest common factor is 2×5, which is 10.

6. **d.** List the multiples of 40 and 50 until one is found in common. Multiples of 50 are 50, 100, 150, 200, 250, . . . , and multiples of 40 are 40, 80, 120, 160, 200, 240, . . . A common multiple is found, namely 200.

7. **b.** The distributive property states that multiplication distributes over addition or subtraction. An illustration of this is choice **b**.

8. **a.** The absolute value symbol serves as a grouping symbol, and grouping symbols are evaluated first. $|-5 \times 3| = 15$ (the absolute value is always positive). Now divide 5 into 100 to get 20. Finally, add $20 + 15 = 35$.

9. **b.** Choice **b** shows an example of the associative property, which states that when all operations in an expression are addition (or multiplication), you can change the grouping symbols to get the same result.

10. **c.** The commutative property states that when all operations are multiplication (or addition) you can change the order of the operands to get the same result.

11. d. To solve this problem, you do not need to solve each expression. Rather, remember the rules for adding or multiplying odd and even numbers. Only odd plus odd (7 + 5) results in an even number.

12. e. $3 \times -7 = -21$, because a positive times a negative always equals a negative. However, the absolute value of -21 is 21.

► Numbers and Operations Posttest

1. d. Multiplication is done before addition in the order of operations. First multiply 15 by 3 and then add 25 to get the result of $45 + 25 = 70$.

2. c. For the order of operations, you must perform division first. This subresult is 5. 5 subtracted from 8 results in positive 3.

3. b. Expressions within parentheses are evaluated first. $6 + 19 = 25$. Now perform multiplication, and $5 \times 25 = 125$.

4. a. First, evaluate parentheses to get $8 + 4 = 12$. Now division is performed before addition: $144 \div 12 = 12$. The final step is to add $12 + 12 = 24$.

5. c. Multiplication and division are done left to right, so first evaluate 120 divided by 5, which is 24. To evaluate multiplication, remember that a positive times a negative is a negative result, and 24 times -2 is -48.

6. c. All of the choices show examples of factors that produce 90, but choice **c** is the only factorization showing all prime numbers.

7. b. The distributive property states that multiplication distributes over addition or subtraction. An illustration of this is choice **b**.

8. e. First find the prime factorization of both 48 and 120, and then look for all common prime factors. $48 = 2 \times 2 \times 2 \times 2 \times 3$ and $120 = 2 \times 2 \times 2 \times 3 \times 5$. The common prime factors are $2 \times 2 \times 2 \times 3 = 24$. The greatest common factor is 24.

9. d. With these numbers, it is easy to just list the multiples of 20 and 30 to find the first one in common. Multiples of 20 are 20, 40, 60, 80, . . . and multiples of 30 are 30, 60, 90, . . . The least common multiple is 60.

10. d. Addition and subtraction are done left to right. Subtraction must be evaluated first. $35 - 5 = 30$. $30 + 7 = 37$. Now find the nearest ten: 37 is between 30 and 40, but closer to 40.

11. e. Remember odd + even always results in an odd number.

12. c. First, do the operations within the absolute symbols: $9 - 4 = 5$. 5 times what number equals -25? $5 \times -5 = -25$.

► Fractions and Decimals Pretest

1. b. The two fractions already have a common denominator, so combine the numerators and keep the denominator. Then simplify. $\frac{4}{9} - \frac{7}{9} = (4 - 7) \div 9 = \frac{-3}{9} \div \frac{3}{3} = -\frac{1}{3}$, in lowest terms.

2. c. First, find a common denominator, the LCM of 15 and 30. The LCM is 30. Convert the first fraction to have a denominator of 30: $\frac{8}{15} \times \frac{2}{2} = \frac{16}{30}$. Now combine to get $\frac{16}{30} + \frac{9}{30} = \frac{25}{30} \div \frac{5}{5} = \frac{5}{6}$.

3. a. Change each mixed number to an improper fraction. $2\frac{3}{4} - 3\frac{2}{4} = \frac{11}{4} - \frac{14}{4}$. The fractions have the same denominator, so combine the numerators and keep the denominator: $\frac{11}{4} - \frac{14}{4} = \frac{11-14}{4} = -\frac{3}{4}$.

4. d. When you multiply fractions, multiply straight across and then simplify: $\frac{7}{9} \times \frac{3}{4} = \frac{21}{36} \div \frac{3}{3} = \frac{7}{12}$.

5. e. Change $4\frac{2}{3}$ and 6 to improper fractions. Then change the operation to multiply by the reciprocal of 6: $\frac{14}{3} \div \frac{6}{1} = \frac{14}{3} \times \frac{1}{6}$. Multiply the numerators and the denominators straight across and simplify: $\frac{14}{3} \times \frac{1}{6} = (14 \times 1) \div (3 \times 6) = \frac{14}{18} \div \frac{2}{2} = \frac{7}{9}$.

6. c. To divide fractions, change the problem to multiply by the reciprocal. Multiply straight across and then simplify: $\frac{3}{4} \div \frac{7}{8} = \frac{3}{4} \times \frac{8}{7} = \frac{24}{28} \div \frac{4}{4} = \frac{6}{7}$.

7. b. Line up the decimal points, and add vertically:

$$\begin{array}{r} 1{,}036.09 \\ 2.40 \\ + 17.00 \\ \hline 1{,}055.49 \end{array}$$

8. a. Multiply as you would with whole numbers; then count the number of digits to the right of the decimal points in the factors. There are three digits, so the decimal place is moved three places to the left in the product.

9. b. The fractions are changed to decimals by dividing: $\frac{7}{12} = 7 \div 12 = 0.58$ and $\frac{5}{7} = 5 \div 7 = 0.71$. Change all numbers to decimal numbers with the same number of digits after the decimal point: 0.5800, 0.7100, 0.0790, 0.6300, 0.0108. The decimal 0.71 is the greatest, which was $\frac{5}{7}$.

10. e. Set up the problem as a long division problem. Because the divisor (2.7) has one digit to the right of the decimal point, you must move the decimal place one place to the right in both the divisor and the dividend (540).

Add a trailing zero onto the dividend as a placeholder. Then, copy the decimal place straight up to the quotient.

▶ Fractions and Decimals Posttest

1. c. To divide fractions, change the operation to multiplication and take the reciprocal of the second fraction. Multiply the numerators and denominators straight across: $\frac{9}{11} \times \frac{22}{7} = \frac{198}{77}$. Change this to an improper fraction by dividing 198 by 77. The result is 2 with remainder 44: $\frac{198}{77} = 2\frac{44}{77}$. Simplify the fractional part: $\frac{44}{77} \div \frac{11}{11} = \frac{4}{7}$.

2. a. First change the numerator to an improper fraction: $1\frac{1}{5} = \frac{6}{5}$. Then change the problem to be a fraction divided by a fraction: $\frac{6}{5} \div \frac{1}{3}$. Dividing fractions is the same as multiplying by the reciprocal of the second fraction. Multiply straight across the numerators and denominators: $\frac{6}{5} \times \frac{3}{1} = \frac{18}{5}$.

3. e. This complex fraction means a fraction divided by a fraction. Change the problem to multiply by the reciprocal of the second fraction. $\frac{2}{3} \times \frac{6}{5} = \frac{12}{15}$. Put the fraction in lowest terms: $\frac{12}{15} \div \frac{3}{3} = \frac{4}{5}$.

4. b. You can convert each fraction to an equivalent fraction, all of which have a common denominator. Find the least common multiple of the denominators: 40 is the LCM: $\frac{5}{8} \times \frac{5}{5} = \frac{25}{40}$, $\frac{17}{20} \times \frac{2}{2} = \frac{34}{40}$, $\frac{1}{2} \times \frac{20}{20} = \frac{20}{40}$, $\frac{7}{10} \times \frac{4}{4} = \frac{28}{40}$, and $\frac{4}{5} \times \frac{8}{8} = \frac{32}{40}$. Now the numerators can be inspected for the greatest, which is $\frac{17}{20} = \frac{34}{40}$.

5. e. Convert all fractions to have a common denominator, which is the LCM = 12. $\frac{1}{3} \times \frac{4}{4} = \frac{4}{12}$, $\frac{2}{6} \times \frac{2}{2} = \frac{4}{12}$, $\frac{5}{12}$, $\frac{1}{2} \times \frac{6}{6} = \frac{6}{12}$, $\frac{1}{4} \times \frac{3}{3} = \frac{3}{12}$. It is sufficient to compare the numerators to find the smallest because the denominators are the same.

6. c. Add the numbers vertically; make sure to line up the decimal points and add trailing zeros when necessary:

$$
\begin{array}{r}
34.70 \\
4.10 \\
+\ 0.03 \\
\hline
38.83
\end{array}
$$

7. d. When subtracting decimals, it is easiest to do the problem vertically, remembering to line up the decimal points:

$$
\begin{array}{r}
125.05 \\
-\ 11.40 \\
\hline
113.65
\end{array}
$$

8. a. Multiply without regard to the decimal points. $168 \times 2 = 336$. Because there are two digits to the right of the decimal points in the factors, place the decimal point two places from the right in the product.

9. d. Use the shortcut when multiplying by 10. Move the decimal point one place to the right, to get the product of 53.4.

10. b. Multiply without regard to the decimal point:

$$
\begin{array}{r}
42.19 \\
\times\ 0.4 \\
\hline
16876
\end{array}
$$

There are three digits to the right of the decimal points in the factors, namely 1, 9, and then 4. Place the decimal point three places from the right in the product.

▶ Measurement Pretest

1. b. Every 3 feet equals 1 yard, so divide: 6 ft. ÷ 3 ft./yd. = 2 yards.

2. c. Every 8 ounces equals 1 cup, so divide: 3 oz. ÷ 8 oz./c. = 0.375 cup.

3. c. Every 36 inches equals 1 yard, so divide: 48 in. ÷ 36 in./yd. = $1\frac{1}{3}$ yards, or $1.\overline{33}$ written as a decimal.

4. e. Each liter equals 0.264 gallon, so for 2 liters: 2 L × 0.264 gal./L = 0.528 gallon. A gallon equals 128 fluid ounces, so multiply: 0.528 gal. × 128 fl. oz./gal. = 67.584 fl. oz. ≈ 67.6 fluid ounces.

5. c. 12 inches equals 1 foot, so divide: 652 in. ÷ 12 in./ft. = 54.333 feet. Because trim is sold by the foot, round up. 55 feet must be purchased so that there is enough trim.

6. c. One foot equals 12 inches so Thomas's height is 6 ft. × 12 in./ft. = 72 in. + 1 in. = 73 inches. His son's height is 3 ft. × 12 in./ft. = 36 in. + 3 in. = 39 inches. The difference between their heights is 73 in. − 39 in. = 34 inches.

7. a. A mile is 5,280 feet, so to find 0.85 mile, multiply: 0.85 mi. × 5,280 ft./mi. = 4,488 feet.

8. b. It takes 5,280 feet to make a mile. To find how many miles are in 33,000 feet, divide: 33,000 ft. ÷ 5,280 ft./mi. = 6.25 miles.

9. d. One cubic yard requires 27 cubic feet. To find the number of cubic yards in 45 cubic feet, divide: 45 ft.^{3} ÷ 27 ft.^{3}/yd.^{3} = $1.\overline{66}$ cubic yards.

10. b. Because the conversion is from smaller units to larger units, division is required. Every 12 inches equals 1 foot, so to figure out the number of feet in the given number of inches, divide by 12. Then, to figure out how many miles are in the calculated number of feet, divide by the number of feet in a mile, 5,280.

11. c. There are 10 millimeters in 1 centimeter: 84 mm ÷ 10 mm/cm = 8.4 cm, not 840 cm.

12. d. Multiply the number of minutes in an hour by the given number of hours. There are 60 minutes in an hour. Therefore, there are 120 minutes in 2 hours. Two hours × 60 minutes = 120 minutes.

13. a. Multiply the number of seconds in a minute by the given number of minutes. There are 60 seconds in one minute. There are 240 seconds in 4 minutes. Four minutes × 60 seconds = 240 seconds.

14. b. To convert 0° F into Celsius, substitute 0 for F in the equation $C = \frac{5}{9}(F - 32)$:
$C = \frac{5}{9}(0 - 32) = \frac{5}{9}(-32) = -\frac{160}{9} = -17.8$;
therefore, $0° F \approx -17.8° C$.

15. b. Set up a proportion based on the ratio of boogie boards to surfboards: $\frac{12}{3} = \frac{84}{s}$. Cross multiply: $3 \times 84 = 12 \times s$, so $252 = 12 \times s$. Divide by 12: $21 = s$. There are 21 surfboards.

16. e. You are given the total number of people (48) and the number of females (16), and are asked to find the ratio of males to females. There are $48 - 16 = 32$ males on the trip. The ratio of males to females is $\frac{32}{16} = \frac{2}{1}$ or 2 to 1.

17. c. Set up a proportion based on the ratio of the smaller number to the larger number: $\frac{5}{8} = \frac{n}{72}$. Cross multiply: $8 \times n = 5 \times 72$, so $8 \times n = 360$. Divide by 8: $n = 45$. The smaller number is 45.

18. c. The proportion of lunch buyers to lunch packers is $\frac{7}{2} = \frac{35}{p}$. Cross multiply to get $2 \times 35 = 7 \times p$. Multiply 2×35 to get 70: $70 = 7 \times p$. Divide 70 by 7 to get 10 lunch packers.

19. a. Set up a ratio of map to real. The proportion is $\frac{0.25}{1} = \frac{6.2}{r}$. Cross multiply to get $1 \times 6.2 = 0.25 \times r$. $6.2 = 0.25 \times r$. Divide 6.2 by 0.25 to get 24.8 miles long.

20. c. Use the formula: interest = principal × rate × time, and substitute known values: interest = $\$700 \times 5\% \times 18$ months. Because the rate is a yearly rate, write 18 months as a number of years: 18 months $= \frac{18}{12}$ years, which reduces to $\frac{3}{2}$ years. Because fractions appear in all the answer choices, change the rate (5%) to a fraction: $\frac{5}{100}$, which reduces to $\frac{1}{20}$. Interest = $\$700 \times \frac{1}{20} \times \frac{3}{2}$. The total will be the principal plus interest: $\$700 + (\$700 \times \frac{1}{20} \times \frac{3}{2})$.

▶ Measurement Posttest

1. e. Each mile equals 5,280 feet. Because there are 4.5 miles, multiply: 4.5 mi. × 5,280 ft./mi. = 23,760 feet.

2. d. The two amounts can be added as they are, but then the sum needs to be simplified. 2 pt. 6 oz. + 1 c. 7 oz. = 2 pints 1 cup 13 ounces. Note that the sum is written with the largest unit first and smallest unit last. To simplify, start with the smallest unit, ounces, and work toward larger units. Every 8 ounces makes 1 cup, so 13 ounces = 1 cup 5 ounces. Replace the 13 ounces with the 1 cup 5 ounces, adding the cup portions together: 2 pints 2 cups 5 ounces. Now note that 2 cups = 1 pint, so the sum can be simplified again combining this pint with the 2 pints in the sum. The simplified total is 3 pints 5 ounces.

3. b. There are 10 millimeters in every centimeter, so divide: 35 mm ÷ 10 mm/cm = 3.5 cm.

4. b. There are 36 inches in a yard. To find the number of inches in 12 yards, multiply: 12 yd. × 36 in./yd. = 432 inches.

5. d. It takes 9 square feet to make a square yard. To find out how many square yards are in 182 square feet, divide: 182 ft.² ÷ 9 ft.²/yd.² = 20.22 square yards. Since Donna cannot purchase part of a square yard, she has to round up. She must purchase 21 square yards to have enough to carpet the room.

6. b. One teaspoon equals 5 milliliters. Therefore, $\frac{3}{4}$ tsp. × 5 mL/tsp. = 3.75 mL.

7. d. One kiloliter equals 1,000 liters: 3.9 kL × 1,000 L/kL = 3,900 L. Each liter equals 1,000 milliliters: 3,900 L × 1,000 mL/L = 3,900,000 mL.

8. c. Each mile is about 1,609.34 meters. Divide to find out how many miles are equivalent to 1,500 meters: 1,500 m ÷ 1,609.34 m/mi. ≈ 0.9321 miles.

9. a. There are 1,000 mm³ in 1 cm³. Divide to determine how many cm³ are in 58.24 mm³: 58.24 mm³ ÷ 1,000 mm³/cm³ = 0.05824 cm³.

10. b. Since one foot equals about 0.3048 meter, 5.5 feet equals: 5.5 ft. × 0.3048 m/ft. = 1.6764 meters. Choice **a** is much too large. Now convert 1.6764 m into the remaining units given in the answer choices. 1.6764 m × 100 cm/m = 167.64 cm, which is very close to choice **b**. 1.6764 m ÷ 1,000 m/km = .0016764 km, which eliminates choices **c** and **e**. 1.6764 m × 1,000 mm/m = 1,676.4 mm, which is much higher than choice **d**. The answer is **b**: 170 cm.

11. e. One meter is approximately 3.281 feet. Therefore, 62.4 m × 3.281 ft./m ≈ 204.73 ft. ≈ 205 feet.

12. c. Multiply the number of years in a decade by the given number of decades. There are 10 years in a decade, so three decades × 10 years = 30 years.

13. e. Multiply the number of minutes in an hour by the given number of hours. There are 60 minutes in each hour. Therefore, there are 720 minutes in 12 hours: 12 hours × 60 minutes = 720 minutes.

14. d. To convert −10° F into Celsius, substitute −10 for F in the equation $C=\frac{5}{9}(F-32)$: $C=\frac{5}{9}(-10-32)=\frac{5}{9}(-42)=-\frac{210}{9}$. C is about equal to −23.3°, so −10° F ≈ −23.3° C.

15. d. Use the formula $D = R \times T$. The distance is D = 390 miles, and the time is T = 6 hours. The speed is the missing term, R. Substitute known values: 390 = R × 6. Then divide by 6: 65 = R. The speed is 65 miles per hour.

16. b. Set up a proportion of quarts of strawberries to price: $\frac{3}{4.98}=\frac{10}{p}$. Cross multiply: 4.98 × 10 = 3 × p, so 49.8 = 3 × p. Divide by 3: 16.6 = p. The total price is $16.60.

17. c. First, determine the distance to drive to work, using the formula $D = R \times T$. Substitute known values and then multiply: $D=60\times\frac{1}{2}$, so D = 30. The distance to work is 30 miles.

Now, determine the time to drive to work at a rate of 40 miles per hour, again using the formula $D = R \times T$. Substitute known values and then divide by 40: 30 = 40 × T, so 0.75 = T. The new time is 0.75 hour, or three-quarters of an hour. The problem asks how much *extra* time it will take to drive. This is the difference between one-half hour and three-quarters of an hour. Subtract the fractions, after changing one-half to two-quarters: $\frac{3}{4}-\frac{2}{4}=\frac{1}{4}$. One-quarter of an hour is 15 minutes.

18. d. A scale is a ratio of model to real, keeping the units consistent. The tower is 986 feet tall, and the replica is 4 inches; 986 feet must be converted to inches, by multiplying by 12: 986 times 12 is 11,832 inches. Set up the ratio of replica to real and simplify: $\frac{4}{11,832}\div\frac{4}{4}=\frac{1}{2,958}$.

19. a. Set up a ratio of length to height. The proportion is $\frac{10}{8}=\frac{l}{5.6}$. Cross multiply to get 8 × l = 10 × 5.6. Multiply 10 times 5.6 to get 8 × l = 56. Divide 56 by 8 to get 7 feet long.

20. d. Use the formula: interest = principal × rate × time, and substitute known values: interest = $5,000 × 8% × 18 months, so interest = $400 × 18 months. Because the rate is a yearly rate, write 18 months as a number of years:

18 months $= \frac{18}{12}$ years, which reduces to $\frac{3}{2}$ years: $400 \times \frac{3}{2} = \$600$. The total will be the principal plus interest: $5,000 + \$600 = \$5,600$.

▶ Percentages Pretest

1. **d.** One method of solution is to set up a proportion: part/whole = percent/100. The whole is 350, and the part is what is being requested in the problem. Substitute the given information: $\frac{n}{350} = \frac{57}{100}$. Cross multiply to get $350 \times 57 = n \times 100$, and then multiply 350 times 57: $19,950 = n \times 100$. Divide 19,950 by 100 to get 199.50 or the equivalent 199.5.

2. **c.** Set up an equation, recalling that *of* means multiply and *is* means equals; make a straight translation using the variable p for percent. $p \times 200 = 68$. Divide both sides by 200 to get $p = 0.34$. This is the answer as a decimal. Change this answer to a percent by multiplying by 100 to get 34%.

3. **b.** Set up a proportion: $\frac{19}{n} = \frac{76}{100}$. In the problem, 19 is the part, 76 is the percent, and the whole is what you need to calculate. Cross multiply to get $n \times 76 = 19 \times 100$. Multiply: $n \times 76 = 1,900$. Now divide 1,900 by 76 to get 25.

4. **b.** Two out of every five indicates a ratio, so use the proportion: $\frac{2}{5} = \frac{p}{100}$. Cross multiply to get $5 \times p = 2 \times 100$. Multiply: $5p = 200$. Now divide both sides by 5 to get $p = 40\%$.

5. **e.** This is a multistep problem, because the sale percentage is a percent decrease, and the sales tax is a percent increase. There are several methods to solve this problem. Remem-

ber that 35% is 0.35 written as a decimal. Set up the equation: discount = percent × original, or $d = 0.35 \times \$89$. Multiply to get the discount, which is $31.15. The sale price is thus $89.00 - \$31.15 = \$57.85$. The sales tax is then calculated based on this sale price: sales tax = percent × sale price. The tax will be $t = 0.06 \times \$57.85$, or $t = \$3.47$, rounded to the nearest cent. Add this to the sale price to find the cost of the hockey stick: $57.85 + \$3.47 = \$61.32$.

6. **a.** This is a percent increase problem, so set up the proportion: change/original = percent/100. The change in attendance is $30 - 25 = 5$. The original attendance is 25 members. The proportion setup is: $\frac{5}{25} = \frac{p}{100}$. Cross multiply to get $25 \times p = 5 \times 100$. Multiply 5 times 100 to get $25 \times p = 500$. Divide both sides by 25 to get $p = 20$. The percent increase is therefore 20%.

7. **c.** The problem asks what percentage are NOT desserts. Because four of the 28 selections are desserts, then $28 - 4 = 24$ selections are NOT desserts. Set up the proportion: part/whole = percent/100, and substitute the correct numbers: $\frac{24}{28} = \frac{p}{100}$. Cross multiply: $28 \times p = 24 \times 100$, or $28 \times p = 2,400$. Divide both sides by 28 to get the percent, rounded to the nearest tenth, of 85.7%.

8. **a.** Twenty-five percent of the 1,032 voters voted for the incumbent. The key word *of* means multiply, and 25% is 0.25 written as a decimal. $0.25 \times 1,032 = 258$ voters.

9. **e.** The tip is a percent increase to the price of the dinner, and 15% can be written as 0.15. $0.15 \times 28 = 4.2$. The tip is $4.20, which is added to the $28.00 to get $32.20.

10. b. Set up an equation, changing 91% to a decimal, 0.91. The key word *of* means multiply and *is* means equals, so translate as $0.91 \times n = 200.2$. Divide 200.2 by 0.91 to get 220.

▶ Percentages Posttest

1. b. Change the fraction $\frac{15}{16}$ to a decimal by long division, to get 0.9375. To change this decimal to a percent, move the decimal point two places to the right, to get 93.75%.

2. c. To change a percent to a decimal, move the decimal point two places to the left: 23.5% = 0.235.

3. d. To change 1.8 to a percent, move the decimal two places to the right. It is necessary to add a trailing zero as a placeholder: 1.8 = 180%.

4. a. To solve this problem, remember that the key word *of* means multiply, and change the percent to a decimal: 12.8% = 0.128. Multiply 0.128 times 405 to get 51.84.

5. e. Set up a proportion, using is/of = percent/100. The term immediately preceding the key word *is* is 272, and the term following the key word *of* is 400. The set up is: $\frac{272}{400} = \frac{p}{100}$. Cross multiply to get $400 \times p = 272 \times 100$. Multiply 272 times 100: $400 \times p = 27,200$. Divide both sides by 400 to get $p = 68$ or 68%.

6. d. You can set up an equation, recalling that *is* means equals and *of* means multiply. For equations, the percent must also be converted to a decimal. A straight translation gives $533 = 0.82 \times n$. Divide both sides by 0.82 to get $n = 650$.

7. c. Change 49% to a decimal to get 0.49. Since the key word *of* means multiply, multiply 0.49 times 3,000 to get 1,470.

8. e. Set up a proportion. 4.25 is the part, since it precedes the key word *is*, and 25 is the whole, as it follows the key word *of*. Use is/of = percent/100. $\frac{4.25}{25} = \frac{p}{100}$. Cross multiply to get $25 \times p = 4.25 \times 100$. Multiply 4.25 times 100: $25 \times p = 425$. Divide both sides by 25 to get $p = 17$ or 17%.

9. d. This is a percent increase problem, so set up a proportion: change/original = percent/100. The change is $1,350 - 1,200 = 150$. The original number is 1,200. $\frac{150}{1,200} = \frac{p}{100}$. Cross multiply to get $1,200 \times p = 150 \times 100$. Multiply 150 times 100: $1,200 \times p = 15,000$. Divide both sides by 1,200 to get $p = 12.5$ or 12.5%.

10. a. For percent decrease, set up a proportion: change/original = percent/100. The change is $25,670 - 24,500 = 1,170$. The original population is 25,670. $\frac{1,170}{25,670} = \frac{p}{100}$. Cross multiply to get $25,670 \times p = 1,170 \times 100$. Multiply 1,170 by 100. $25,670 \times p = 117,000$. Divide both sides by 25,670 to get $p =$ approximately 4.5578%, which rounds to the nearest tenth as 4.6%.

▶ Exponents and Roots Pretest

1. e. $7^2 = 7 \times 7$, and $7 \times 7 = 49$.

2. d. When there is a negative exponent, take the reciprocal of the base and raise it to the positive power. $2^{-3} = (\frac{1}{2})^3$, and $\frac{1^3}{2^3} = \frac{1}{8}$.

3. b. $\sqrt[3]{27}$ is the cube root of 27; what number multiplied by itself twice equals 27? Because $3 \times 3 \times 3 = 27$, the answer is 3.

4. e. An exponent of $\frac{1}{2}$ means the second root or square root of 25. Because $5 \times 5 = 25$, the answer is 5.

5. a. When you multiply two numbers with the same base, you keep the base and add the exponents. $2^2 \times 2^3 = 2^{2+3} = 2^5$.

6. c. Ten with a negative exponent of 4 dictates that you move the decimal point four places to the left.

7. b. Change the large number to be a decimal number between 1 and 10, followed by multiplication by a power of 10. By doing this, you have moved the decimal point eight places to the left.

8. c. Divide: $5.4 \div 9 = 0.6$. Then, use the law of exponents: $10^{16} \div 10^{14} = 10^{16-14} = 10^2$. So this is $0.6 \times 10^2 = 60$ by moving the decimal point two places to the right.

9. d. Evaluate the exponent first and then evaluate the negative sign: $5^2 = 5 \times 5$, which is 25, so the answer is -25.

10. c. For order of operations, parentheses would have been evaluated first, but there are no parentheses. Evaluate exponents next to get $700 + 25 - 25 \times 2$. Multiplication is performed next: $700 + 25 - 50$. Now, addition and subtraction are done left to right for a result of $725 - 50 = 675$.

▶ Exponents and Roots Posttest

1. b. For this problem, the exponent is handled first. Eleven squared is 11 times 11, which is 121, and then the negative sign is evaluated to get the answer of -121.

2. b. The exponent of $\frac{1}{4}$ means the fourth root of 81; what factor multiplied by itself three times will yield 81? Trial and error will show that $3 \times 3 \times 3 \times 3 = 81$. The root is 3.

3. a. The problem is asking for the cube root of 64; what number multiplied by itself twice will give the product of 64? Because $4 \times 4 \times 4 = 64$, the cube root is 4.

4. a. The problem is asking for the square root of 169. Because 13 times 13 equals 169, the root is 13.

5. c. Combine these radicals by multiplying the radicands together: $\sqrt{48 \times 3} = \sqrt{144}$. The square root of 144 is 12, because 12 times 12 equals 144.

6. e. Break this fractional radicand up into two separate radicals and then simplify what can be simplified. $\sqrt{\frac{3}{9}} = \frac{\sqrt{3}}{\sqrt{9}}$. The $\sqrt{3}$ is simplified, and $\sqrt{9} = 3$. So, the answer is $\frac{\sqrt{3}}{3}$.

7. b. The exponent of 7 on the power of 10 dictates that you move the decimal point in 2.701 seven places to the right. Three of the places will be taken up by the digits 7, 0, and 1, and then four more zeros will follow to result in 27,010,000.

8. c. The negative exponent, -5, on the power of 10 means that you must move the decimal point five places to the left. The number 4.09 has only one digit to the left of the decimal point. Four leading zeros must be added as placeholders: 0.0000409.

9. c. For this problem, you use the commutative and associative properties of multiplication and change the order of the factors to get $(2.5 \times 3.0) \times (10^{-4} \times 10^8)$. 2.5 times 3 equals 7.5. For the powers of 10, when you multiply two powers with the same base, you keep the base and add the exponents, which results in $10^{-4} \times 10^8 = 10^{-4+8} = 10^4$. Now, $7.5 \times 10^4 = 75,000$ because you move the decimal point four places to the right, one place being the 5 (in the tenths place) followed by three trailing zeros for placeholders.

10. c. First, perform the addition enclosed in the parentheses: $5 - (-10)2 \times 3$. Now, take negative 10 and square it, which is $-10 \times -10 = 100$, so the problem becomes $5 - 100 \times 3$. Now, multiply: $5 - 300$. Finally, subtract to get -295.

▶ Algebra and Functions Pretest

1. d. Subtract the like terms by subtracting the coefficients of the terms: $9a - 5a = 4a$. $4a$ and $12a^2$ are not like terms, so they cannot be combined any further: $9a + 12a^2 - 5a = 12a^2 + 4a$.

2. a. Multiply the coefficients of the terms in the numerator, and add the exponents of the bases: $(3a)(4a) = 12a^2$. Do the same with the terms in the denominator: $6(6a^2) = 36a^2$. Finally, divide the numerator by the denominator. Divide the coefficients of the terms and subtract the exponents of the bases: $\frac{12a^2}{36a^2} = \frac{1}{3}$.

3. c. To find the product of two binomials, multiply the first term of each binomial, the outside terms, the inside terms, and the last terms. Then, add the products: $(x - 3)(x + 7) = x^2 + 7x - 3x - 21 = x^2 + 4x - 21$.

4. d. To find the product of two binomials, multiply the first term of each binomial, the outside terms, the inside terms, and the last terms. Then, add the products: $(x - 6)(x - 6) = x^2 - 6x - 6x + 36 = x^2 - 12x + 36$.

5. b. To find the factors of a quadratic, begin by finding two numbers whose product is equal to the constant of the quadratic. Of those numbers, find the pair that adds to the coefficient of the x term of the quadratic:

-3 and 2 multiply to -6 and add to -1. Therefore, the factors of $x^2 - x - 6$ are $(x - 3)$ and $(x + 2)$.

6. c. To solve the equation, subtract 5 from both sides of the equation, then divide both sides by 9: $9a + 5 = -22$, $9a + 5 - 5 = -22 - 5$, $9a = -27$, $a = -3$.

7. d. Begin with the innermost function: find $g(-3)$ by substituting -3 for $\times$ in the function $g(x)$: $g(-3) = (-3)^2 = 9$. Then, substitute the result of that function for x in $f(x)$: $f(9) = 2(9) - 1 = 18 - 1 = 17$.

8. b. Begin with the innermost function: find $f(-2)$ by substituting -2 for x in the function $f(x)$: $f(-2) = 3(-2) + 2 = -6 + 2 = -4$. Then, substitute the result of that function for x in $g(x)$: $g(-4) = 2(-4) - 3 = -8 - 3 = -11$.

9. a. The domain of the function is all real numbers; any real number can be substituted for x. There are no x values that can make the function undefined. The range of a function is the set of all possible outputs of the function. Because the x term is squared, then made negative, the largest value that this term can equal is 0 (when $x = 0$). Every other x value will result in a negative value for $f(x)$. The range of $f(x)$ is all real numbers less than or equal to 0.

10. c. The square root of a negative value is imaginary, so the value of $4x - 1$ must be greater than or equal to 0. $4x - 1 \geq 0$, $4x \geq 1$, $x \geq \frac{1}{4}$. The domain of $f(x)$ is all real numbers greater than or equal to $\frac{1}{4}$. Because x must be greater than or equal to $\frac{1}{4}$, the smallest value of $f(x)$ is the square root of 0, which is 0. The range of the function is all real numbers greater than or equal to 0.

► Algebra and Functions Posttest

1. d. The terms $5a$ and $7b$ have unlike bases; they cannot be combined any further. Add the terms in the denominator: $b + 2b = 3b$. Divide the b term in the numerator by the $3b$ in the denominator: $\frac{b}{3b} = \frac{1}{3}$. $(5a + 7b)(\frac{1}{3}) = \frac{5a + 7b}{3}$.

2. b. Multiply $2x^2$ and $4y^2$ by multiplying the coefficients of the terms: $(2x^2)(4y^2) = 8x^2y^2$. $8x^2y^2$ and $6x^2y^2$ have like bases, so they can be added. Add the coefficients: $8x^2y^2 + 6x^2y^2 = 14x^2y^2$.

3. a. First, multiply $(x + 2)$ by 4: $4(x + 2) = 4x + 8$. Then, subtract $3x$ from both sides of the inequality and also subtract 8 from both sides of the inequality:
$3x - 6 \leq 4x + 8$
$3x - 6 - 3x \leq 4x + 8 - 3x$
$-6 \leq x + 8$
$-6 - 8 \leq x + 8 - 8$
$x \geq -14$

4. a. To find the product of two binomials, multiply the first term of each binomial, the outside terms, the inside terms, and the last terms. Then, add the products. $(x - 1)(x + 1) = x^2 + x - x - 1 = x^2 - 1$.

5. e. $(x + c)^2 = (x + c)(x + c)$. To find the product of two binomials, multiply the first term of each binomial, the outside terms, the inside terms, and the last terms. Then, add the products. $(x + c)(x + c) = x^2 + cx + cx + c^2 = x^2 + 2cx + c^2$.

6. d. To find the factors of a quadratic, begin by finding two numbers whose product is equal to the constant of the quadratic. Of those numbers, find the pair that adds to the coefficient of the x term of the quadratic.

However, this quadratic has no x term; the sum of the products of the outside and inside terms of the factors is 0. −2 and 2 multiply to −4 and add to 0. Therefore, the factors of $x^2 - 4$ are $(x - 2)$ and $(x + 2)$.

7. e. Begin with the innermost function: find $f(3)$ by substituting 3 for x in the function $f(x)$: $f(3) = 2(3) + 1 = 6 + 1 = 7$. Next, substitute the result of that function for x in $g(x)$: $g(7) = 7 - 2 = 5$. Finally, substitute 5 for x in $f(x)$: $f(5) = 2(5) + 1 = 10 + 1 = 11$.

8. c. Begin with the innermost function. You are given the value of $f(x)$: $f(x) = 6x + 4$. Substitute this expression for x in the equation $g(x)$: $g(x) = x^2 - 1$; $g(6x + 4) = (6x + 4)^2 - 1 = 36x^2 + 24x + 24x + 16 - 1 = 36x^2 + 48x + 15$. Therefore, $g[f(x)] = 36x^2 + 48x + 15$.

9. b. The domain of a function is the set of all possible inputs to the function. All real numbers can be substituted for x in the function $f(x) = \frac{1}{x^2 - 9}$, excluding those that make the fraction undefined. Set the denominator equal to 0 to find the values of x that make the fraction undefined. These values are not in the domain of the function. $x^2 - 9 = 0$, $(x - 3)(x + 3) = 0$, $x - 3 = 0$, $x = 3$; $x + 3 = 0$, $x = -3$. The domain of $f(x)$ is all real numbers excluding 3 and −3.

10. e. The range of a function is the set of all possible outputs of the function. All real numbers can be substituted for x in the function $f(x) = x^2 - 4$, so the domain of the function is all real numbers. Because the x term is squared, the smallest value that this term can equal is 0 (when $x = 0$). Therefore, the smallest value that $f(x)$ can have is when $x = 0$. When $x = 0$, $f(x) = 0^2 - 4 = -4$. The range of $f(x)$ is all real numbers greater than or equal to −4.

► Geometry Pretest

1. d. Angles 2, 4, 6, and 7 are alternating (vertical) angles. Therefore, their measures are equal. Angles 7 and 8 are supplementary. Therefore, angles 2 and 8 are also supplementary. $12x + 10 + 7x − 1 = 180$, $19x + 9 = 180$, $19x = 171$, $x = 9$. Because $x = 9$, the measure of angle 2 is $12(9) + 10 = 108 + 10 = 118$ degrees.

2. e. Angles 5 and 6 are supplementary. Therefore, the sum of their measures is 180 degrees. If the measure of angle 6 is x, then the measure of angle 5 is $5x$. $5x + x = 180$, $6x = 180$, $x = 30$. The measure of angle 6 is 30 degrees, and the measure of angle 5 is $5(30) = 150$ degrees.

3. c. Angles 4 and 7 are alternating angles. Therefore, their measures are equal: $6x + 20 = 10x − 40$, $4x = 60$, $x = 15$. Because $x = 15$, the measure of angles 4 and 7 is $6(15) + 20 = 90 + 20 = 110$. Notice that replacing x with 15 in the measure of angle 7 also yields 110: $10(15) − 40 = 150 − 40 = 110$. Because angles 6 and 7 are vertical angles, the measure of angle 6 is also 110 degrees.

4. a. If angle 3 measures 90 degrees, then angles 1, 6, and 7 must also measure 90 degrees, because they are alternating angles. Angles 3 and 4 are supplementary, because these angles form a line. Therefore, the measure of angle 4 is equal to $180 − 90 = 90$ degrees. Angles 3 and 4 are congruent and supplementary. Because angles 2, 4, 5, and 8 are alternating angles, they are all congruent to each other. Every numbered angle measures 90 degrees. Therefore, every numbered angle is congruent and supplementary to every other numbered angle. Angles 5 and 7 are in fact adjacent, because they share a common

vertex and a common ray. However, angles 1 and 2 are not complementary—their measures add to 180 degrees, not 90 degrees.

5. b. Angles 2 and 6 are alternating angles. Therefore, their measures are equal. $8x + 10 = x^2 − 38$, $x^2 − 8x − 48 = 0$. Factor $x^2 − 8x − 48$ and set each factor equal to 0. $x^2 − 8x − 48 = (x + 4)(x − 12)$, $x + 4 = 0$, $x = −4$. $x − 12 = 0$, $x = 12$. An angle cannot have a negative measure, so the −4 value of x must be discarded. If $x = 12$, then the measure of angle 2 is $8(12) + 10 = 106$ degrees. Notice that replacing x with 12 in the measure of angle 6 also yields 106: $(12)^2 − 38 = 144 − 38 = 106$. Angles 6 and 8 are supplementary, so the measure of angle 8 is equal to $180 − 106 = 74$ degrees.

6. e. If x is the width of the rectangle, then $2x − 4$ is the length of the rectangle. Because opposite sides of a rectangle are congruent, the perimeter of the rectangle is equal to $2x − 4 + x + 2x − 4 + x = 6x − 8$.

7. c. One face of a cube is a square. The area of a square is equal to the length of one side of the square multiplied by itself. Therefore, the length of a side of this square (and edge of the cube) is equal to $\sqrt{9x}$ or $3\sqrt{x}$ units. Because every edge of a cube is equal in length and the volume of a cube is equal to e^3, where e is the length of an edge (or *lwh*, *l* is the length of the cube, *w* is the width of the cube, and *h* is the height of the cube, which in this case, are all $3\sqrt{x}$ units), the volume of the cube is equal to $(3\sqrt{x})^3 = 27x\sqrt{x}$ cubic units.

8. d. The circumference of a circle is equal to $2\pi r$. Because the radius of a circle is half the diameter of a circle, $2r$ is equal to the diameter, d, of a circle. Therefore, the circumference of a circle is equal to πd. If the diameter is doubled, the circumference becomes $\pi 2d$, or two times its original size.

9. b. If the base of the triangle is b, then the height of the triangle is $\frac{1}{2b}$. The area of a triangle is equal to $\frac{1}{2}bh$. Therefore, the area of this triangle is equal to $\frac{1}{2}[b(\frac{1}{2}b)] = \frac{1}{4}b^2$.

10. e. Use the Pythagorean theorem: $(x-3)^2 + (x+4)^2 = (2x-3)^2$, $x^2 - 6x + 9 + x^2 + 8x + 16 = 4x^2 - 12x + 9$, $2x^2 + 2x + 25 = 4x^2 - 12x + 9$, $2x^2 - 14x - 16 = 0$, $x^2 - 7x - 8 = 0$, $(x-8)(x+1) = 0$, $x = 8$. Disregard the negative value of x, because a side of a triangle cannot be negative. Because $x = 8$, the length of the hypotenuse is $2(8) - 3 = 16 - 3 = 13$.

11. b. The slope of a line is the difference between the y values of two points divided by the difference between the x values of those two points: $(4-6) \div 7 - (-3) = \frac{-2}{10} = -\frac{1}{5}$.

12. b. The midpoint of a line segment is equal to the average of the x values of the endpoints and the average of the y values of the endpoints:

$$\left(\frac{0+(-8)}{2}, \frac{-8+0}{2}\right) = \left(\frac{-8}{2}, \frac{-8}{2}\right) = (-4, -4).$$

13. c. To find the distance between two points, use the distance formula:

$$D = \sqrt{(x_2 - x_1)^2 + (y_2 - y_1)^2}$$
$$D = \sqrt{(2-(-6))^2 + (17-2)^2} = \sqrt{8^2 + (15)^2}$$
$$= \sqrt{64 + 225} = \sqrt{289} = 17 \text{ units.}$$

▶ Geometry Posttest

1. a. Perpendicular lines cross at right angles. Therefore, angle AOC is 90 degrees. Because angles 1 and 2 combine to form angle AOC, the sum of the measures of angles 1 and 2 must be 90 degrees. Therefore, they are complementary angles.

2. d. AE is perpendicular to OC, so angles AOC and EOC are both 90 degrees. Because angles 1 and 2 combine to form angle AOC and angles 3 and 4 combine to form angle EOC, these sums must both equal 90 degrees. Therefore, angle 1 + angle 2 = angle 3 + angle 4. Angles 1, 2, 3, and 7 form a line, as do angles 4, 5, and 6. Therefore, the measures of angles 1, 2, 3, and 7 add to 180 degrees, as do the measures of angles 4, 5, and 6. In the same way, angles 2, 3, 4, and 5 form a line, so the sum of the measures of those angles is also 180 degrees. Angles GOF and BOD are vertical angles. Therefore, their measures are equal. Angle 6 is angle GOF and angles 2 and 3 combine to form angle BOD, so the measure of angle 6 is equal to the sum of the measures of angles 2 and 3. However, the sum of angle 1 and angle 7 is not equal to the sum of angle 2 and angle 3. In fact, the sum of angles 2 and 3 is supplementary to the sum of angles 7 and 1, because angle 6 is supplementary to the sum of angles 7 and 1, and the sum of angles 2 and 3 is equal to the measure of angle 6.

3. c. Because AE is perpendicular to OC, angle EOC is a right angle (measuring 90 degrees). Angles 3 and 4 combine to form angle EOC; therefore, their sum is equal to 90 degrees: $2x + 2 + 5x - 10 = 90$, $7x - 8 = 90$, $7x = 98$,

$x = 14$. Angle 4 is equal to $5(14) - 10 = 70 - 10 = 60$ degrees. Because angles 4 and 7 are vertical angles, their measures are equal, and angle 7, too, measures 60 degrees.

4. b. Because AE is perpendicular to OC, angle EOC is a right angle (measuring 90 degrees). Angles 3 and 4 combine to form angle EOC; therefore, their sum is equal to 90 degrees: $90 - 57 = 33$. Angle 3 measures 33 degrees. Angle AOC is also a right angle, with angles 1 and 2 combining to form that angle. Therefore, the measure of angle 2 is equal to: $90 - 62 = 28$ degrees. Angle 6 and angle BOD are vertical angles; their measures are equal. Because angles 2 and 3 combine to form angle BOD, the measure of BOD (and angle 6) is equal to: $33 + 28 = 61$ degrees.

5. b. Because AE is perpendicular to OC, angle EOC is a right angle (measuring 90 degrees). Angles 3 and 4 combine to form angle EOC; therefore, their sum is equal to 90 degrees: $5x + 3 + 15x + 7 = 90$, $20x + 10 = 90$, $20x = 80$, $x = 4$. Therefore, the measure of angle 4 is equal to: $15(4) + 7 = 67$ degrees. Angles 4, 5, and 6 form a line; therefore, the sum of their measures is 180 degrees. If x is the sum of angles 5 and 6, then $67 + x = 180$, and $x = 113$ degrees.

6. a. If the square and the rectangle share a side, then the width of the rectangle is equal to the length of the square. If the length of the square is x, then $x + x + x + x = 2$, $4x = 2$, $x = \frac{1}{2}$. Because the width of the rectangle is equal to the length of the square and the length of the rectangle is 4 times the length of the square, the width of the rectangle is $\frac{1}{2}$ and the length is $4(\frac{1}{2}) = 2$. Therefore, the perimeter of the rectangle is equal to: $\frac{1}{2} + 2 + \frac{1}{2} + 2 = 5$ units.

7. c. The area of a rectangle is equal to its length times its width. Therefore, the width of the rectangle is equal to its area divided by its length: $\frac{x^2 + 7x + 10}{x + 2}$. $x^2 + 7x + 10$ can be factored into $(x + 2)(x + 5)$. Cancel the $(x + 2)$ terms from the numerator and denominator of the fraction. The width of the rectangle is $x + 5$ units.

8. e. The volume of a rectangular solid is equal to lwh, where l is the length of the solid, w is the width of the solid, and h is the height of the solid. If x represents the width (and therefore, the height as well), then the length of the solid is equal to $2(x + x)$, or $2(2x) = 4x$. Therefore, $(4x)(x)(x) = 108$, $4x^3 = 108$, $x^3 = 27$, and $x = 3$. If the width and height of the solid are each 3 inches, then the length of the solid is $2(3 + 3) = 2(6) = 12$ inches.

9. d. Use the Pythagorean theorem: $8^2 + x^2 = (8\sqrt{5})^2$, $64 + x^2 = 320$, $x^2 = 256$, $x = 16$ (x cannot equal -16 because the side of a triangle cannot be negative).

10. b. The measures of the angles of a triangle add to 180 degrees. Therefore, $3x + 4x + 5x = 180$, $12x = 180$, and $x = 15$.

11. e. To find the distance between two points, use the distance formula:
$$D = \sqrt{(x_2 - x_1)^2 + (y_2 - y_1)^2}$$
$$= \sqrt{(4 - 0)^2 + [4 - (-4)]^2}$$
$$= \sqrt{4^2 + 8^2} = \sqrt{16 + 64} = \sqrt{80} = \sqrt{16}\sqrt{5} = 4\sqrt{5} \text{ un}$$

12. c. The midpoint of a line segment is equa' the average of the x values of the en' and the average of the y values of endpoints:
$$\left(\frac{6 + 15}{2}, \frac{-4 + 8}{2}\right) = \left(\frac{21}{2}, \frac{4}{2}\right)$$

13. c. The slope of a line is the difference between the y values of two points divided by the difference between the x values of those two points: $[-5 - (-5)] \div -5 - 5 = \frac{0}{-10} = 0$.

► Data Analysis, Statistics, and Probability Pretest

1. b. To find the mean of a set of data, add up all the numbers and divide by the amount of data. $96 + 90 + 78 + 90 + 92 = 446$. There are five data items. $446 \div 5 = 89.2$, choice **b**.

2. c. To find the mean fuel efficiency, add up the six numbers and divide by 6: $16 + 22 + 14 + 28 + 16 + 12 = 108$, and $108 \div 6 = 18$ miles per gallon.

3. c. To answer this question, calculate the mean, median, and mode of the set of numbers. First, arrange the numbers in ascending order: 26, 27, 27, 27, 29, 29, 30, 30. There are eight numbers; add them together and divide by 8 for the mean: $26 + 27 + 27 + 27 + 29 + 29 + 30 + 30 = 225$, and 225 divided by 8 is 28.125, which is the mean. The mode is the number that occurs most often, which is 27. The median is the middle number; since there are eight entries, it is the average of the two middle numbers: $27 + 29 = 56$, and 56 divided by 2 is 28. Knowing the three measures can lead to the only right conclusion, which is that the median is greater than the mode, choice **c**.

4. b. There is no number value repeated, so there is no mode.

5. a. Probability is a ratio of number of favorable outcomes/number of total outcomes. There are six sides to a die, so there are six total outcomes, one of which is a 3. The probability is therefore $\frac{1}{6}$.

6. b. The steepest rise on the graph was from April 23 to April 30. The symbol indicates that it was in the Midwest.

7. d. The prices for the West Coast have been rising steadily by 2 or 3 cents each week. On May 7, the price on the West Coast is a little beneath $2.80. If it rises 2 or 3 cents, it should be at about $2.82 by the following week. The question gives no reason to expect a sudden decline in price or a sharp increase.

8. e. Look for the first year in which the bar that represents the number of women receiving bachelor's degrees is taller than the bar that represents the number of men receiving bachelor's degrees.

The first time this occurs is for 1989–1990.

9. c. To solve the problem, first find how many women and how many men received bachelor's degrees in 1989–1990. For women, the height of the bar is a little past the middle between 500,000 and 600,000, at approximately 560,000. For men, the bar is at approximately 500,000. Subtract the estimates: $560,000 - 500,000 = 60,000$. Approximately 60,000 more women received bachelor degrees in 1989–1990.

▶ Data Analysis, Statistics, and Probability Posttest

1. **b.** To find the mean, add up all of the data values, and divide by the number of items, which is eight: $32 + 34 + 34 + 35 + 37 + 38 + 34 + 42 = 286$; 286 divided by 8 is 35.75.

2. **e.** There are two modes for this data set. Both 71 and 68 appear in the set twice.

3. **a.** First, arrange the data into increasing order: 8, 9, 9, 9, 10, 10, 11, 12, 13, 17. There is an even number of data values, so the median is the mean of the two middle values. They are both 10, so the median is 10. The middle values are $10 + 10 = 20$, and 20 divided by 2 is 10.

4. **b.** The range is the difference between the highest and lowest values in the set of data. The highest temperature is 84° and the lowest temperature is 42°: $84° - 42° = 42°$.

5. **e.** Use a table to find all of the possible sum outcomes when rolling two dice. From a table, you will see that there are 36 total outcomes, five of which generate a sum of 8. The sums of 8 are circled on the chart: 6 and 2, 2 and 6, 3 and 5, 5 and 3, and 4 and 4. The probability is therefore: number of favorable outcomes/number of total outcomes $= \frac{5}{36}$.

6. **a.** Subtract hourly earnings of previous year from given year.
   a: $1992–1991 = \$10.57 - \$10.32 = \$0.25$
   b: $1994–1993 = \$11.12 - \$10.83 = \$0.29$
   c: $1996–1995 = \$11.82 - \$11.43 = \$0.39$
   d: $1997–1996 = \$12.28 - \$11.82 = \$0.46$
   e: $1998–1997 = \$12.77 - \$12.28 = \$0.49$
   Compare differences to find the least difference. $0.25 is the least difference, which means 1992 had the least increase in hourly earnings from the previous year.

7. **c.** Subtract to find the amount of increase.
   1996 hourly earnings – 1990 hourly earnings
   $\$11.82 - \$10.01 = \$1.81$
   Write a ratio comparing the amount of increase to the original amount: $\frac{\$1.81}{\$10.01}$.
   Change to a percent by first expressing the faction as decimal and then changing the decimal to a percent.
   $1.81 \div 10.01 \approx = 0.1808$
   $0.1808 = 18.08\% \approx 18\%$

8. **c.** Use the table to find the total number of cars sold in the United States in 1998.
   total sales in 1998 = 8,141,721
   Use the bar graph to find what percent of total car sales in 1998 small cars represented.
   small car sales in 1998 = 24.7%
   Estimate 24.7% of 8,141,721 to find the approximate number of cars sold.
   $24.7\% \approx 25\% = \frac{1}{4}$
   $8,141,721 \approx 8,000,000$
   $\frac{1}{4} \times 8,000,000 = 2,000,000$
   Approximately 2,000,000 small cars were sold in 1998.

9. **d.** Use the graph to find the percent of sales for midsize, luxury, and large cars.
   midsize: 52.7%
   luxury: 16.5%
   large: 7.6%
   Find the sum of the percentages of luxury and large car sales.
   $16.5 + 7.6 = 24.1$
   Find the ratio of midsize car sales to the sum of luxury and large car sales.
   52.7:24.1
   This is about 2 to 1. About twice as midsize cars as luxury and large bined were sold in 1998.

▶ Posttest

1.

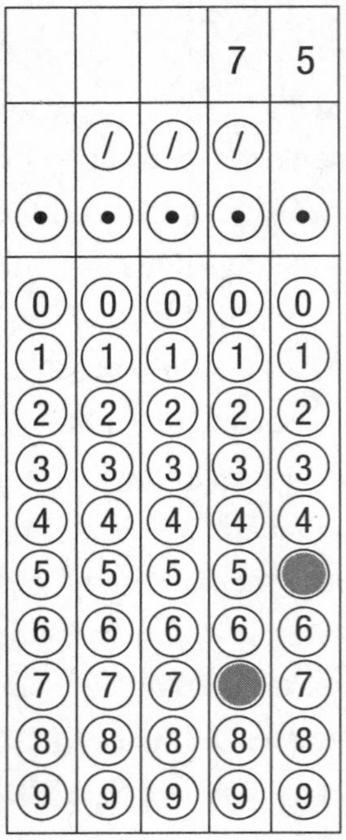

(grid answer showing 7 5)

Nine out of 12 notebooks are gray. $\frac{9}{12} = \frac{3}{4}$.
$\frac{3}{4} \times 100\% = \frac{300\%}{4} = 75\%$.

2. d. Rounding to the nearest hundred, $(600 + 500 + 600 + 500 + 700 + 700) \div 6 = 600$.

3. a. $\$0.1165 - \$0.095 = \$0.0215$.

4. a.
$$5 + \frac{\sqrt{5^2 - 4 \times 2 \times 2}}{3} = 5 + \frac{\sqrt{25 - 16}}{3}$$
$$= 5 + \frac{\sqrt{9}}{3} = 5 + \frac{3}{3} = 6$$

If you use a calculator to solve this, solve for the value inside the square root sign and then take the square root.

5. d. $(\$15.95 \times 2) + \$5.97 = \$37.87$. The cost of standard shipping for this order is $7.95. $\$37.87 + \$7.95 = \$45.82$.

6. a. The cost for three DVDs is $43.50. One-day shipping would be $26.95 and standard shipping would be $7.95. Find the difference: $\$26.95 - \$7.95 = \$19.00$.

7. c. 1 mile = 1,760 yards $(5,280 \div 3)$. 100 yards = $100 \div 1,760$ yards/mile = 0.056818181 mile, which is about 0.06 mile.

8. d. Let c = the number of calories in 4 ounces. Calories/ounces: $\frac{c}{4} = \frac{230}{1.2}$. $c = \frac{230 \times 4}{1.2} = \frac{920}{1.2} = 766.666\ldots$, which is about 770.

9. d. It is easier to solve this problem using decimals, rather than fractions or percents: $\$2,000 \times 0.12 \times 1.5 = \$240 \times 1.5 = \$360$.

10. d. The actual length is 24 inches $\times 1\frac{3}{4} = 24 \times \frac{7}{4} = 6 \times \frac{7}{1} = 42$. 42 inches is also 3 feet 6 inches.

11.

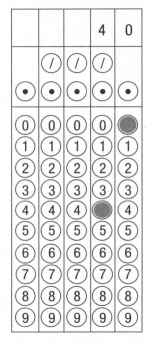

$3,140 \div 80 = 39\frac{1}{4}$. To complete the job, Herman must buy 40 packages.

12. c. The three roses sections have 90-degree angles which, when added, total 270 degrees. Subtract the total of the roses sections from the total degrees in a circle: $360 - 270 = 90$. The lily sections total 90 degrees, or $\frac{90}{360} = \frac{1}{4}$ of the garden.

13. d. Angle $PNO = 180 - (90 + 50) = 180 - 140 = 40°$.

14. **e.** Without knowing the measure of angle *MNO*, there is no way to know the measure of angle *NMO*.

15. **d.** The area of the walkway equals the area of the outer rectangle minus the area of the pool. Notice that the outer rectangle has a length of 60 feet $(50 + 5 + 5)$ and a width of 40 feet $(30 + 5 + 5)$. The area of the walkways equals $(60 \times 40) - (50 \times 30) = 2,400 - 1,500 = 900$ square feet.

16. **a.** $V = \frac{1}{3} \times \pi \times r^2 \times h = \frac{1}{3} \times 3.14 \times 4^2 \times 4$, which is about equal to 66.987 or 70 cubic feet.

17. **c.** The ratio of rent in Wycoff to South Orange in 2000 $= \frac{600}{450} = \frac{4}{3}$.

18. **e.** Between 1980 and 2000, rent in South Orange increased from about $250 to $450. Percent increase = $(\$450 - \$250) \div \$250 = \frac{4}{5} = 80\%$.

19.

	4	0	0	0
		/	/	/
•	•	•	•	•
0	0	●	●	●
1	1	1	1	1
2	2	2	2	2
3	3	3	3	3
4	●	4	4	4
5	5	5	5	5
6	6	6	6	6
7	7	7	7	7
8	8	8	8	8
9	9	9	9	9

The total interest paid on a 30-year loan at 6% is about $118,000. To find the average: $118,000 \div 3 = \$3,933$, which rounds to $4,000.

20. **a.** To raise the average profit per quarter to $5,000, Two Scoops Ice-Cream Parlor would need to earn a total yearly profit of $20,000. You can see above the circle graph that the total yearly profit is $18,000. $20,000 - $18,000 = $2,000.

21. **a.** The probability that the next pizza will be pepperoni is $\frac{8}{20}$, which rounds to $\frac{2}{5}$ or 40%.

22. **c.** The probability that the next pizza will be cheese is $\frac{4}{20}$, which reduces to $\frac{1}{5}$. Of the next 15 pizzas, $\frac{1}{5} \times 15$ are likely to be cheese. $\frac{1}{5} \times 15 = 3$.

23. **a.** Try this rule on the sequence and you will see that it predicts each next number in this sequence. This is not true for any of the other rules.

24. **a.** A ticket package costs $2.25 and is good for three rides. A single ride costs $2.25 \div 3$, or $0.75.

25. **b.** $V = \pi \times r^2 \times h$. $\pi = \frac{V}{r^2 h} = \frac{124}{2^2} \times 10 = \frac{124}{40} = 3.1$.

26. **c.** 4,289 rounded to the nearest hundred is 4,300; 289 rounds up to 300, not down to 200.

27. **d.** Add the prices of what Joey bought together: $2.25 + $0.75. This total amount must be subtracted from $10.00: $10.00 - ($2.25 + $0.75).

28. **e.** Subtract to find the weight of the cans and then divide by two dozen to find the weight of one can.

29.

		3	/	4
	○/	○/	●	
⊙	⊙	⊙	⊙	⊙
0	0	0	0	0
1	1	1	1	1
2	2	2	2	2
3	3	●	3	3
4	4	4	4	●
5	5	5	5	5
6	6	6	6	6
7	7	7	7	7
8	8	8	8	8
9	9	9	9	9

$147\frac{1}{2} - 146\frac{3}{4} = \frac{3}{4}$ pound. You could solve using decimals: $147.5 - 146.75 = 0.75$, which as a fraction is expressed as $\frac{3}{4}$.

30. d. $\frac{2}{3} \times 100\%$ is about 67%. You can also eliminate the other answer choices easily if you figure out that $\frac{2}{3}$ is the only fraction listed that is greater than $\frac{1}{2}$ (50%).

31. a. Materials/labor $= \frac{25}{75} = \frac{25 \div 25}{75 \div 25} = \frac{1}{3}$.

32. b. A centimeter is about the length of a ladybug. A millimeter would be the measure of a small ant, while a meter is a little longer than a yard. Liters measure capacity, not length.

33. d. In 45 minutes, the time will be 11:30 and, if you add one more hour, the time will be 12:30, the time shown on the clock: 45 minutes + 1 hour = 1 hour 45 minutes.

34. a. The ratio is amount earned/number of hours worked. On Saturday, this ratio is $\frac{\$48}{5}$, and on Sunday $\frac{b}{3}$.

35. c. The actual distance is 15 miles $\times 2\frac{1}{2} = 15 \times \frac{5}{2}$ = 37.5 miles.

36. d. The angle shown is larger than a right angle, which is 90 degrees, but less than a straight angle, which is 180 degrees.

37. a. The formula for the area of a triangle is $\frac{1}{2} \times$ base $\times$ height $= \frac{1}{2} \times 12 \times 20 = 120$ square yards.

38. c. Any coordinates in this shaded area would have negative x and y values.

39. e. This point is three units to the left of the y-axis and four units above the x-axis.

40. d. Slope = change in y value/change in x value $= (1 - 0) \div (5 - 2)$.

41.

			6	9
	○/	○/	○/	
⊙	⊙	⊙	⊙	⊙
0	0	0	0	0
1	1	1	1	1
2	2	2	2	2
3	3	3	3	3
4	4	4	4	4
5	5	5	5	5
6	6	●	6	6
7	7	7	7	7
8	8	8	8	8
9	9	9	●	●

Identify the point on the line of best fit that lies directly above 10.5 on the horizontal axis. This point is directly across from 69 on the vertical axis.

42. a. Identify the point on the line of best fit that lies directly across from 62 on the vertical axis. This point is directly above 8 on the horizontal axis.

43. **c.** You need to find the average of the two middle foot lengths. Both of these points are 10 inches; there are seven points to the left and seven points to the right. The median is 10 inches.

44. **c.** The probability that the next call is for Mr. Rivera is $\frac{10}{15}$ (or $\frac{2}{3}$) $\times 6 = 4$.

45. **e.** The number of men is represented by m; the number of women is represented by $n - m$. The ratio of men to women can be written as the fraction $\frac{m}{n-m}$.

46. **e.** The cost of the tennis balls = 1.75×8. The cost of the golf balls = $g \times 12 = 12g$. The cost of the golf balls is $32.50 minus the cost of the tennis balls, or $12g = \$32.50 - \$1.75 \times 8$.

47. **e.** Each guest beyond the first person pays $1.75 to be admitted to the beach. For a total of five people, the total cost is $4.50 + ($1.75 $\times 4$), or $11.50.

48. **d.** When $p = 3$, $y = 6(3) - 23 = 18 - 23 = -5$. When $p = 4$, $y = 6(4) - 23 = 24 - 23 = 1$.

49. **d.** Substitute $x = 3$ and $y = 1$ into the equation. Only choice d results in a true statement: $1 = (\frac{2}{3})3 - 1 = 2 - 1 = 1$.

50. **c.** When the diameter doubles, so does the radius. If r increases from 1 to 2 units, r^2 increases from 1 to 4 units. The area of a circle quadruples when r doubles.

Formula Cheat Sheet

Area

Square: $A = \text{side}^2$

Rectangle: $A = \text{length} \times \text{width}$

Parallelogram: $A = \text{base} \times \text{height}$

Triangle: $A = \frac{1}{2} \times \text{base} \times \text{height}$

Trapezoid: $A = \frac{1}{2}(\text{base}_1 + \text{base}_2) \times \text{height}$

Circle: $A = \pi \times \text{radius}^2$; π is approximately equal to 3.14.

Circumference

Circle: $C = \pi \times \text{diameter}$; π is approximately equal to 3.14.

Distance between Points on a Coordinate Plane

Distance between points: $\sqrt{(x_2 - x_1)^2 + (y_2 - y_1)^2}$; (x_1, y_1) and (x_2, y_2) are two points on the line.

Distance Formula

Distance $= \text{rate} \times \text{time}$

Measures of Central Tendency

Mean: $(x_1 + x_2 + \ldots + x_n - x_1) \div n$, where x's are values for which a mean is desired and n is the total number of values for x

Median: the middle value of an odd number of ordered scores, and halfway between the two middle values of an even number of ordered scores

Perimeter

Square: $P = 4 \times \text{side}$

Rectangle: $P = 2 \times \text{length} + 2 \times \text{width}$

Triangle: $P = \text{side}_1 + \text{side}_2 + \text{side}_3$

Pythagorean Theorem

$a^2 + b^2 = c^2$; a and b are legs, and c is the hypotenuse of a right angle.

Simple Interest Formula

Interest $= \text{principal} \times \text{rate} \times \text{time}$

Slope of a Line on a Coordinate Plane

Slope of a line: $(y_2 - y_1) \div (x_2 - x_1)$; (x_1, y_1) and (x_2, y_2) are two points on the line.

Total Cost

Total cost = number of units × price per unit

Volume

Cube: $V = \text{edge}^3$

Rectangular solid: $V = \text{length} \times \text{width} \times \text{height}$

Square pyramid: $V = \frac{1}{3} \times (\text{base edge})^2 \times \text{height}$

Cone: $V = \frac{1}{3} \times \pi \times \text{radius}^2 \times \text{height}$; π is approximately equal to 3.14.

Cylinder: $\pi \times \text{radius}^2 \times \text{height}$; π is approximately equal to $3.14 V = B \times h$ (the area of the base times the height).

Rectangular solid: $V = l \times w \times h$

Cylinder: $V = \pi \times r^2 \times h$

Glossary ▶

THE FOLLOWING GLOSSARY is meant as a tool to prepare you for the GED. You will not be asked any vocabulary questions on the GED Mathematics Exam, so there is no need to memorize any of these terms or definitions. However, reading through this list will familiarize you with general math words and concepts, as well as terms you may encounter in the GED questions.

▶ A

absolute value   For a number, this is the distance, or number of units from the origin, on a number line. Absolute value is the size of the number and is always positive.

area   a measure of how many square units it takes to cover a closed figure

associative property   This property is used when grouping symbols are present. This property states that when you perform a string of addition operations, or all multiplication operations you can change the grouping. In other words, $(a \times b) \times c = a \times (b \times c)$.

▶ B

base   A number used as a repeated factor in an exponential expression. In 8^5, 8 is the base number.

▶ C

circle   the set of all points equidistant from one given point, called the *center*. The center point defines the circle, but it is not on the circle.

circumference   the distance around the outside of a circle

coefficient   the number in front of the variable(s)

commutative property This property states that when performing a string of addition operations or a string of multiplication operations, the *order* does not matter. In other words, $a + b = b + a$.

composite number any integer that can be divided evenly by a number other than itself and 1. All numbers are either prime or composite.

coordinate plane a graph formed by two lines that intersect to create right angles

counting numbers all whole numbers, with the exception of 0

▶ D

decimal a number in the base-10 number system. Each place value in a decimal number is worth ten times the place value of the digit to its right.

denominator the bottom number in a fraction. The denominator of $\frac{1}{2}$ is 2.

diameter a chord that passes through the center of a circle and has endpoints on the curve of the circle

difference the result of subtracting one number from another

distributive property This property states that multiplication distributes over addition or subtraction.

dividend The number in a division problem that is being divided. In $32 \div 4 = 8$, 32 is the dividend.

divisible by capable of being evenly divided by a given number, without a remainder

▶ E

equation two equal expressions. Examples: $2 + 2 = 1 + 3$ and $2x = 4$.

even number a counting number that is divisible by 2

expanded notation a method of writing numbers as the sum of their units (hundreds, tens, ones, etc.). The expanded notation for 378 is $300 + 70 + 8$.

exponent a number that indicates an operation of repeated multiplication. For instance, 3^2 indicates that the number 3 should be multiplied by itself once; 3^5 indicates it should be multiplied by itself four times.

▶ F

factor one of two or more numbers or variables that are being multiplied together

fraction the result of dividing two numbers. When you divide 3 by 5, you get $\frac{3}{5}$, which equals 0.6. A fraction is a way of expressing a number that involves dividing a top number (the numerator) by a bottom number (the denominator).

▶ H

hexagon a polygon with six sides

hypotenuse the side of a right triangle that is opposite the right angle

▶ I

improper fraction a fraction whose numerator is the same size as or larger than its denominator. Improper fractions are equal to or greater than 1.

inequality two expressions that are not equal and are described by an inequality symbol such as $<$, $>$, $\leq$, $\geq$, or $\neq$

integer all of the whole numbers and negatives, too. Examples are $-3, -2, -1, 0, 1, 2$, and 3. Note that integers *do not* include fractions or decimals.

interest the amount of money that is paid for using someone else's money

► L

like terms   terms that have the same variable(s) with the same exponent(s), such as $3x^2y$ and $5x^2y$

linear equation   a linear equation always graphs into a straight line. The variable in a linear equation cannot contain an exponent greater than 1. This type of equation cannot have a variable in the denominator, and the variables cannot be multiplied.

► M

mixed number   a number with an integer part and a fractional part. Mixed numbers can be converted into improper fractions.

monomial   an expression with one term

multiple of   a multiple of a number has that number as one of its factors; 35 is a multiple of 7; it is also a multiple of 5.

► N

negative number   a real number whose value is less than zero

numerator   the top number in a fraction. The numerator of $\frac{1}{4}$ is 1.

► O

octagon   a polygon with eight sides

odd number   a counting number that is not divisible by 2

order of operations   the sequence of performing steps to get the correct answer. The order you follow is

1. Simplify all operations within grouping symbols such as parentheses, brackets, braces, and fraction bars.

2. Evaluate all exponents.
3. Do all multiplication and division in order from left to right.
4. Do all addition and subtraction in order from left to right.

ordered pair   two numbers in a specific sequence that represent a point on a coordinate plane. The numbers are enclosed in parentheses with the x-coordinate first and the y-coordinate second; for example, (2,3).

origin   the starting point, or zero, on a number line. On a coordinate plane, the origin is the point where the x-axis and y-axis intersect. The coordinates of the origin are (0,0).

► P

parallelogram   a quadrilateral with two pairs of parallel sides

pentagon   a polygon with five sides

percent   a ratio or fraction whose denominator is assumed to be 100, expressed using the % sign; 98% is equal to $\frac{98}{100}$.

perimeter   the distance around the outside of a polygon

polygon   a closed two-dimensional shape made up of several line segments that are joined together

polynomial   a number, variable, or combination of a number and a variable. Examples: 5, $3x$, and $2x + 2$.

positive number   a real number whose value is greater than zero

prime number   a real number that is divisible by only two positive factors: 1 and itself

product   the result when two numbers are multiplied together

proper fraction   a fraction whose denominator is larger than its numerator. Proper fractions are equal to less than 1.

proportion   a relationship between two equivalent sets of fractions in the form $\frac{a}{b} = \frac{c}{d}$

Pythagorean theorem the theorem stating that in all right triangles, the sum of the squares of the two legs is equal to the square of the hypotenuse: $\text{leg}^2 + \text{leg}^2 = \text{hypotenuse}^2$

▶ Q

quadrants the four equal parts of a coordinate plane. A number names each quadrant. The upper-right-hand area is quadrant I. You proceed counterclockwise to name the other quadrants.

quadrilateral a polygon with four sides

quotient the result when one number is divided into another

▶ R

radical the symbol used to signify a root operation

radius any line segment from the center of a circle to a point on the curve of the circle. The radius of a circle is equal to half the diameter.

rate a ratio comparing two items with unlike units

ratio the relationship between two things, expressed as a proportion

real numbers numbers that include fractions and decimals in addition to integers

reciprocal one of two numbers that, when multiplied together, give a product of 1. For instance, because $\frac{3}{2} \times \frac{2}{3}$ is equal to 1, $\frac{3}{2}$ is the reciprocal of $\frac{2}{3}$.

rectangle a parallelogram with four right angles

remainder the amount left over after a division problem using whole numbers. Divisible numbers always have a remainder of zero.

rhombus a parallelogram with four equal and congruent sides

root (square root) one of two (or more) equal factors of a number. The square root of 36 is 6 because $6 \times 6 = 36$. The cube root of 27 is 3 because $3 \times 3 \times 3 = 27$.

▶ S

scale a special ratio used for models of real-life items

scientific notation a special notation used as a shorthand for large numbers

signed number a number with a positive or negative sign in front of it

simplify terms to combine like terms and reduce an equation to its most basic form

slope the steepness of a line. Slope is the rise or decline over the run or the change in y over the change in x.

slope-intercept form $y = mx + b$. It is also known as $y =$ form.

square a parallelogram with both four equal and right angles and four congruent sides. A square is a rhombus, a rectangle, a parallelogram, and a quadrilateral.

sum the result of adding two numbers together

surface area the measurment of the area of each face of an object

▶ T

trapezoid a quadrilateral with one pair of parallel sides

triangle a polygon with three sides

trinomial an expression with three terms; for example, $a + b + c$

► **V**

variable   a letter, often *x*, used to represent an unknown number value in a problem

volume   a cubic measurement that measures how many cubic units it takes to fill a solid figure

► **W**

whole numbers   0, 1, 2, 3, and so on. They do not include negatives, fractions, or decimals.

► **X**

***x*-axis**   the horizontal line that passes through the origin on the coordinate plane

► **Y**

***y*-axis**   the vertical line that passes through the origin on the coordinate plane

***y*-intercept**   the point where a line graphed on the coordinate plane intersects the *y*-axis

NOTES

NOTES

NOTES

$x = 14$. Angle 4 is equal to $5(14) - 10 = 70 - 10 = 60$ degrees. Because angles 4 and 7 are vertical angles, their measures are equal, and angle 7, too, measures 60 degrees.

4. b. Because AE is perpendicular to OC, angle EOC is a right angle (measuring 90 degrees). Angles 3 and 4 combine to form angle EOC; therefore, their sum is equal to 90 degrees: $90 - 57 = 33$. Angle 3 measures 33 degrees. Angle AOC is also a right angle, with angles 1 and 2 combining to form that angle. Therefore, the measure of angle 2 is equal to: $90 - 62 = 28$ degrees. Angle 6 and angle BOD are vertical angles; their measures are equal. Because angles 2 and 3 combine to form angle BOD, the measure of BOD (and angle 6) is equal to: $33 + 28 = 61$ degrees.

5. b. Because AE is perpendicular to OC, angle EOC is a right angle (measuring 90 degrees). Angles 3 and 4 combine to form angle EOC; therefore, their sum is equal to 90 degrees: $5x + 3 + 15x + 7 = 90$, $20x + 10 = 90$, $20x = 80$, $x = 4$. Therefore, the measure of angle 4 is equal to: $15(4) + 7 = 67$ degrees. Angles 4, 5, and 6 form a line; therefore, the sum of their measures is 180 degrees. If x is the sum of angles 5 and 6, then $67 + x = 180$, and $x = 113$ degrees.

6. a. If the square and the rectangle share a side, then the width of the rectangle is equal to the length of the square. If the length of the square is x, then $x + x + x + x = 2$, $4x = 2$, $x = \frac{1}{2}$. Because the width of the rectangle is equal to the length of the square and the length of the rectangle is 4 times the length of the square, the width of the rectangle is $\frac{1}{2}$ and the length is $4(\frac{1}{2}) = 2$. Therefore, the perimeter of the rectangle is equal to: $\frac{1}{2} + 2 + \frac{1}{2} + 2 = 5$ units.

7. c. The area of a rectangle is equal to its length times its width. Therefore, the width of the rectangle is equal to its area divided by its length: $\frac{x^2 + 7x + 10}{x + 2}$. $x^2 + 7x + 10$ can be factored into $(x + 2)(x + 5)$. Cancel the $(x + 2)$ terms from the numerator and denominator of the fraction. The width of the rectangle is $x + 5$ units.

8. e. The volume of a rectangular solid is equal to lwh, where l is the length of the solid, w is the width of the solid, and h is the height of the solid. If x represents the width (and therefore, the height as well), then the length of the solid is equal to $2(x + x)$, or $2(2x) = 4x$. Therefore, $(4x)(x)(x) = 108$, $4x^3 = 108$, $x^3 = 27$, and $x = 3$. If the width and height of the solid are each 3 inches, then the length of the solid is $2(3 + 3) = 2(6) = 12$ inches.

9. d. Use the Pythagorean theorem: $8^2 + x^2 = (8\sqrt{5})^2$, $64 + x^2 = 320$, $x^2 = 256$, $x = 16$ (x cannot equal -16 because the side of a triangle cannot be negative).

10. b. The measures of the angles of a triangle add to 180 degrees. Therefore, $3x + 4x + 5x = 180$, $12x = 180$, and $x = 15$.

11. e. To find the distance between two points, use the distance formula:

$$D = \sqrt{(x_2 - x_1)^2 + (y_2 - y_1)^2}$$
$$= \sqrt{(4-0)^2 + [4-(-4)]^2}$$
$$= \sqrt{4^2 + 8^2} = \sqrt{16 + 64} = \sqrt{80} = \sqrt{16}\sqrt{5} = 4\sqrt{5} \text{ units}$$

12. c. The midpoint of a line segment is equal to the average of the x values of the endpoints and the average of the y values of the endpoints:

$$\left(\frac{6+15}{2}, \frac{-4+8}{2}\right) = \left(\frac{21}{2}, \frac{4}{2}\right) = (10.5, 2).$$

13. **c.** The slope of a line is the difference between the y values of two points divided by the difference between the x values of those two points: $[-5 - (-5)] \div -5 - 5 = \frac{0}{-10} = 0$.

▶ Data Analysis, Statistics, and Probability Pretest

1. **b.** To find the mean of a set of data, add up all the numbers and divide by the amount of data. $96 + 90 + 78 + 90 + 92 = 446$. There are five data items. $446 \div 5 = 89.2$, choice **b.**

2. **c.** To find the mean fuel efficiency, add up the six numbers and divide by 6: $16 + 22 + 14 + 28 + 16 + 12 = 108$, and $108 \div 6 = 18$ miles per gallon.

3. **c.** To answer this question, calculate the mean, median, and mode of the set of numbers. First, arrange the numbers in ascending order: 26, 27, 27, 27, 29, 29, 30, 30. There are eight numbers; add them together and divide by 8 for the mean: $26 + 27 + 27 + 27 + 29 + 29 + 30 + 30 = 225$, and 225 divided by 8 is 28.125, which is the mean. The mode is the number that occurs most often, which is 27. The median is the middle number; since there are eight entries, it is the average of the two middle numbers: $27 + 29 = 56$, and 56 divided by 2 is 28. Knowing the three measures can lead to the only right conclusion, which is that the median is greater than the mode, choice **c.**

4. **b.** There is no number value repeated, so there is no mode.

5. **a.** Probability is a ratio of number of favorable outcomes/number of total outcomes. There are six sides to a die, so there are six total outcomes, one of which is a 3. The probability is therefore $\frac{1}{6}$.

6. **b.** The steepest rise on the graph was from April 23 to April 30. The symbol indicates that it was in the Midwest.

7. **d.** The prices for the West Coast have been rising steadily by 2 or 3 cents each week. On May 7, the price on the West Coast is a little beneath $2.80. If it rises 2 or 3 cents, it should be at about $2.82 by the following week. The question gives no reason to expect a sudden decline in price or a sharp increase.

8. **e.** Look for the first year in which the bar that represents the number of women receiving bachelor's degrees is taller than the bar that represents the number of men receiving bachelor's degrees.

The first time this occurs is for 1989–1990.

9. **c.** To solve the problem, first find how many women and how many men received bachelor's degrees in 1989–1990. For women, the height of the bar is a little past the middle between 500,000 and 600,000, at approximately 560,000. For men, the bar is at approximately 500,000. Subtract the estimates: $560,000 - 500,000 = 60,000$.

Approximately 60,000 more women received bachelor degrees in 1989–1990.

► Data Analysis, Statistics, and Probability Posttest

1. **b.** To find the mean, add up all of the data values, and divide by the number of items, which is eight: 32 + 34 + 34 + 35 + 37 + 38 + 34 + 42 = 286; 286 divided by 8 is 35.75.

2. **e.** There are two modes for this data set. Both 71 and 68 appear in the set twice.

3. **a.** First, arrange the data into increasing order: 8, 9, 9, 9, 10, 10, 11, 12, 13, 17. There is an even number of data values, so the median is the mean of the two middle values. They are both 10, so the median is 10. The middle values are 10 + 10 = 20, and 20 divided by 2 is 10.

4. **b.** The range is the difference between the highest and lowest values in the set of data. The highest temperature is 84° and the lowest temperature is 42°: 84° − 42° = 42°.

5. **e.** Use a table to find all of the possible sum outcomes when rolling two dice. From a table, you will see that there are 36 total outcomes, five of which generate a sum of 8. The sums of 8 are circled on the chart: 6 and 2, 2 and 6, 3 and 5, 5 and 3, and 4 and 4. The probability is therefore: number of favorable outcomes/number of total outcomes = $\frac{5}{36}$.

6. **a.** Subtract hourly earnings of previous year from given year.
   a: 1992–1991 = $10.57 − $10.32 = $0.25
   b: 1994–1993 = $11.12 − $10.83 = $0.29
   c: 1996–1995 = $11.82 − $11.43 = $0.39
   d: 1997–1996 = $12.28 − $11.82 = $0.46
   e: 1998–1997 = $12.77 − $12.28 = $0.49
   Compare differences to find the least difference. $0.25 is the least difference, which means 1992 had the least increase in hourly earnings from the previous year.

7. **c.** Subtract to find the amount of increase.
   1996 hourly earnings − 1990 hourly earnings
   $11.82 − $10.01 = $1.81
   Write a ratio comparing the amount of increase to the original amount: $\frac{\$1.81}{\$10.01}$.
   Change to a percent by first expressing the faction as decimal and then changing the decimal to a percent.
   1.81 ÷ 10.01 ≈ = 0.1808
   0.1808 = 18.08% ≈ 18%

8. **c.** Use the table to find the total number of cars sold in the United States in 1998.
   total sales in 1998 = 8,141,721
   Use the bar graph to find what percent of total car sales in 1998 small cars represented.
   small car sales in 1998 = 24.7%
   Estimate 24.7% of 8,141,721 to find the approximate number of cars sold.
   24.7% ≈ 25% = $\frac{1}{4}$
   8,141,721 ≈ 8,000,000
   $\frac{1}{4}$ × 8,000,000 = 2,000,000
   Approximately 2,000,000 small cars were sold in 1998.

9. **d.** Use the graph to find the percent of sales for midsize, luxury, and large cars.
   midsize: 52.7%
   luxury: 16.5%
   large: 7.6%
   Find the sum of the percentages of luxury and large car sales.
   16.5 + 7.6 = 24.1
   Find the ratio of midsize car sales to the sum of luxury and large car sales.
   52.7:24.1
   This is about 2 to 1. About twice as many midsize cars as luxury and large cars combined were sold in 1998.

▶ **Posttest**

1.

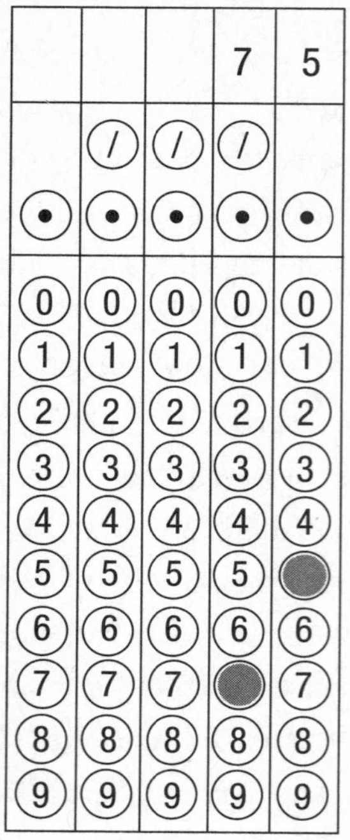

(grid showing 7 5 entered, with bubbles filled)

Nine out of 12 notebooks are gray. $\frac{9}{12} = \frac{3}{4}$. $\frac{3}{4} \times 100\% = \frac{300\%}{4} = 75\%$.

2. d. Rounding to the nearest hundred, $(600 + 500 + 600 + 500 + 700 + 700) \div 6 = 600$.

3. a. $0.1165 - \$0.095 = \$0.0215$.

4. a.
$$5 + \frac{\sqrt{5^2 - 4 \times 2 \times 2}}{3} = 5 + \frac{\sqrt{25 - 16}}{3}$$
$$= 5 + \frac{\sqrt{9}}{3} = 5 + \frac{3}{3} = 6$$

If you use a calculator to solve this, solve for the value inside the square root sign and then take the square root.

5. d. $(\$15.95 \times 2) + \$5.97 = \$37.87$. The cost of standard shipping for this order is $7.95. $37.87 + \$7.95 = \$45.82$.

6. a. The cost for three DVDs is $43.50. One-day shipping would be $26.95 and standard shipping would be $7.95. Find the difference: $26.95 - \$7.95 = \$19.00$.

7. c. 1 mile = 1,760 yards $(5,280 \div 3)$. 100 yards = $100 \div 1,760$ yards/mile = 0.056818181 mile, which is about 0.06 mile.

8. d. Let c = the number of calories in 4 ounces. Calories/ounces: $\frac{c}{4} = \frac{230}{1.2}$. $c = \frac{230 \times 4}{1.2} = \frac{920}{1.2} = 766.666\ldots$, which is about 770.

9. d. It is easier to solve this problem using decimals, rather than fractions or percents: $\$2,000 \times 0.12 \times 1.5 = \$240 \times 1.5 = \$360$.

10. d. The actual length is 24 inches $\times 1\frac{3}{4} = 24 \times \frac{7}{4} = 6 \times \frac{7}{1} = 42$. 42 inches is also 3 feet 6 inches.

11.

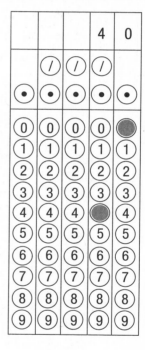

$3,140 \div 80 = 39\frac{1}{4}$. To complete the job, Herman must buy 40 packages.

12. c. The three roses sections have 90-degree angles which, when added, total 270 degrees. Subtract the total of the roses sections from the total degrees in a circle: $360 - 270 = 90$. The lily sections total 90 degrees, or $\frac{90}{360} = \frac{1}{4}$ of the garden.

13. d. Angle $PNO = 180 - (90 + 50) = 180 - 140 = 40°$.

14. e. Without knowing the measure of angle
MNO, there is no way to know the measure
of angle *NMO*.

15. d. The area of the walkway equals the area of
the outer rectangle minus the area of the
pool. Notice that the outer rectangle has a
length of 60 feet (50 + 5 + 5) and a width of
40 feet (30 + 5 + 5). The area of the walkways
equals $(60 \times 40) - (50 \times 30) = 2,400 - 1,500 =$
900 square feet.

16. a. $V = \frac{1}{3} \times \pi \times r^2 \times h = \frac{1}{3} \times 3.14 \times 4^2 \times 4$, which is
about equal to 66.987 or 70 cubic feet.

17. c. The ratio of rent in Wycoff to South Orange
in 2000 $= \frac{600}{450} = \frac{4}{3}$.

18. e. Between 1980 and 2000, rent in South
Orange increased from about $250 to $450.
Percent increase = ($450 − $250) ÷ $250 =
$\frac{4}{5} = 80\%$.

19.

The total interest paid on a 30-year loan at
6% is about $118,000. To find the average:
$118,000 ÷ 3 = $3,933, which rounds to
$4,000.

20. a. To raise the average profit per quarter to
$5,000, Two Scoops Ice-Cream Parlor would
need to earn a total yearly profit of $20,000.
You can see above the circle graph that
the total yearly profit is $18,000.
$20,000 − $18,000 = $2,000.

21. a. The probability that the next pizza will be
pepperoni is $\frac{8}{20}$, which rounds to $\frac{2}{5}$ or 40%.

22. c. The probability that the next pizza will be
cheese is $\frac{4}{20}$, which reduces to $\frac{1}{5}$. Of the next
15 pizzas, $\frac{1}{5} \times 15$ are likely to be cheese.
$\frac{1}{5} \times 15 = 3$.

23. a. Try this rule on the sequence and you will see
that it predicts each next number in this
sequence. This is not true for any of the
other rules.

24. a. A ticket package costs $2.25 and is good for
three rides. A single ride costs $2.25 ÷ 3, or
$0.75.

25. b. $V = \pi \times r^2 \times h$. $\pi = \frac{V}{r^2 h} = \frac{124}{2^2} \times 10 = \frac{124}{40} = 3.1$.

26. c. 4,289 rounded to the nearest hundred is
4,300; 289 rounds up to 300, not down to
200.

27. d. Add the prices of what Joey bought together:
$2.25 + $0.75. This total amount must be
subtracted from $10.00: $10.00 − ($2.25 +
$0.75).

28. e. Subtract to find the weight of the cans and
then divide by two dozen to find the weight
of one can.

29.

		3	/	4

36. d. The angle shown is larger than a right angle, which is 90 degrees, but less than a straight angle, which is 180 degrees.

37. a. The formula for the area of a triangle is $\frac{1}{2} \times$ base $\times$ height $= \frac{1}{2} \times 12 \times 20 = 120$ square yards.

38. c. Any coordinates in this shaded area would have negative x and y values.

39. e. This point is three units to the left of the y-axis and four units above the x-axis.

40. d. Slope = change in y value/change in x value $= (1 - 0) \div (5 - 2).$

41.

			6	9

Identify the point on the line of best fit that lies directly above 10.5 on the horizontal axis. This point is directly across from 69 on the vertical axis.

42. a. Identify the point on the line of best fit that lies directly across from 62 on the vertical axis. This point is directly above 8 on the horizontal axis.

$147\frac{1}{2} - 146\frac{3}{4} = \frac{3}{4}$ pound. You could solve using decimals: $147.5 - 146.75 = 0.75$, which as a fraction is expressed as $\frac{3}{4}$.

30. d. $\frac{2}{3} \times 100\%$ is about 67%. You can also eliminate the other answer choices easily if you figure out that $\frac{2}{3}$ is the only fraction listed that is greater than $\frac{1}{2}$ (50%).

31. a. Materials/labor $= \frac{25}{75} = \frac{25 \div 25}{75 \div 25} = \frac{1}{3}$.

32. b. A centimeter is about the length of a ladybug. A millimeter would be the measure of a small ant, while a meter is a little longer than a yard. Liters measure capacity, not length.

33. d. In 45 minutes, the time will be 11:30 and, if you add one more hour, the time will be 12:30, the time shown on the clock: 45 minutes + 1 hour = 1 hour 45 minutes.

34. a. The ratio is amount earned/number of hours worked. On Saturday, this ratio is $\frac{\$48}{5}$, and on Sunday $\frac{b}{3}$.

35. c. The actual distance is 15 miles $\times 2\frac{1}{2} = 15 \times \frac{5}{2} = 37.5$ miles.

43. c. You need to find the average of the two middle foot lengths. Both of these points are 10 inches; there are seven points to the left and seven points to the right. The median is 10 inches.

44. c. The probability that the next call is for Mr. Rivera is $\frac{10}{15}$ (or $\frac{2}{3}$) $\times 6 = 4$.

45. e. The number of men is represented by m; the number of women is represented by $n - m$. The ratio of men to women can be written as the fraction $\frac{m}{n-m}$.

46. e. The cost of the tennis balls $= \$1.75 \times 8$. The cost of the golf balls $= g \times 12 = 12g$. The cost of the golf balls is $32.50 minus the cost of the tennis balls, or $12g = \$32.50 - \$1.75 \times 8$.

47. e. Each guest beyond the first person pays $1.75 to be admitted to the beach. For a total of five people, the total cost is $4.50 + ($1.75 \times 4$), or $11.50.

48. d. When $p = 3$, $y = 6(3) - 23 = 18 - 23 = -5$. When $p = 4$, $y = 6(4) - 23 = 24 - 23 = 1$.

49. d. Substitute $x = 3$ and $y = 1$ into the equation. Only choice d results in a true statement: $1 = (\frac{2}{3})3 - 1 = 2 - 1 = 1$.

50. c. When the diameter doubles, so does the radius. If r increases from 1 to 2 units, r^2 increases from 1 to 4 units. The area of a circle quadruples when r doubles.

Formula Cheat Sheet

Area

Square: $A = \text{side}^2$

Rectangle: $A = \text{length} \times \text{width}$

Parallelogram: $A = \text{base} \times \text{height}$

Triangle: $A = \frac{1}{2} \times \text{base} \times \text{height}$

Trapezoid: $A = \frac{1}{2}(\text{base}_1 + \text{base}_2) \times \text{height}$

Circle: $A = \pi \times \text{radius}^2$; π is approximately equal to 3.14.

Circumference

Circle: $C = \pi \times \text{diameter}$; π is approximately equal to 3.14.

Distance between Points on a Coordinate Plane

Distance between points: $\sqrt{(x_2 - x_1)^2 + (y_2 - y_1)^2}$; (x_1, y_1) and (x_2, y_2) are two points on the line.

Distance Formula

Distance $= \text{rate} \times \text{time}$

Measures of Central Tendency

Mean: $(x_1 + x_2 + \ldots + x_n - x_1) \div n$, where x's are values for which a mean is desired and n is the total number of values for x

Median: the middle value of an odd number of ordered scores, and halfway between the two middle values of an even number of ordered scores

Perimeter

Square: $P = 4 \times \text{side}$

Rectangle: $P = 2 \times \text{length} + 2 \times \text{width}$

Triangle: $P = \text{side}_1 + \text{side}_2 + \text{side}_3$

Pythagorean Theorem

$a^2 + b^2 = c^2$; a and b are legs, and c is the hypotenuse of a right angle.

Simple Interest Formula

Interest $= \text{principal} \times \text{rate} \times \text{time}$

Slope of a Line on a Coordinate Plane

Slope of a line: $(y_2 - y_1) \div (x_2 - x_1)$; (x_1, y_1) and (x_2, y_2) are two points on the line.

Total Cost

Total cost = number of units × price per unit

Volume

Cube: $V = \text{edge}^3$

Rectangular solid: $V = \text{length} \times \text{width} \times \text{height}$

Square pyramid: $V = \frac{1}{3} \times (\text{base edge})^2 \times \text{height}$

Cone: $V = \frac{1}{3} \times \pi \times \text{radius}^2 \times \text{height}$; π is approximately equal to 3.14.

Cylinder: $\pi \times \text{radius}^2 \times \text{height}$; π is approximately equal to 3.14 $V = B \times h$ (the area of the base times the height).

Rectangular solid: $V = l \times w \times h$

Cylinder: $V = \pi \times r^2 \times h$

Glossary ▶

THE FOLLOWING GLOSSARY is meant as a tool to prepare you for the GED. You will not be asked any vocabulary questions on the GED Mathematics Exam, so there is no need to memorize any of these terms or definitions. However, reading through this list will familiarize you with general math words and concepts, as well as terms you may encounter in the GED questions.

▶ A

absolute value   For a number, this is the distance, or number of units from the origin, on a number line. Absolute value is the size of the number and is always positive.

area   a measure of how many square units it takes to cover a closed figure

associative property   This property is used when grouping symbols are present. This property states that when you perform a string of addition operations, or all multiplication operations you can change the grouping. In other words, $(a \times b) \times c = a \times (b \times c)$.

▶ B

base   A number used as a repeated factor in an exponential expression. In 8^5, 8 is the base number.

▶ C

circle   the set of all points equidistant from one given point, called the *center*. The center point defines the circle, but it is not on the circle.

circumference   the distance around the outside of a circle

coefficient   the number in front of the variable(s)

commutative property   This property states that when performing a string of addition operations or a string of multiplication operations, the *order* does not matter. In other words, $a + b = b + a$.

composite number   any integer that can be divided evenly by a number other than itself and 1. All numbers are either prime or composite.

coordinate plane   a graph formed by two lines that intersect to create right angles

counting numbers   all whole numbers, with the exception of 0

▶ **D**

decimal   a number in the base-10 number system. Each place value in a decimal number is worth ten times the place value of the digit to its right.

denominator   the bottom number in a fraction. The denominator of $\frac{1}{2}$ is 2.

diameter   a chord that passes through the center of a circle and has endpoints on the curve of the circle

difference   the result of subtracting one number from another

distributive property   This property states that multiplication distributes over addition or subtraction.

dividend   The number in a division problem that is being divided. In $32 \div 4 = 8$, 32 is the dividend.

divisible by   capable of being evenly divided by a given number, without a remainder

▶ **E**

equation   two equal expressions. Examples: $2 + 2 = 1 + 3$ and $2x = 4$.

even number   a counting number that is divisible by 2

expanded notation   a method of writing numbers as the sum of their units (hundreds, tens, ones, etc.). The expanded notation for 378 is $300 + 70 + 8$.

exponent   a number that indicates an operation of repeated multiplication. For instance, 3^2 indicates that the number 3 should be multiplied by itself once; 3^5 indicates it should be multiplied by itself four times.

▶ **F**

factor   one of two or more numbers or variables that are being multiplied together

fraction   the result of dividing two numbers. When you divide 3 by 5, you get $\frac{3}{5}$, which equals 0.6. A fraction is a way of expressing a number that involves dividing a top number (the numerator) by a bottom number (the denominator).

▶ **H**

hexagon   a polygon with six sides

hypotenuse   the side of a right triangle that is opposite the right angle

▶ **I**

improper fraction   a fraction whose numerator is the same size as or larger than its denominator. Improper fractions are equal to or greater than 1.

inequality   two expressions that are not equal and are described by an inequality symbol such as $<$, $>$, $\leq$, $\geq$, or $\neq$

integer   all of the whole numbers and negatives, too. Examples are $-3, -2, -1, 0, 1, 2$, and 3. Note that integers *do not* include fractions or decimals.

interest   the amount of money that is paid for using someone else's money

▶ L

like terms   terms that have the same variable(s) with the same exponent(s), such as $3x^2y$ and $5x^2y$

linear equation   a linear equation always graphs into a straight line. The variable in a linear equation cannot contain an exponent greater than 1. This type of equation cannot have a variable in the denominator, and the variables cannot be multiplied.

▶ M

mixed number   a number with an integer part and a fractional part. Mixed numbers can be converted into improper fractions.

monomial   an expression with one term

multiple of   a multiple of a number has that number as one of its factors; 35 is a multiple of 7; it is also a multiple of 5.

▶ N

negative number   a real number whose value is less than zero

numerator   the top number in a fraction. The numerator of $\frac{1}{4}$ is 1.

▶ O

octagon   a polygon with eight sides

odd number   a counting number that is not divisible by 2

order of operations   the sequence of performing steps to get the correct answer. The order you follow is

1. Simplify all operations within grouping symbols such as parentheses, brackets, braces, and fraction bars.

2. Evaluate all exponents.

3. Do all multiplication and division in order from left to right.

4. Do all addition and subtraction in order from left to right.

ordered pair   two numbers in a specific sequence that represent a point on a coordinate plane. The numbers are enclosed in parentheses with the x-coordinate first and the y-coordinate second; for example, (2,3).

origin   the starting point, or zero, on a number line. On a coordinate plane, the origin is the point where the x-axis and y-axis intersect. The coordinates of the origin are (0,0).

▶ P

parallelogram   a quadrilateral with two pairs of parallel sides

pentagon   a polygon with five sides

percent   a ratio or fraction whose denominator is assumed to be 100, expressed using the % sign; 98% is equal to $\frac{98}{100}$.

perimeter   the distance around the outside of a polygon

polygon   a closed two-dimensional shape made up of several line segments that are joined together

polynomial   a number, variable, or combination of a number and a variable. Examples: 5, $3x$, and $2x + 2$.

positive number   a real number whose value is greater than zero

prime number   a real number that is divisible by only two positive factors: 1 and itself

product   the result when two numbers are multiplied together

proper fraction   a fraction whose denominator is larger than its numerator. Proper fractions are equal to less than 1.

proportion   a relationship between two equivalent sets of fractions in the form $\frac{a}{b} = \frac{c}{d}$

Pythagorean theorem the theorem stating that in all right triangles, the sum of the squares of the two legs is equal to the square of the hypotenuse: $\text{leg}^2 + \text{leg}^2 = \text{hypotenuse}^2$

▶ **Q**

quadrants the four equal parts of a coordinate plane. A number names each quadrant. The upper-right-hand area is quadrant I. You proceed counterclockwise to name the other quadrants.

quadrilateral a polygon with four sides

quotient the result when one number is divided into another

▶ **R**

radical the symbol used to signify a root operation

radius any line segment from the center of a circle to a point on the curve of the circle. The radius of a circle is equal to half the diameter.

rate a ratio comparing two items with unlike units

ratio the relationship between two things, expressed as a proportion

real numbers numbers that include fractions and decimals in addition to integers

reciprocal one of two numbers that, when multiplied together, give a product of 1. For instance, because $\frac{3}{2} \times \frac{2}{3}$ is equal to 1, $\frac{3}{2}$ is the reciprocal of $\frac{2}{3}$.

rectangle a parallelogram with four right angles

remainder the amount left over after a division problem using whole numbers. Divisible numbers always have a remainder of zero.

rhombus a parallelogram with four equal and congruent sides

root (square root) one of two (or more) equal factors of a number. The square root of 36 is 6 because $6 \times 6 = 36$. The cube root of 27 is 3 because $3 \times 3 \times 3 = 27$.

▶ **S**

scale a special ratio used for models of real-life items

scientific notation a special notation used as a short-hand for large numbers

signed number a number with a positive or negative sign in front of it

simplify terms to combine like terms and reduce an equation to its most basic form

slope the steepness of a line. Slope is the rise or decline over the run or the change in y over the change in x.

slope-intercept form $y = mx + b$. It is also known as $y =$ form.

square a parallelogram with both four equal and right angles and four congruent sides. A square is a rhombus, a rectangle, a parallelogram, and a quadrilateral.

sum the result of adding two numbers together

surface area the measurment of the area of each face of an object

▶ **T**

trapezoid a quadrilateral with one pair of parallel sides

triangle a polygon with three sides

trinomial an expression with three terms; for example, $a + b + c$

► **V**

variable a letter, often x, used to represent an unknown number value in a problem

volume a cubic measurement that measures how many cubic units it takes to fill a solid figure

► **W**

whole numbers 0, 1, 2, 3, and so on. They do not include negatives, fractions, or decimals.

► **X**

x-axis the horizontal line that passes through the origin on the coordinate plane

► **Y**

y-axis the vertical line that passes through the origin on the coordinate plane

y-intercept the point where a line graphed on the coordinate plane intersects the y-axis

NOTES

NOTES

NOTES

NOTES

NOTES

NOTES